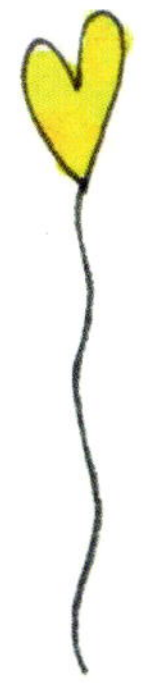

First published in Great Britain in 2020 by Jackanory Communications Ltd.

Copyright © 2020 Anna James

Cover illustration by Roxanne Knott

Pre-production by Lynn Forbes

Printed and bound by Gemini Print

IBSN 978-1-5272-7582-9

A CIP catalogue record for this book is available from the British Library.

NHS CHARITIES
TOGETHER

ALL PROFITS FROM THE SALE OF THIS BOOK GO TO GOOD CAUSES

When sold at the full recommended retail price, NHS Charities Together will receive a minimum of £2.50 from the sale of every book with at least another £2.50 being shared between other good causes nominated by the contributors. Stockists also have the option to donate their retailer's margin to a local charity or good cause of their choice.

and so shines
a good deed
in a weary world...

(attributed to both William Shakespeare and Willy Wonka, although we'd guess Shakespeare said it first!)

NHS CHARITIES
TOGETHER

COVID KINDNESS UK:2020

A celebration of hard work, adaptability and kindness

Jackanory
COMMUNICATIONS

2020 was an unprecedented year, with the monumental challenges and heart-breaking sadnesses of the global Covid-19 pandemic. But it was also a year of exceptional hard work, adaptability and kindness. Our humanity and community spirit shone in the darkness.

There isn't a book big enough to include all of the people who deserve to be mentioned, so this celebrates the stories of a few on behalf of the many.

This book is for everyone who worked really hard, everyone who made someone else smile and everyone who just about held it together. You are all heroes. We are Great, Britain.

At the time of going to print, the UK was just heading into a second full national Lockdown. I hope the stories in this book give you some comfort and encouragement for the difficult winter months ahead. Stay safe and be kind.

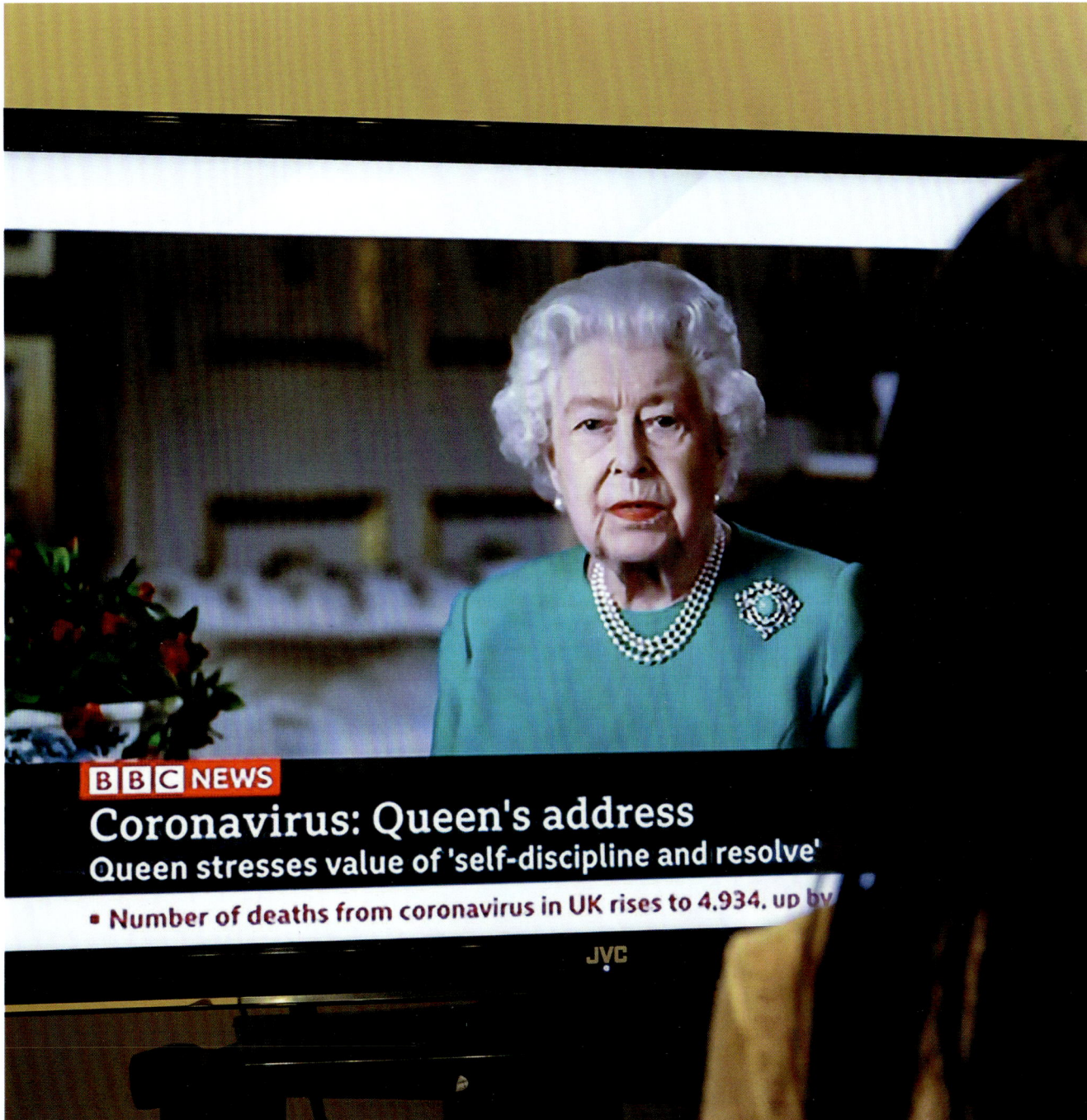

NHS CHARITIES TOGETHER

NHS Charities Together is the umbrella organisation that brings together all the official charities of the NHS. In response to the Covid-19 emergency, NHS Charities Together launched an urgent appeal to support NHS staff and volunteers during this time.

As the official charity partner to the NHS, it worked with member NHS Charities on a nationally co-ordinated response.

Its national appeal acknowledges and supports NHS staff and volunteers caring for Covid-19 patients and has been put together in liaison with NHS charities, national bodies and national giving platforms.

The money raised is funding grants to help NHS charities support NHS staff, volunteers and patients in ways above and beyond what NHS funding can ordinarily provide, from meeting immediate and urgent needs to supporting the long-term recovery from the impact of the crisis.

This can mean providing somewhere comfortable so staff and volunteers can take a break and get nutritious food and drink. It can also mean providing electronic tablets so patients, staff and volunteers can stay in contact with loved ones, as well as offering counselling support to protect mental health and help staff and volunteers process what they are dealing with.

Funds are also supporting vital partnerships outside hospitals, such as hospices, community healthcare and social care, making sure patients returning home have access to the care they need to recover. NHS Charities Together is also working with member NHS charities to identify where additional support is most urgently needed, with a particular focus on support for people who are disproportionately affected by the Covid crisis.

> Helping the NHS support staff, volunteers and patients in ways above and beyond what NHS funding can ordinarily provide.

I am speaking to you at what I know is an increasingly challenging time. A time of disruption in the life of our country: a disruption that has brought grief to some, financial difficulties to many, and enormous changes to the daily lives of us all.

I want to thank everyone on the NHS front line, as well as care workers and those carrying out essential roles, who selflessly continue their day-to-day duties outside the home in support of us all.

I am sure the nation will join me in assuring you that what you do is appreciated and every hour of your hard work brings us closer to a return to more normal times.

I also want to thank those of you who are staying at home, thereby helping to protect the vulnerable and sparing many families the pain already felt by those who have lost loved ones.

Together we are tackling this disease, and I want to reassure you that if we remain united and resolute, then we will overcome it.

I hope in the years to come everyone will be able to take pride in how they responded to this challenge. And those who come after us will say the Britons of this generation were as strong as any. That the attributes of self-discipline, of quiet good-humoured resolve and of fellow-feeling still characterise this country.

The pride in who we are is not a part of our past, it defines our present and our future.

The moments when the United Kingdom has come together to applaud its care and essential workers will be remembered as an expression of our national spirit; and its symbol will be the rainbows drawn by children.

Across the Commonwealth and around the world, we have seen heart-warming stories of people coming together to help others, be it through delivering food parcels and medicines, checking on neighbours, or converting businesses to help the relief effort.

And though self-isolating may at times be hard, many people of all faiths, and of none, are discovering that it presents an opportunity to slow down, pause and reflect, in prayer or meditation.

It reminds me of the very first broadcast I made, in 1940, helped by my sister. We, as children, spoke from here at Windsor to children who had been evacuated from their homes and sent away for their own safety.

Today, once again, many will feel a painful sense of separation from their loved ones. But now, as then, we know, deep down, that it is the right thing to do.

While we have faced challenges before, this one is different. This time we join with all nations across the globe in a common endeavour, using the great advances of science and our instinctive compassion to heal.

We will succeed – and that success will belong to every one of us.

We should take comfort that while we may have more still to endure, better days will return: we will be with our friends again; we will be with our families again; we will meet again.

Her Majesty The Queen / Message to the Nation

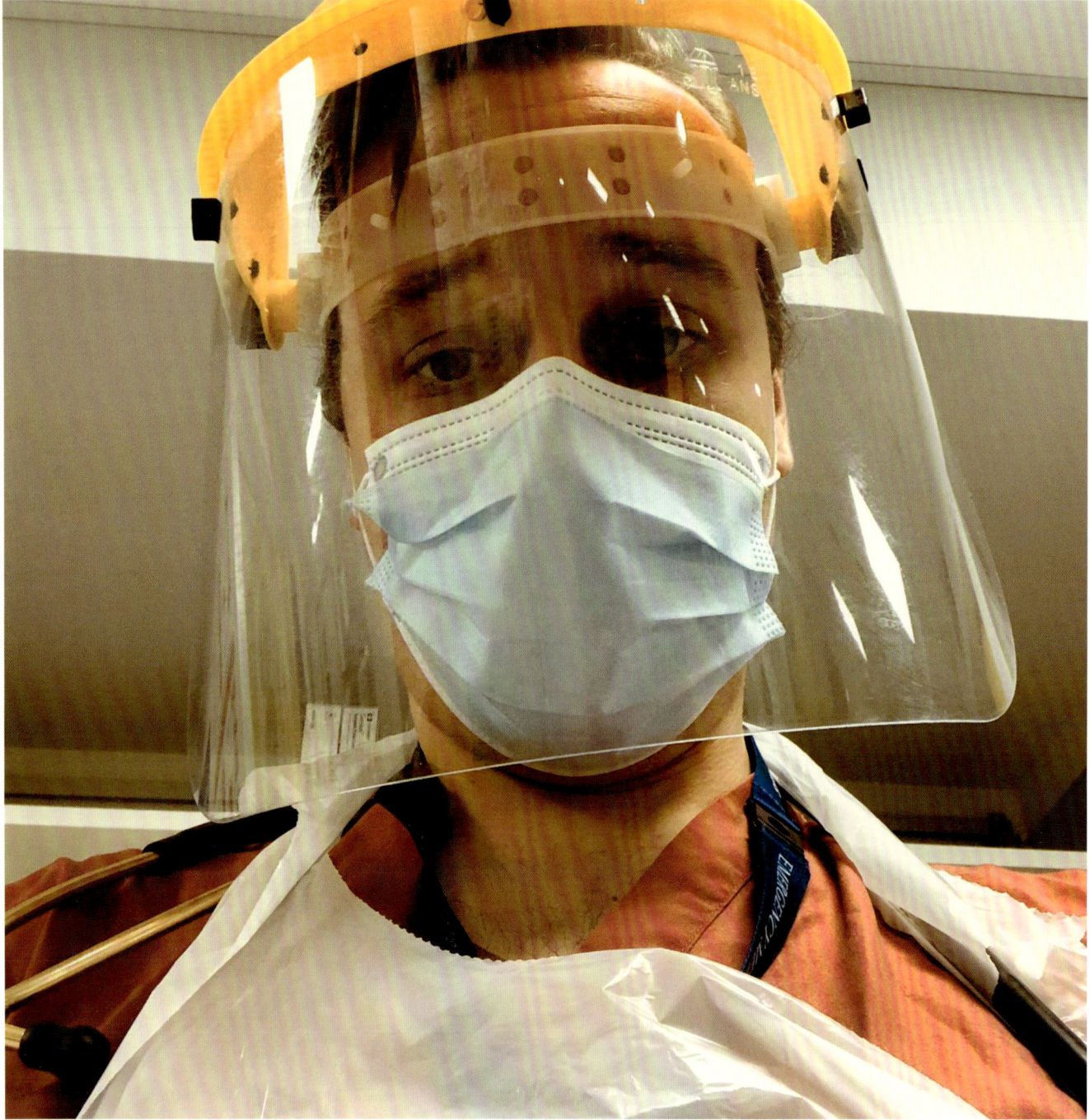

DR HARRISON CARTER
Doctor / Central London Emergency Department

I was interested in studying medicine as it provided a huge number of opportunities to intervene directly in peoples' lives to look after them and keep them safe. I also have an insatiable intellectual curiosity and medicine is a broad subject where you can learn about lots of different things whilst also contributing to other peoples' lives.

A normal day working in the Emergency Department (or a normal night!) is spending time assessing patients who either come into the hospital through the ED waiting area or by ambulance in an emergency. I talk to patients, examine them, make diagnoses and initiate a management plan. Working patterns are early, late and night shifts.

Part of my job is sometimes helping people who are very distressed and need to be comforted and listened to. On other occasions the patients may have stopped breathing or their heart may have stopped so we work very closely as a team to provide the best possible advanced life support – which can be very demanding in full personal protective equipment.

Covid meant total re-organisation of the department where I work. The majority of patients we looked after had suspected Covid-19. We worked very closely with specialist teams based in the department to support those that needed swift interventions to help their breathing; like being put on a ventilator.

The most difficult part of the job was that conversations with families about the care of their loved ones changed dramatically. Families were not allowed in the hospital. It highlighted just how important it was to keep families in the loop. We had to phone them to provide updates and this changed the type of doctor-patient and family relationship.

Sometimes patients were really scared that their families couldn't see them and so were the families. We had a very important role to be honest, to provide hope where we could but crucially to be clear, compassionate and kind in all of our conversations. To hold a hand if we needed to. To spend time with our patients in lieu of their families.

It was busier when patients started to come into the hospital more unwell. The emotional, mental and physical turmoil associated with the job was much greater. Constantly wearing PPE caused a sore face, dry mouth and banging headaches after a long shift.

Work was extremely tiring and busy. It was important to be highly focused on the individual tasks at hand to make it safe for patients. The world was changing by the day but we had to maintain focus on the important task of helping, caring for and treating patients.

It was difficult to be away from home – I missed my family and friends and my usual ways of relaxing. I also didn't see my partner for over three months as we didn't live together when the Lockdown started.

However, I became a doctor to help people in situations like this one. I felt a personal responsibility to stand up during trying times to play my part to look after the country.

The camaraderie made it better – we tried to keep our morale high and all pulled together. We ensured that we were all rested and took our breaks. We spoke about our experiences and how they had affected us. I'd never want to relive those experiences but in working together to save lives I have made some of my closest friends.

> 66
> The world was changing by the day but we had to maintain focus on helping, caring for and treating patients.

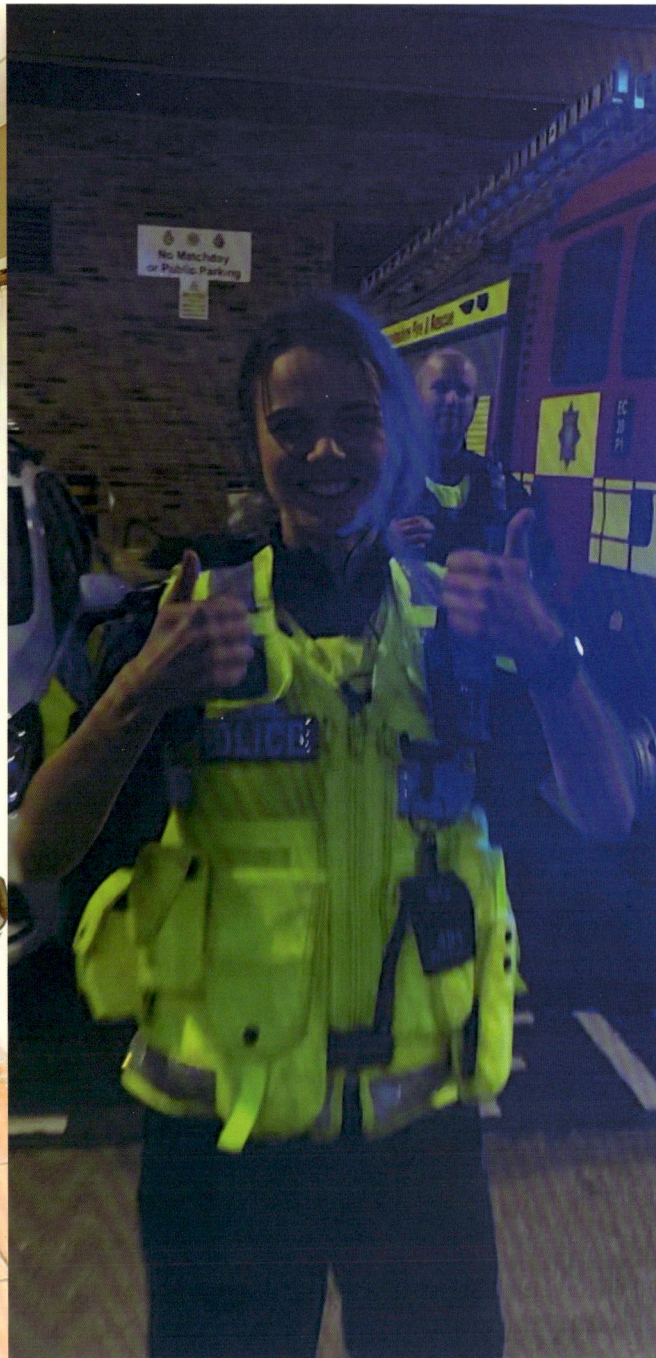

ELISE KEYWORTH
University Student & Sports Therapist / Lincoln

I'd usually be at university studying Sports Therapy and Rehabilitation and working in sports therapy, offering sports massage to athletes and other people. I am also a Police Special Constable for Lincolnshire Police.

My job has certainly changed because I can't be hands on with clients so I had to stop working – that's why I applied to work at Tesco. I'm also still working for Lincolnshire police as a special constable at the same time.

I'm a personal shopper at Tesco, so I pick the shopping for all the online orders for vulnerable people or people who can't get to the store. Tesco have worked really hard to keep essentials on the shelves. They've taken on lots of extra staff like me to help with picking the online ordering and they've also done lots of things instore to ensure social distancing and all the extra cleaning.

I also have to wear more PPE for the police.

It is very difficult because I'm getting up at 2 a.m., 4 days a week for work whilst also trying to get out and help keep the public safe policing, but it's a challenge I'm enjoying. When I see how thankful people are at the end of the day – in both jobs – it really makes everything worthwhile. I love helping people and that's what drives me to do it.

Due to Covid-19, it makes both jobs difficult when trying to talk and interact with customers at Tesco and support victims of crime and people that need help in Lincoln because we are unable to get close to them.

Working as part of a team – both at Tesco and with the police – makes it a bit easier as we can all support each other whilst this pandemic is going on as we are all in the same boat, knowing how it's affecting everybody's day to day lives.

I'm still working at Tesco, but have just found out I've passed my police interviews so next year I'll be a full time Police Constable!

> " I love helping people and when I see how thankful people are in both jobs, it really makes everything worthwhile.

LEANNE O'HAGAN
OPG Tyneside Mail Centre / Tyneside

We're a 24-hour operation with multiple shifts that run across the working day. I work on the outward operation which means we get the mail posted from around the area and process it so it can be delivered around the country to every location the next working day.

On a normal working day, we process almost 2 million items in the plant, with over 1,000 people employed in the operation. However, during the Covid-19 outbreak those numbers vastly increased to over the usual Christmas levels and this continued throughout the pandemic. I think people were trapped at home so they needed things like sporting equipment and other things that usually they wouldn't normally need so the demand for parcels shot up.

Our workload increased significantly with lots of changes in the workplace too – new rules to follow and different ways of working. We had to have regular announcements telling people to remain 2 metres apart and introduced a one-way system around the building among many other new safety protocols. It was difficult to adapt quickly, but you could tell the team wanted to make it work. There are numerous PPE stations placed around the building with sanitisers, gloves and facemasks for the teams.

Obviously, at first there was uncertainty. We saw higher sick levels through people showing symptoms or having loved ones showing symptoms, and also those who had health conditions that needed to be shielded. We also had higher stress and anxiety absences brought on by the worry of the difficult circumstances the globe found itself in.

The whole operation had changed, we had to work differently and we had to process high levels of mail with huge restriction on how we did it. We had to adapt as we knew we were a key part of keeping the country running, so felt like we had a duty and responsibility to carry on.

I think we found the responsibility of what we do and how we connect the country rewarding. We found that the general public appreciated our efforts along with all the other key workers. We had letters and pictures coming through from children and little motifs on letters thanking us for our efforts. We've also had little messages on parcels from Grandparents who are sending their Grandchildren little gifts, it was heart-warming, but also motivating.

Over the last few weeks when we had the 8 p.m. clap for carers every Thursday. Before the clap, the staff were addressed by one of the team leaders. This was often a very solemn speech given what was happening around the country, but with this and the clap, I think this lifted the moral of the staff and gave us a sense of unity. When the granddaughter of a colleague, 11-year-old Myah, came in and sang 'Somewhere Over the Rainbow' the whole Mail Centre stopped, we were all amazed and honoured to have such talent sing to us. It was a very touching moment and came at a time when things were starting to improve in terms of lock down. I think in that moment with that song the whole Mail Centre's emotions lifted, it was such an amazing moment, something that I would regard as a highlight of my time at Royal Mail and something that I will remember forever.

If anything, out of all this I think we all realised the worth and culture we bring to the country. We deliver to every house in the nation and are the heart of the community to whom we serve. I think that in itself can bring us a great sense of worth and I'm proud to work for Royal Mail and be part of what we have achieved during these last few months.

> 66
>
> Sometimes we forget what we do in terms of how we connect people. This pandemic brought things back into perspective of how much of an essential service we provide to the country.

M&S

EST. 1884

We're all in this together

M&S

M&S has been operating since 1884, including through two world wars. In times of crisis, we have a longstanding history of stepping up to support the communities we serve – and during the Covid-19 pandemic, this was no different: our resolve and determination to do our bit for the nation was as strong as ever.

From the outset, it became clear that the NHS was the cause that mattered most to our customers and colleagues so we set out to understand how we could best help. After speaking to our hospital partners, we quickly responded with the largest support package in M&S history. We redirected food supplies into our hospital stores to help NHS workers access the products they need; we were the first retailer to introduce priority shopping hours for NHS workers and we introduced a free food delivery service for at our longstanding hospital partners at St Mary's Hospital and Great Ormond Street Hospital

We donated thousands of specially branded t-shirts as part of the uniform pack for the Nightingale frontline teams and delivered clothing care packs to the NHS Nightingale Hospitals in London, Glasgow, Cardiff, Belfast and Birmingham to help provide comfort and dignity for discharged patients. We also donated over 4,000 pyjamas to NHS Derbyshire to be used as scrubs, located near our Castle Donington distribution centre.

However, it was clear our customers wanted to play their part too so we quickly established ways for them to contribute to our fund-raising efforts. We switched the NHS Charities Together Covid-19 Urgent Appeal on as a Sparks charity – meaning M&S donated every time customers shop. Over 25,000 customers have selected it as their chosen charity.

We were the first to introduce a 'Thank you NHS' bag for life and we launched a series of bespoke 'All in This Together' T-shirts which became the fastest-selling T-shirt in M&S history, selling out within 24 hours with one t-shirt selling every second and some well known faces supporting them.

Across these different initiatives – with the support of our customers – we raised £8 million for NHS Charities Together in less than six months.

We have a longstanding partnership with community platform Neighbourly which connects all of our stores with deserving causes in their local community. As the pandemic began, we knew this would be more important than ever, so we accelerated the rollout of our app to make it as easy as possible for stores to donate leftover food. In the first few weeks, we doubled our food donation rate in our stores, supporting over 1,500 community causes across the UK with over 5.4 million meals.

Alongside this, we set up a brand-new emergency fund with a start-up donation of £100k providing instant support to Neighbourly's existing network of charity and community groups. We also added the fund to our list of Sparks charities and in the first few months alone, more than 6,000 customers selected Neighbourly as their chosen charity, supporting more than 150,000 people and 622 grassroot causes.

Given the unprecedented times we were operating in, we also wanted to make it as easy as possible for our customers to access the products they needed. We were the first to introduce dedicated shopping hours for NHS staff, as well as elderly and more vulnerable customers, emergency service workers, and health & social care workers. We also launched an online Food Box delivery business in under two weeks to cater for customers that were shielding at home.

Our colleagues really stepped up to help us support our customers and the NHS, and we gave a pay reward to all store & distribution centre colleagues that continued working during the Lockdown period.

Like so many other colleagues, I have never been prouder to work for M&S. The care and commitment our colleagues have shown to our customers, their teammates and our communities has been inspiring to see; we really have been #AllInThisTogether.

Carmel McQuaid / Head of Sustainable Business

> In times of crisis, we have a longstanding history of stepping up to support the communities we serve.

We shared social media posts like this, so that we'd get a yearly reminder ...

Prime Minister Boris Johnson started lockdown on the evening of 23rd of March 2020 🚫

On the 5th April he was admitted to hospital after 10 days self isolating with the Corona Virus 🧪

On the 6th April he is in intensive care with deteriorating symptoms 🩺

The Queen addressed the nation at 8pm on 5th April 👑

Excel now known as NHS Nightingale and will be a hospital for up to 4,000 patients, most of whom are on ventilators. Similar venues being used in cities across the country. Opened by Prince Charles at 11am on 3rd April 🏥

Community support groups established, to support the vulnerable, elderly, immunocompromised and people in enforced isolation due to exposure, in their community 👵👴

Schools are closed and parents must teach children at home.

Fuel prices drop a record amount.

Governments close borders to all but non-essential travel.

Panic buying 🛒 sets in and we have limits on toilet paper 🧻 disinfecting supplies, paper towels, staple foods 🥗 hand sanitizer 🧴 Flour is hard to get because the packaging comes from China 🇨🇳 and borders are closed 🚧

Manufacturers 🏭 distilleries and other businesses 🏢 switch their lines to help make visors, masks 😷 hand sanitizer 🧴 and PPE 🧤

Fines are established for breaking lockdown rules 🤑

Stadiums 🏟 and recreation facilities overseas open up for the overflow of Covid-19 🦠 patients.

Public Park 🏕 areas turned into caravan parks for stranded tourists to self isolate 🚐

Press conferences daily from the PM 👱 and other government 🏛 officials. Daily updates on new cases, recoveries, and deaths ⚰

Government 🏛 incentives to stay home.
with many people placed on furlough

Tape on the floors at grocery stores ❌ and others to help distance shoppers 🛒 (2 mtrs) from each other.

Limited number of people inside stores, therefore, lineups outside the store doors 🏬

Non-essential stores and businesses mandated closed 🚫 People who can work 👩‍💻 👨‍💻 from home 🏡

Parks 🏕 trails, entire cities 🏛 closed or restricted to locals only in their bubble.

Entire sports ⚽ 🏈 🎾 seasons cancelled.

Olympics postponed to 2021. 🔵 🟡 ⚫ 🟢 🔴

Concerts 🎫 tours 🚌 festivals 👷 entertainment events 💃 cancelled 🚫

Weddings 👰 🤵 family celebrations 🥳 holiday gatherings 👨‍👩‍👧 even funerals ⚰️ cancelled 🚫

No masses, churches ⛪ are closed 🚫

No gatherings of 50 or more, then 20 or more, then 10 or more. Now, Don't socialize with anyone outside of your home bubble 🛌

People wearing masks 😷 and gloves outside 🧤

Essential service workers are terrified to go to work 👮 💁 🙍

Medical field workers 👩‍⚕️ are afraid to go home to their families 👨‍👧‍👦

82,195 deaths globally so far.

This is the Novel Coronavirus 🦠 (Covid-19) Pandemic, WHO declared March 11th, 2020.

Why, you ask, do I write 📝 this status?

One day it will show up in my memory 🕯 feed, and it will be a yearly reminder that life is precious and not to take the things we dearly love for granted 💕

We have so much! 🙌
Be thankful. Be grateful 😌
Be kind to each other - love one another - support everyone 🥰

We are all one! ❤️ 🧡 💛 💚 💙 💜 🤎 🖤 🤍

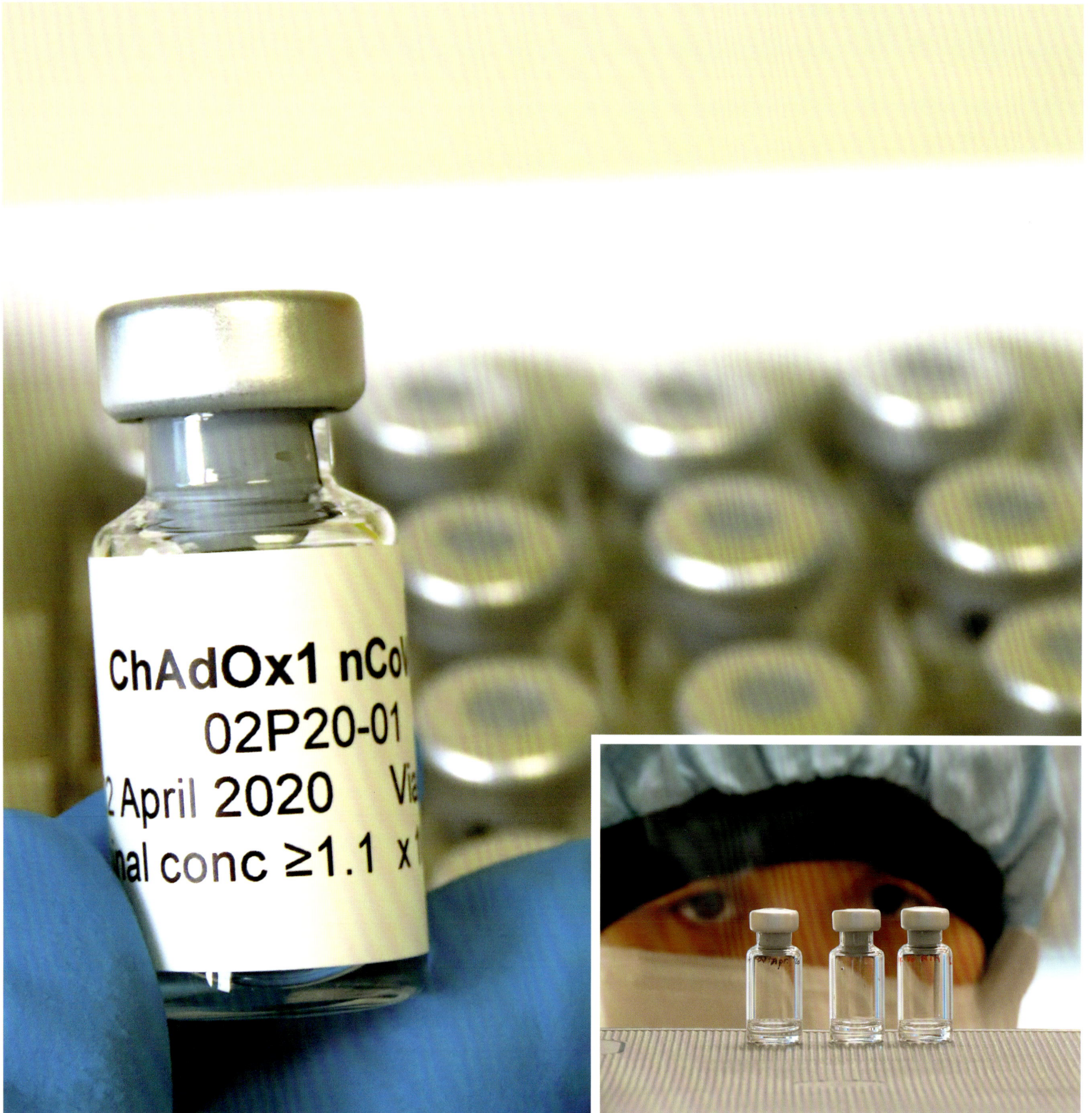

DR SEAN ELIAS
Post-Doctoral Immunologist / Jenner Institute / University of Oxford

I am very much a lab scientist, based at the Jenner Institute at the University of Oxford. A normal working day is usually centred around running experiments to look at the human immune response to infection or vaccination – for the past 4 years I have been working on Salmonella disease.

Since Covid, our lab work is now focused on developing a vaccine. I've also been tasked with documenting our vaccine work from the inside so we have content to share with the public and the media without need to have external photographers and film crews on site. The change of role has been challenging at times but rewarding, especially seeing my photos shared in the worldwide news.

The trials process, especially the logistics of planning such a big series of studies in a short period of time, has probably been the biggest challenge for the team as a whole. I think the best way to describe it is, that it's like our normal work, just scaled up and fast forwarded beyond anything we could ever have imagined.

But, although it sounds like a cliché, knowing you are part of something that can genuinely help everyone in the world is pretty good for motivation. We also have a fantastic camaraderie in our team (one the reasons I have been working at the institute for over 12 years) which if anything is even stronger now.

The photos show a very important job being performed by my colleague Chang – checking each individual vaccine vial to make sure it has the correct volume and no contaminants. This process is performed in a clean room so this picture was taken through a hatch where the final, approved vials are eventually passed through.

The larger photo shows Vial 1 from Box 1 of the first batch of vaccine approved for use in the Phase 1 vaccine trial. I managed to get a shot of this before the box went into the freezer. We have kept the vial and hope to put it in a museum at some point.

> It's like our normal work, just scaled up and fast forwarded beyond anything we could ever have imagined but knowing you are part of something that can genuinely help everyone in the world is pretty good for motivation.

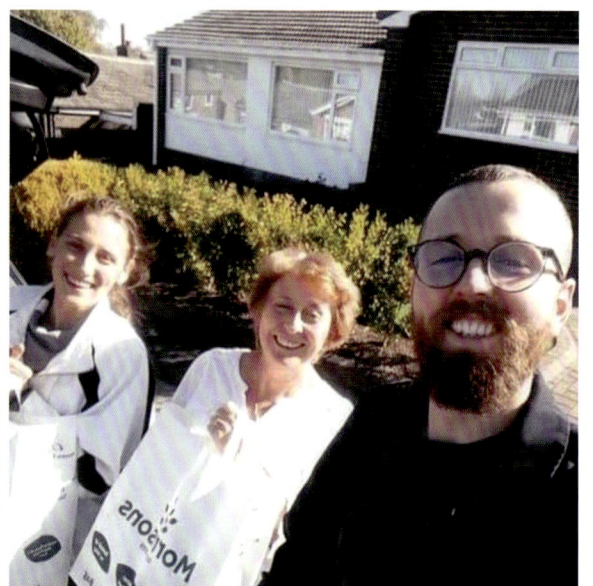

AGE UK GATESHEAD

With the onset of Covid, thousands of our clients had to self-isolate. They saw some sudden and big life changes. The services we provide, and that so many rely on, had to change too – and fast. We'd usually provide buses and take people to places but we can't do that now. Services have to be delivered in their front room, in person or virtually.

People need people and the littlest things can make the biggest difference. We've taken people a hot meal and ended up sitting with them for hours. With one lady, she was laid on her bed with her teddy because she was so scared about the virus. But we made her smile.

We also saw a big increase in demand with almost 25% of all requests to Gateshead Council being referred to us. In the first 100 days, we had over 20,000 calls. At peak, that was around 5 calls every minute. This helped us identify and create 14 new services to help the community, from food and prescription services to mental health support.

We also made over 100,000 friendship and welfare calls to vulnerable clients to offer human contact and a listening ear.

Rather than close, our team worked hard to find new ways to deliver the support people now need. But with more than half of our 150 volunteers having to isolate, it soon proved a strain on resources.

However, within days, our volunteer base saw a massive increase to over 2,000 and we were joined by 17 mutual aid groups and partners. There were so many people coming together to support others. It was simply about people,

With the amazing support of our volunteers and partners, our dedicated staff were able to keep supporting our 15,000 local clients. We delivered food and hot meals, we collected prescriptions, we dealt with energy suppliers and we provided talking therapies and online fitness.

The demand for our specialist services grew too, including living with and beyond cancer. Our 'mental health matters' provided more help at the point of crisis, with suicide threats rising from about three a month to eight a week. The need for our bereavement services increased alarmingly too.

Following the guidelines, we've also made sure we could relaunch and safely continue our face-to-face services. We've got PPE and deep cleaning on our transport services, with buses limited to six people. All of our venues comply with social distancing and track and trace, with temperature checking, hand sanitiser and PPE. We're prepared for local Lockdowns too.

How we live, work and socialise has changed and so have we – but we're still here when you need us, now and in the future. The way we've delivered our service has changed but putting clients health and wellbeing first, hasn't.

Ian Wolstenholme / CEO

> 66
>
> People need people, and the littlest things can make the biggest difference.

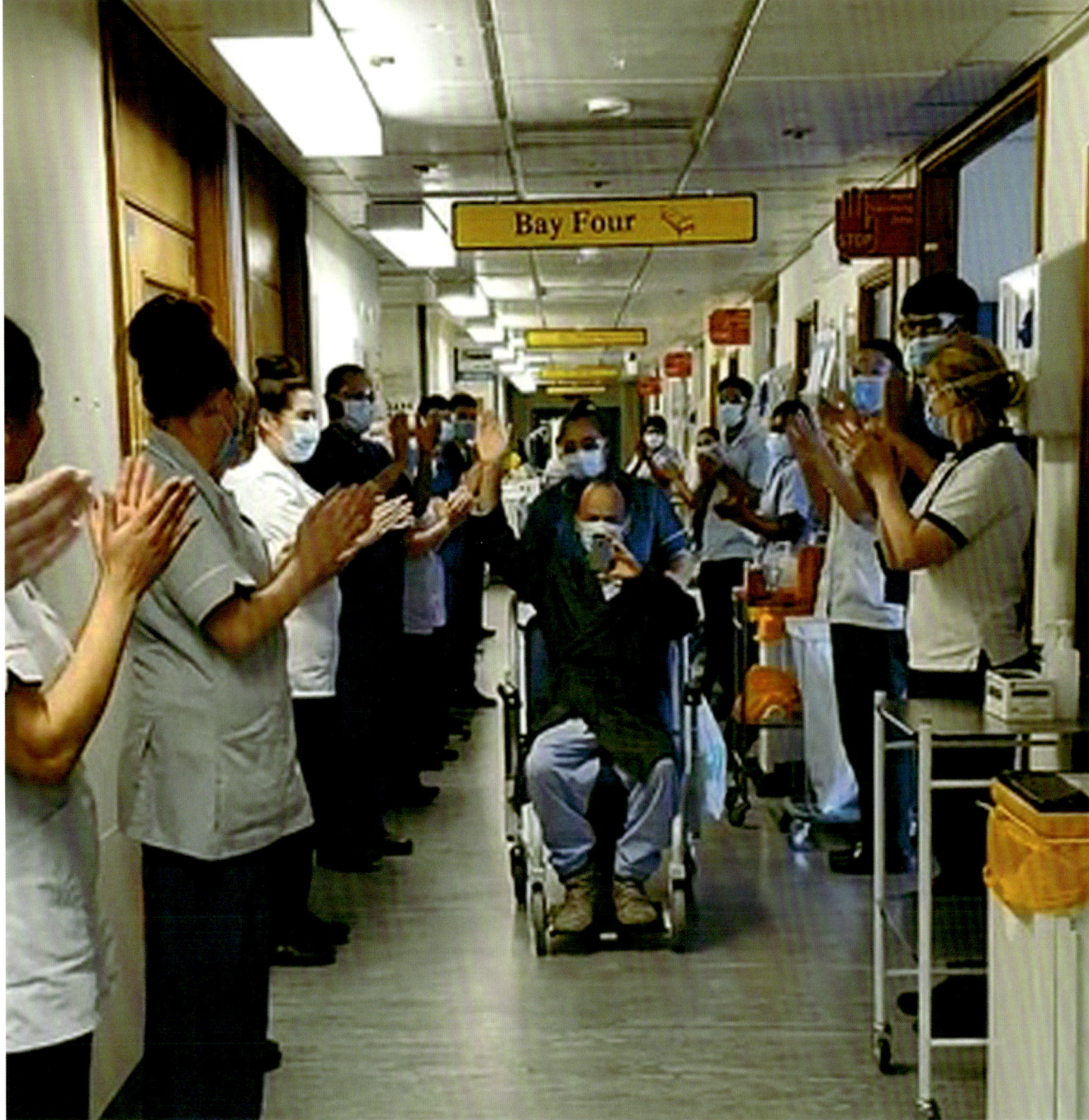

HYLTON MURRAY-PHILIPSON
Covid Survivor / Leicestershire

I'd been feeling unwell for a few days with a high temperature and a cough, when I was admitted to hospital fighting for breath.

I was hospitalised for 12 days, five of which were spent in intensive care fighting for my life. There were moments of great distress, great panic.

I spent my birthday recovering on the ward and the nurses asked me what I would like for my birthday – when you've just come through a fight for your life, it's hard to think of something.

I told them I'd really like a shave. I sat in the chair as they gave me a shave and after, they all stood around my bed with a piece of birthday cake with a candle in it. I cried like a baby, I was so overcome with emotion.

When I was discharged, I was given a guard of honour by staff. It was filmed and shown on TV, hence the rather blurry picture!

I am so grateful to be alive. When you have battled for every breath, everything just feels incredible. My journey can, I think, be divided into three themes: faith, hope and charity.

To begin with, faith. Of all the images that came to me in intensive care, the strongest of all was that of Jesus calming the storm on the Sea of Galilee. At the time, if I coughed I was unable to perform a following in-breath as my lungs were so full of infection. I was being kept alive by a respirator forcing air into my lungs and this inability to breathe quickly turns to panic. The appearance of Christ rising from sleep in the bow of the boat to calm the waters was precisely what I needed to calm the storm in my throat.

I was also aware of a world-wide web of friends and family – together with many I've never met – praying for my recovery. In calm moments, I focused this energy as light and bought it into my body.

However, by Day Four, I started to feel physically exhausted and doubt began creeping in. For how much longer could I hold out? The temptation to call it a day was certainly there but various things kicked in to keep me going – hope was one of them.

First and foremost, having lost my darling wife four years ago, I wanted to live for my boys. I wanted to see them, hold them, smell them as any parent would.

Secondly, my father had died the day before I was taken to hospital. I had to watch the funeral from my hospital bed. I'd already planned to plant some walnut trees on the farm and now, getting them in the ground at the same time as my father's burial became an obsession.

Then an even wider hope kicked in. I've been an environmentalist for nearly 25 years and, as chairman of Global Canopy, I am focused on the urgent need to bring deforestation in the tropics to a halt, especially in the Amazon. In short, now aged 61, I feel I have a contribution to make and a reason to be here.

And finally, charity. For many years I have admired the Dalai Lama; I've read many books and listened to many talks on compassion, but I have never witnessed compassion being lived, day in day out, as it is lived by the doctors and nurses of the NHS. When you are as ill as I was, you return to a childlike state of total dependence on the kindness of others.

I would not be here without the professionalism and dedication of the staff of the NHS. But my abiding memory of that time is of human kindness and compassion. A nurse bringing a cup of tea in the middle of the night; giving me a shave on my birthday; whispering in my ear "It's going to be OK". In my hour of need, I reached out and found the hand of the NHS holding mine.

> " In my hour of need, I reached out and found the hand of the NHS holding mine.

CRYSTAL STANLEY
'The Rainbow Lady' / Suffolk

The purpose of the *Rainbow Trail* is to make a rainbow and place it in your window, to spread hope, positivity and togetherness during this hard time. It's a way of making a person smile and to take their mind off Covid-19.

I'd spotted a similar post on Facebook from Italy and thought it would help keep my 3 year old daughter entertained and to distract us from Covid-19. I put my own ideas to it and started the a Facebook group for Ipswich where I live. Within 24 hours we had over 4,000 people join.

We had people from over the UK wanting to join so we changed the group to all over the UK – and then we had people ask to join from all over the world, making my rainbow trail worldwide.

As I am writing this we are close to 200,000 members worldwide in our group. They are all are so creative with so many different types of rainbows from rainbow hair, glass rainbows, rainbows made from everyday objects, rainbow food. It's just amazing! As well as doing the rainbows, we are also raising funds for children's charities to help during Covid-19.

It's an incredible, unreal feeling about how much the *Rainbow Trail* has taken off. It's not just in peoples homes, it's in hospital, hospices, shops, places of work, farms – you name it and I'm sure there will be a rainbow there.

> 66
> The purpose of the Rainbow Trail is to spread hope, positivity and togetherness.

BANKSY

Street artist Banksy donated a new painting 'Game Changer' to Southampton General Hospital, paying tribute to NHS staff as heroes. He left a note with it that said, "Thanks for all you're doing. I hope this brightens the place up a bit".

Gail Byrne, Chief Nursing Officer, University Southampton Hospital, NHS Foundation Trust said, "The fact that Banksy chose the University Southampton Hospital as the venue to recognise the outstanding contribution of the NHS is a huge honour. Equally, to have the masked hero depicted as a nurse feels a fitting dedication to the extraordinary response of all our brilliant frontline staff throughout the pandemic. The painting has provided a focal point for who everyone in the hospital as a place to stop, pause and reflect and appreciate this beautiful piece of art. It's also been a massive boost to morale for everyone who works and is cared for at our hospital".

The new artwork will be on public display at the hospital during Lockdown and then be auctioned to raise money for the NHS charities.

THE JOLLY HOG

We make sausages and bacon for supermarkets, we cook and sell them at events and we have a restaurant called Pigsty. When we started hearing rumblings of this pandemic, we began to wonder "What if we end up having to go into a Lockdown?", "What if we have to shut down some of the business?".

And we did. We shut Pigsty on 19th March and I'll never forget that day. We deliberated offering takeaway and Deliveroo options but quickly decided it was safer to close temporarily whilst we assessed the situation. We also shut the train station kiosk we'd just opened at Bath Spa. Twelve months of hard work turned into just 12 days of trade. It was heart-breaking. And of course, we couldn't trade at any events – from Glastonbury to Tough Mudder, they were all cancelled. We calculated that the expected loss of income would leave us with at least a £600k hole in our turnover. A totally devastating thought for our small family business.

Luckily for us, our sausages and bacon were getting panic bought by customers right up there with loo roll and flour so, thankfully, the lost sales were getting covered by the uplift in retail.

We told staff to work from home. There was no way we could afford to pay everyone's wages with hardly any income so the furlough scheme was a huge relief. My brothers and I all took a pay cut and used the money to top up the furlough. We relocated to our old dairy barn and it was back to the old days of three fat lads doing literally anything and everything to make it work.

As a business, we believe in doing 'Jolly Good Deeds' and this seemed a particularly apt time to try and do some good. We donated some surplus stock to a fabulous local charity – the Square Food Foundation – who were donating their time to cook food for the vulnerable.

I also spoke to a friend who works at our local hospital. He was really stressed and tired and told us how difficult things were for staff. Southmead has a very special place in our hearts, with all 3 of us brothers – and all our children – being born there; and family and friends have received life-saving treatment there.

We offered to spread some love in the best way we know, with sausages and bacon! We took our airstream trailer, Miss Piggy, down to the hospital and I can honestly say it was one of the most unforgettable things I have ever done. We spent the day handing out bacon rolls and speaking to all the key workers, who were just the best people working in the toughest of environments. We ended up staying all day and gave out 500 bacon rolls.

We thought it was going to be a one off but quickly decided we'd go back 3 times a week. This was all before clap for carers started, but when that kicked off and people saw what we'd been doing, we had a huge influx of people who wanted to help. It was amazing. We had cash donations from companies to help towards stock and a local bakery donated all the rolls. My mother in law was even baking cupcakes for us to hand out.

One of the most memorable donations was right at the start when our old generator packed up. We put an SOS on Twitter and Ryan from Falcon Power offered to lend us a generator for the first session. We met him at 6 a.m. at the hospital and when asked where he'd come from, thinking it would be somewhere local, he said he'd driven down from Manchester! He'd left his house at 1 a.m., stayed until we'd given out all the food and then towed it home. When he found out we were going back, Falcon lent us a generator for the full 3 months and a farmer donated the diesel.

So far, we've given out almost 25,000 free bacon and sausage baps – and we're still going down there once a month. We've decided to continue our legacy with Southmead Hospital Charity by donating some of the proceeds from all of our 'Jolly Good (Scotch) Eggs' to support the amazing work done by their researchers on the after-effects of Covid-19.

Who knows what life is going to be like for anyone after Covid. I know it will never be the same for us. It's certainly taught us to look after your people, to have diversity in your business and to do a little bit of good if you can. We'll certainly be doing a lot more Jolly Good Deeds.

Max Kohn / Co-Founder

66

It was truly a special time of people and businesses coming together to do the right thing for the people looking after us.

OUR HEROES

I'll tell you a tale, that's been recently written,
Of a powerful army, so Great it saved Britain.
They didn't have bombs and they didn't have planes,
They fought with their hearts and they fought with their brains.

They didn't have bullets, armed just with a mask,
We sent them to war, with one simple task.
To show us the way, to lead and inspire us,
To protect us from harm and fight off the virus.

It couldn't be stopped by our bulletproof vests,
An invisible enemy, invaded our chests.
So we called on our weapon, our soldiers in blue,
"All Doctors, All Nurses, Your Country Needs You".

We clapped on our streets, hearts bursting with pride,
As they went off to war, while we stayed inside.
They struggled at first, as they searched for supplies,
But they stared down the virus, in the whites of its eyes.

They leaped from the trenches and didn't think twice,
Some never came back, the ultimate price.
So tired, so weary, yet still they fought on,
As the virus was beaten and the battle was won.

The many of us, owe so much, to so few,
The brave and the bold, our heroes in blue.
So let's line the streets and remember our debt ,
We love you, our heroes, Lest We Forget.

// WRITTEN BY MATT KELLY
READ BY CHRISTOPHER ECCLESTON

DAVID TILLYER
Paramedic / North Norfolk

In my job, there is no such thing as a normal day. It's one of the great things about being a Paramedic. That being said, every day prior to Covid-19 was similar in one way – it was relentless. Job after job with very little down time. We cover a wide range of health and social issues and not all the jobs we do are strictly appropriate for the ambulance service. But, we are always there for people and more often than not we can help. Sometimes, those jobs that are not strictly what we were trained for can be the most satisfying as we can sometimes be the ones that are able to listen, help and effect change in their lives.

Covid changed things in some expected and unexpected ways. We expected confusion and fear from many people out there and to some degree we were learning as we went along just like the public. Covid doesn't present like other illnesses we see and it wasn't always clear if some symptoms were as a result of the virus or not. The main improvement we saw was in the number of calls we dealt with overall. At least in the area where I work. We saw an increase in downtime for crews and I personally noticed a decrease in the number of jobs for people who didn't need an ambulance or the types of jobs where we suffer abuse/assault.

I'd say the biggest challenge was trying to adapt to a new virus and one that we were not used to treating – learning to identify the signs and deal with them appropriately and trying to manage the inherent fear in the public because the early days were confusing for everyone. On a personal level, not having a social outlet when not at work was hard but I'm thankful I was able to continue working and work kept me sane.

> It felt heart-warming that people are grateful to everyone on the front line.

What makes it better – one of the constants in my job are my colleagues. We support each other, tease each other and generally act as a team.

Being able to continue working and seeing different people every day (at work) helped me no end. I live alone, most of my close friends live 20-30 minutes away and my family is spread across the UK. Therefore, my days off were often painfully solitary during Lockdown. Without my job I may have suffered with some of the mental health issues that we've seen so many people go through. I'm grateful for that. I'm also grateful for on demand TV!

Why do I do it? It's my job.

One day, after finishing a night shift, I needed to pick up some food for my next few shifts as my fridge was empty. I went to the nearest supermarket to our ambulance station, just as it was about to open. There was a line of people outside and I joined the end of the queue. One by one they let me past and just as I got the door someone shouted "Let's all give him a round of applause". I was humbled and embarrassed. I must have gone bright red. Once I'd pottered around the shop and picked up my food, I joined the queue for the checkout. I got chatting to a lovely lady and a young couple. They asked me about my job and how it was all going. Once all my items had been scanned though, the lady I'd been talking to ran up and swiped her card on the card reader. I tried to say please don't but she smiled and said "It's done, you can't stop me now". She paid for the food that kept me fed for the next week.

I put a thank you on Facebook to try and reach her – and it was shared over 75,000 times. So, thank you to the lady that did that and thank you to all the shoppers who made me feel special after a tough run of shifts.

I felt humbled and a bit emotional and it felt really heart-warming that people really do respect what we do and that they're grateful to everyone on the front line for what we're doing at the moment. So often in my job we get treated with contempt and often violence. I've been physically assaulted more times than I can remember and verbally abused pretty much every other day. This reminded me that those people are actually the minority and most people are grateful for what the NHS does.

JO KENNET
Headteacher / Halesowen

A 'normal' work day is usually mad busy – since Covid, it's still busy but I'm also now managing a three-way schooling system.

It's been challenging to keep up with the ever-changing guidance around staff and pupil welfare and the organisation of a school system. We often only knew the changes when the nation did!!

As we are close to town and the QE/Universities, we inevitably have a lot of Key Workers whose children have had to come into school. We have managed the rising numbers but it has been really tricky and affected the staff rotas especially when our 'bubbles' were groups of 8. The definition of a Key Worker also caused us a few anxieties.

Home schooling has been an evolving phenomenon, with staff increasing in confidence with online systems. We started by just uploading to the school website but then developed our BGFL online learning platform. We've also had some live lessons using Zoom – Eddy the school teddy would often make an appearance, holding a sign to remind the children that "we're all in this together".

Our staff called parents to check on their access to the internet and then we had to deliver some work to the house in a paper form as not all parents have reliable access to wifi or devices for each child to work on.

Our poor Year 6 children didn't have their end of year production or leaving discos and some children have lost family members – especially grandparents – to Covid.

I also had to juggle staffing levels, with higher levels of absence for many differing reasons. Many staff wanted to return but couldn't because of the guidance and I would not have let them return if they were in a 'risk' category.

Whilst it was sad that emails often replaced conversations, we were really grateful for the range of mediums that helped make communication with our families still possible. We all learnt new skills with technology and became more efficient in cutting down travel time to meetings.

But everyone is in the same boat and head teachers have been working together as well as sharing ideas and concerns.

And, despite the challenges, we've all felt that we were doing our bit – playing our part in support of Key Workers, especially our parents working in the NHS. I have a great team of staff, who were rolling up their sleeves and willing to do anything that was needed. We were rewarded with Key Worker children coming in to school every day with a big smile.

We saw an overwhelming appreciation of school from parents and children. The need for its structure and friendships and a new appreciation for teachers. A number of our children became entrepreneurs too, raising money for the NHS – Millie made masks and Leo made tie-dye t-shirts.

We've always been open for Key Workers, Reception, Year 1 and Year 6 and we are planning to reopen fully in September, with staggered opening and closing times and dedicated IN and OUT gates. Children will operate in year group bubbles which will have breaktimes and lunchtimes together, and assemblies will be virtual. There will still be challenges but this will be easier to organise than the three-tier home-schooling!

> 66
> We felt we were doing our bit – rolling up our sleeves and willing to do anything that was needed.

ANIS ALI
Volunteer / South West London

I'm a Heathrow Express Train Driver at Great Western Railway. To tell you the truth, in my job, no two days are the same. My shift patterns determine the structure of my day as sometimes when I am on early shifts, I become nocturnal!

I've been volunteering with NHS Volunteer Responders since the start of the pandemic as a 'Check-in and Chat' volunteer, so I call people who are isolating alone and have a friendly chat with them to help them feel less alone.

I knew that I wanted to do something to support others in the pandemic. Not being a health or frontline worker, I felt that I really wanted to do my bit and this was the perfect solution. I have very sadly lost people I love to Covid-19 and I think this made me particularly motivated to help those in need. My workplace are also very supportive of my volunteering and always encourage me to keep doing it.

So far I have done over 700 calls and I have found it incredibly rewarding. We take so much for granted and since volunteering I have found that the smallest acts of kindness can make a huge difference to those who need it.

I think it really hit home how difficult the pandemic has been for so many. I am lucky to have a fantastic support network of family and friends but there are so many out there who don't, and these are the people who need their community now more than ever.

The thing that makes it all worthwhile for me is when people tell me that I've made their day. It's so lovely to hear that you have made a difference to people and it lets you know that you are doing something really special.

It was also overwhelming to be recognised by Oxford Street as one of their 2020 heroes and have my name in lights on the famous street. Apparently I have done the most volunteering as an NHS Volunteer Responder in London, which I was certainly not expecting. I never see it as a chore, it's something I love to do and I will continue to help people for as long as I'm needed.

I was incredibly proud to do it. It's such a fantastic scheme to be part of and although I didn't know what to expect, I have found it to be really rewarding. I always say this, but I think it has honestly helped me as much as the people I am calling! It's lovely to have a friendly chat in times like this and I always end up having a laugh and a joke which is really nice – especially at the moment.

> The smallest act of kindness can make a huge difference to those who need it. I will continue to help for as long as I'm needed.

JASON BAIRD
The Stockport Spider-Man

I started in martial arts when I was 5, competing for GB and becoming World Champion when I was 12. I went on to win 18 World Championships and now run my own martial arts school in Stockport. We teach children from the age of 2 and I love helping people lose weight, gain confidence and getting the kids off the streets.

When Covid struck, I lost half of my students really quite quickly and then, because we're a contact sport, we closed completely in March and didn't reopen until July. I still did some stuff for people remotely to keep that interaction going and to give them motivation but I had to learn how to do it all and of course there were often wifi glitches! It was a really tough time.

One day, after so many more memberships had been cancelled, I really hit rock-bottom. I just sat on the floor in my lounge and cried. One of my coaches, Andrew Baldock, had really cheered our students up by doing one of his Zoom classes dressed as Spider-Man and he suggested it might cheer me up too, as well as giving other people something to smile at. I had nothing to lose so we went out for my daily exercise dressed as Spider-Man.

After the first photo of us had appeared online, it went viral all around the world. We kept running. We'd go out for an hour every day, taking a different route each day and, in total, covered over 450 miles during Lockdown. It gave me an hour every day feeling happier and not thinking about the business.

People were coming out to clap us, playing the theme tune from their front doors and putting posters in their windows. Even the police and ambulance crews were beeping us and asking for selfies. We were featured in 'The Times' and interviewed by Phil and Holly live on 'This Morning' which was amazing. I felt like I really was Spider-Man!

We found ourselves heading up loads of other characters wanting to get involved – from other superheroes to Disney princesses – so we set up a WhatsApp group to co-ordinate appearances locally. It grew across the country and the team have created a superhero chat so we've made friendships out of this as well, which is nice.

We decided to try and do something good with all the publicity and started a JustGiving page to raise money for the NHS.

Someone donated £25,000 using the pseudonym 'Peter Parker' and a message that said: "Read about this in 'The Times' this morning. Inspirational stuff. Might have to give my outfit a dusting down and get out myself".

People are suggesting that it might be Tom Holland who played Spider-Man, some people are saying it's Keith Lemon because he followed my academy on Instagram around that same time. He's not said it's him, but he was then seen in a Spider-Man uniform the day after on his YouTube channel so it's just speculation, but it could be anybody really.

We've raised over £50,000 so far, we've got over 10,000 in our Facebook group and we're still going. It's amazing, we're bringing smiles to people and raising money for the NHS.

This is what superheroes have always been about. Superheroes are there to give us hope, to make us feel that it's not all doom and gloom. There's always that person that will be there to save the day. And that's why we call the NHS the true superheroes.

> It's amazing – we're bringing smiles to people and raising money for the NHS.

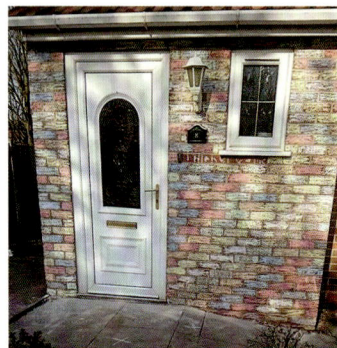

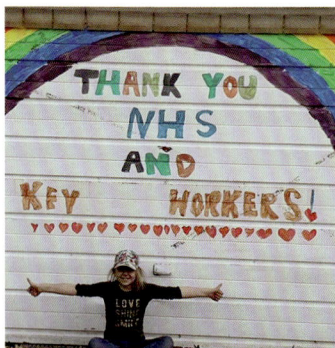

In an expression of hope and appreciation for key workers, the whole country burst into colour with rainbows of all shapes and sizes popping up in windows, on walls and more ...

TO THE DOCTORS NURSES CARERS AND EVERYONE ON THE FRONT LINE
TO THE UTILITIES WORKERS KEEPING OUR COUNTRY GOING
TO THE VOLUNTEERS AND HELPERS KEEPING SPIRITS UP
AND THE PICKERS PACKERS SUPPLIERS DRIVERS
AND THE CLEANERS WORKING AT AMAZON
TO EVERYONE STAYING AT HOME

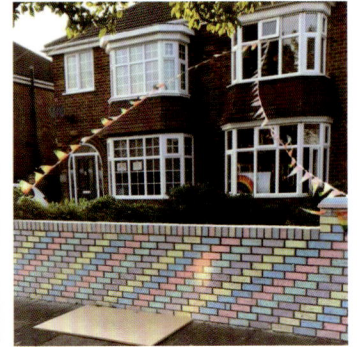

THANK YOU

FARESHARE

FareShare is the UK's largest charity fighting hunger and food waste, redistributing donated and surplus food to almost 11,000 local charities and community groups nationwide.

Before the pandemic, we worked with around 500 food partners to divert food that would have otherwise been wasted to frontline charities such as homeless hostels, food banks, breakfast clubs for children and domestic violence refuges. As the coronavirus began to impact, we saw a steep rise in applications from charities and community groups across the UK, with many charities reporting they were running low on essential food supplies.

Following the overnight shutdown of the food service sector in March, and England footballer Marcus Rashford's public plea to the food industry to support FareShare in getting food to those most affected by the crisis, we've signed up 25% more food businesses to help. The Government also made £16 million available so FareShare could purchase food and divert it onto frontline charities and community groups.

With the support of new and existing partners, we've doubled the amount of food we distribute, now providing enough food for 2 million meals every week. We teamed up with XPO Logistics and hauliers Nagel Langdons to help meet the sky-rocketing demand and partnered with the British Red Cross to get emergency food parcels to people. What was amazing is that in just one week in April, more people signed up to volunteer to sort, pack and deliver food for FareShare than in the whole of last year.

> 66
> With support like this, we stand ready to continue supporting those families and children that seek help to access good, healthy food this winter.

During the pandemic, we saw some amazing examples of companies stepping up to help: Asda donated £5 million; Barber's donated an extra 4 tonnes of cheese and butter; Brakes increased the volume of food it diverts to us to the equivalent of over 500,000 meals; food producer G's diverted enough surplus veg to help create more than a million meals; Nestle donated 650,000 bowls of cereal; Pink Lady donated thousands of apples; UK Fisheries donated over a tonne of frozen cod and, as a result of the closure of their restaurants, Whitbread donated over 140 tonnes of food. And many many more.

We've been humbled and overwhelmed by the support shown by our volunteers, corporate supporters, partners, funders, and by the thousands of people who have donated to our emergency appeal. It is because of them we have been able to rapidly scale up our response, supplying more frontline charities with food, getting more delivery vans on the road, opening new warehouses, and moving vital food supplies up and down the UK. With support like this, we stand ready to provide all the food we can obtain, so we can continue supporting those families and children that seek help to access good, healthy food this winter.

Lindsay Boswell / CEO

The real superstars in this country can be found in the heart of most cities, towns and villages, working tirelessly to support our most vulnerable across the UK. When we stumble, there will always be a community to wrap their arms around us and pick us back up.

For many of us, that is FareShare or the local food bank and, as we approach one of the toughest winters on record with demand likely to be higher than ever before, it is important that I lend my support wherever it is needed.

I encourage everyone to stop and listen. The time for action is now. I'm proud and I'm humbled to see such a reaction and commitment from the food industry, and I am confident that together we can help change the lives of those most vulnerable for the better.

Marcus Rashford

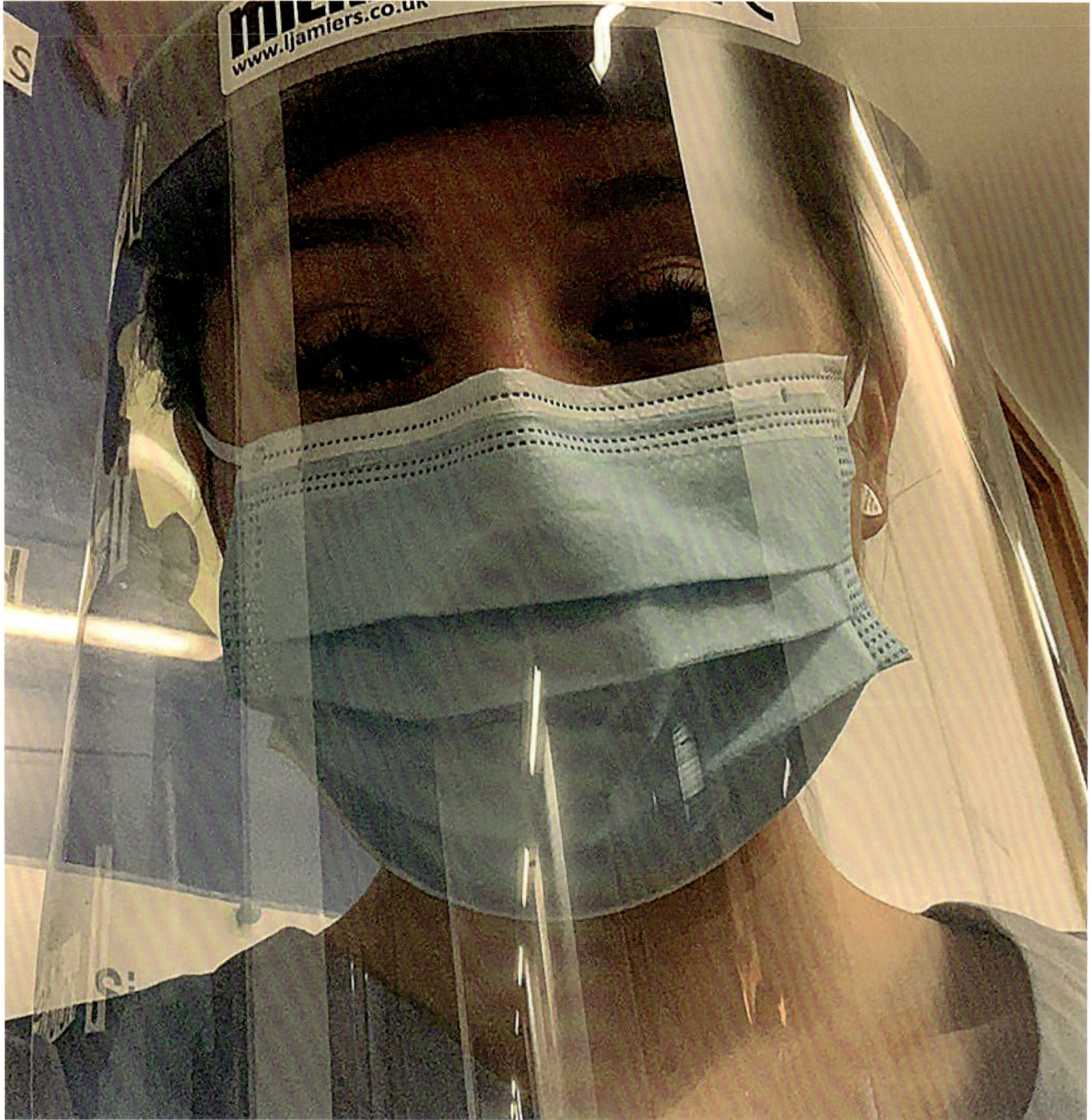

SAMMIE HARRISON
Healthcare Assistant / Bristol

I work on a ward which provides care specifically for older people, and my role involves providing personal care and emotional support to patients. I've been doing this for almost a year and absolutely love it. It was something I'd thought about for years and years – I love the caring side of it, making patients smile and making a change to their day.

It's been a challenging time for everyone but we have definitely rallied round and pulled together as a team, and we are really lucky to have that. Our team has such a great manager who supports us so much, and we've just tried to keep positive.

Mornings always start by getting patients up and ready for breakfast and at the moment there is a lot more emotional support too, just being there for them – naturally they want to turn to their families.

Emotions are so high. We've had to step up our focus on emotional support for patients – their own loved ones are unable to visit due to the restrictions so we are the only people they can have face-to-face interaction with. We've been using phones to FaceTime families and it's so emotional, especially for the elderly. They think the technology is absolutely amazing.

We've also helped several patients to mark milestone birthdays on the ward, including a 100-year-old woman who survived Coronavirus. We made homemade cakes and arranged for some balloons. She absolutely loved it. We just wanted to make it special for her. She was doing so well and just kept fighting.

The Clap for Carers on Thursday nights made us feel so valued and appreciated. It's really emotional, to feel that everyone is proud. It's amazing.

Of course getting the virus is a worry but the main focus is on the patients. It's always at the back of your mind but the main priority is putting patients first. We've had all the PPE we needed so I've felt quite safe throughout.

Seeing patients get through it is so uplifting but it's awful when patients die – although as healthcare assistants we are perhaps prepared for the loss of patients to a certain extent, and some days are harder than others. You just put yourself in the family's shoes and try to provide them some comfort.

You just need to keep spirits high and day by day we will work through it – fingers crossed, if everyone is safe and keeps doing what they're doing.

> 66
> It's been a challenging time and emotions are so high but we have rallied round and pulled together as a team.

THE UDDER FARM SHOP

We're a family run farm shop and restaurant on the edge of the Blackmore Vale in Dorset. When we first started hearing about Covid, we began making some contingency plans but it then all happened really quite suddenly.

I remember when we had to shut our restaurant. We'd only just reopened after months of hard work extending and refurbishing it. It was the week before Mother's Day and we were fully booked so we stood to lose a lot of business but even worse, we had to ring people to cancel their tables. Everyone understood but you knew they were really disappointed. It was horrendous and I just stood in that beautiful, empty space and sobbed. We then also closed the shop for a bit – we didn't have to but we wanted to be as safe as we could be. No one really knew what the days or weeks ahead were going to be like.

We continued to provide a service though, introducing temporary phone and collect and free delivery options. Almost overnight. What a challenge! It wasn't easy – we had to invent and adapt everything, from order forms to re-jigging our phone lines to cope with the extra calls. We even had to buy a new van to be able to offer the delivery service.

We kept as many people on as we could but we had to furlough some staff from the restaurant which was really sad. I feel really responsible for my team – they and their families rely on their wages from my business, so the Government furlough helped with that worry a bit, but we still really missed them. Those of us that were still there worked bloody hard. We were really busy, it was very stressful and people were doing jobs that wouldn't be what they'd usually do – taking phone orders, picking shopping and even jumping in their cars to make deliveries. But we muddled through and the team formed a really special bond.

Why did we do it? We felt we had a duty to serve our community. A lot of our older and more vulnerable customers couldn't go to a supermarket and couldn't get a delivery slot either. In those first few weeks we were quite often literally the only place they were able to get supplies. We were also getting calls from across the country with people ordering on behalf of their elderly family in the area. We had so many emotional and grateful "thank you" messages which made us feel like we were doing something that was really making a difference.

It was wonderful when we were finally able to welcome people back in store, and then later into the restaurant. We'd really missed our customers and it was great to feel a buzz about the place again. Obviously we've got all the social distancing measures in place but we're trying really hard to make it feel as normal and enjoyable as it always did.

Jane Down / Owner

66

Thank you so much for your thoughtfulness – just what we would have expected from you! My wife and I who frequently shop with you are both octogenarians and it's really comforting to know we can turn to you for help and support.

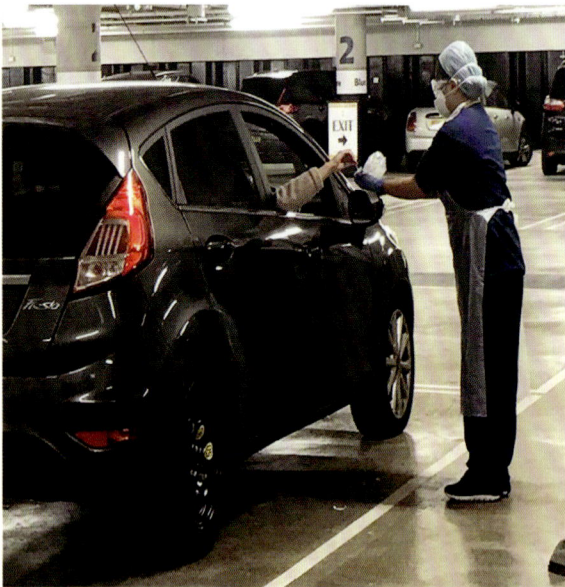

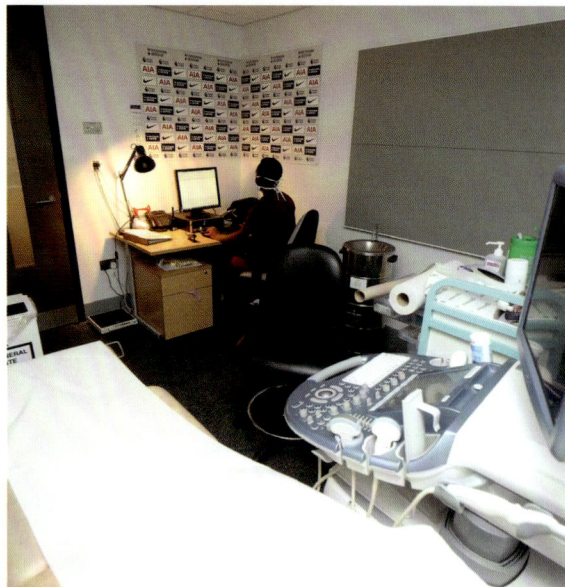

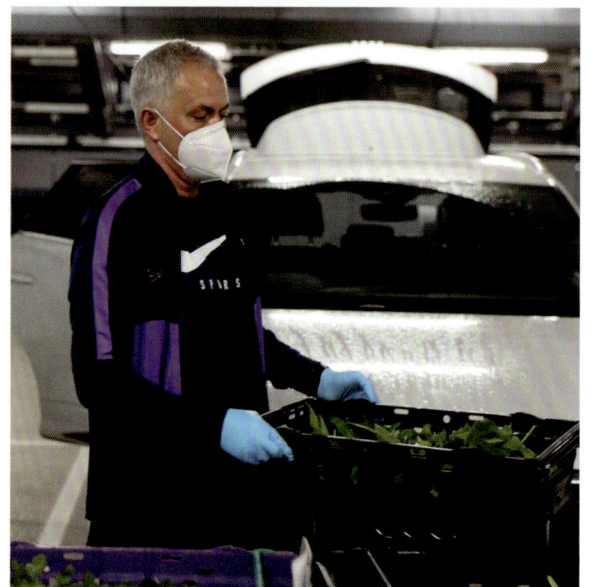

TOTTENHAM HOTSPUR FC

We were the first Premier League ground to offer stadium facilities for NHS use during the pandemic – our huge basement car park was used for drive-thru Covid-19 testing and swabbing.

The hospital's Women's Outpatient Services also relocated to the stadium to free up much-needed capacity at the hospital so they could treat patients facing Covid symptoms, whilst also supporting the redirection of pregnant women away from the hospital during the pandemic.

Recognisable areas of our stadium were transformed for clinical use. Our Media Entrance and Café were used as a main reception and welfare area for visitors and NHS staff whilst the NFL Away Changing Room areas were used as a Maternal Day Unit. Our Flash Interview Rooms off of the players' tunnel – where post-match TV interviews are normally conducted – as well as the referees' area, were used as consultation and scanning rooms, and the Away Dressing Room area was used as a Midwives Clinical Room and staff Admin Office.

We helped provide food to those most in need within the local community – the stadium's 'pitch pocket' was used as a storage base by the London Food Alliance, a scheme set up by the capital's three largest food surplus distributors to ensure food supplies for the most vulnerable people within the capital during the Covid-19 pandemic. We'd already been working with

> *We are absolutely committed to supporting the NHS and our communities during these unprecedented times.*

The Felix Project both before and at the start of the pandemic, donating surplus food and drink intended for use at our postponed fixture against Manchester United in March.

Fresh produce taken from our Kitchen Garden at the Club's Training Centre in Enfield – and which usually serves the First Team restaurant throughout the football season – was taken to the Haringey food distribution hub that was operating at the stadium and Jose Mourinho volunteered his time to make the weekly deliveries, that included potatoes, carrots, strawberries and tomatoes.

Our Foundation is continuing to deliver its programmes online where possible, including virtual yoga sessions for those on our cancer rehabilitation programme, virtual seated exercise classes delivered in local elderly care homes, and virtual Kicks sessions for local teenagers. We're also continuing to provide employment advice, up-skilling and personal development activities.

We are continuing to keep our fans engaged, with players past and present making birthday calls to elderly and isolated Season Ticket Holders over the age of 70. Fans have also been involved across our digital channels, with exclusive content and archive footage, interacting via the #SpursAtHome hashtag.

Through our sponsorship of The London Academy of Excellence Tottenham Sixth Form, we're assisting in the production of protective equipment as they use equipment we've funded to produce protective face shields for NHS staff on the front-line of the pandemic at our local hospitals and GP surgeries.

We illuminated the stadium in 'NHS blue' colours alongside other iconic landmarks across the capital and of course we all supported the national campaign encouraging people step outside of their homes and applaud the heroic efforts of NHS staff and other key workers at 8 p.m. every Thursday.

In a world where
you can be anything,
be kind.

// UNKNOWN

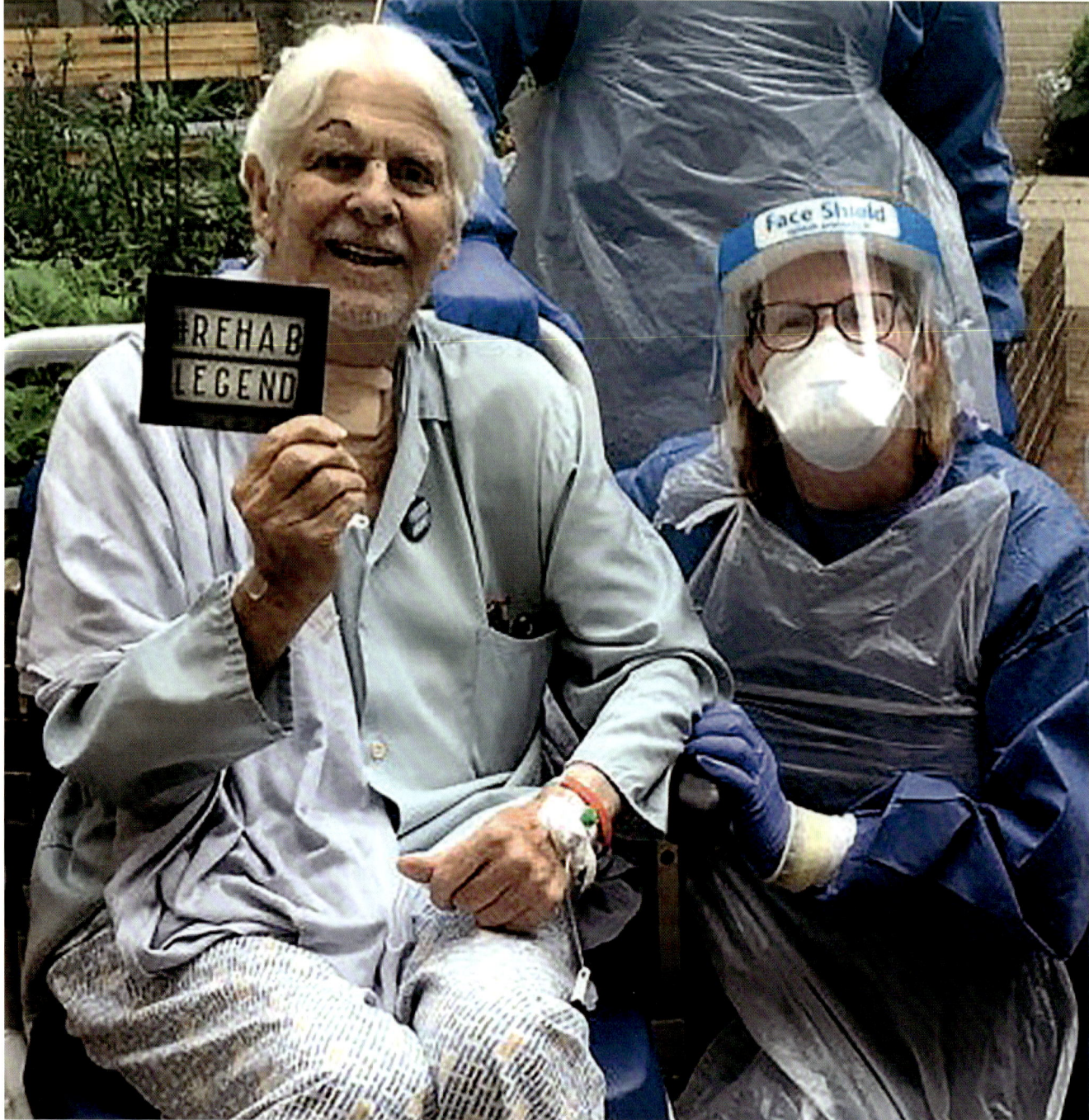

KATE TANTAM BEM
Specialist Sister in Rehabilitation in Critical Care / Plymouth

On a 'normal day', I usually get up at 6.30 a.m., get the kids to school and get to work at about 7.45 a.m. In the mornings, I follow up our ICU patients after ICU discharge, supporting their recovery and planning their rehabilitation goals. Often this means supporting them do normal things like go outside, have a shower, wash their hair, go to the shop.

In the afternoons, I see the patients in ICU, supporting our longer-term patients with their rehab, goal setting and going out into our ICU Rehab Secret Garden. I also work particularly with patients who are delirious.

Since Covid, I have been doing many of the same roles but just in full PPE. We have also had the extra pressure of patient numbers and the challenge of managing the general anxiety of Covid.

I have helped teams with the education of staff, simulation training and procurement of space and equipment as well as supporting them with the care of patients post Covid.

I believe that people who work in health care (irrespective of role) do it for one reason – it's a vocation. They care fundamentally about people and their health. That means that coming to work is something that I do because I love it. I just feel so lucky to work with such amazing patients, loved ones and colleagues.

I feel just so, so proud of the people I get to work with and care for everyday and I get to meet and work with utter #Rehablegends.

My family and my colleagues have been amazing, we have all supported each other so much. The team work, camaraderie, humour, love and care has been phenomenal.

I feel incredibly shocked and overwhelmed to have been on the Honours List. It was a total surprise and I just feel so proud that our work with improving patients experience during Covid and fresh air spaces has been recognised. For me, supporting patients to get outside irrespective of injury or illness is such an important part of their recovery.

> 66
>
> I believe that people who work in health care do it for one reason. They care fundamentally about people and their health.

JUSTIN MOORHOUSE
Comedian / Manchester (and around the world!)

My bread and butter comes from hosting corporate shows and awards – that's the regular work that pays the bills. But at heart, I'm a comedian. I work the Comedy Store around the country or will be on tour all over the world.

Even before Covid struck, one by one all my gigs were cancelled. People were getting the vibe – especially from international sponsors who were a bit ahead of us with the pandemic – that this wasn't going to be great. My last gig was actually just before Lockdown in a cellar venue in Liverpool which was probably the worst place to be, packed in a small, underground space.

I was still really busy for the first few weeks – cancelling things! I was lucky not to be too worried about feeling the effect financially as I was still owed money from jobs I'd already done.

My first worry was actually a loss of identity. Who was I if I wasn't a comedian, performing? I love it so much that even if I didn't do it as a living, I'd do it anyway. It's part of my self-expression, it lifts my mental health and now I couldn't do it. I had a massive loss of adrenalin and a sense of depression.

I did a week of feeling sorry for myself and doing lots of dog walks. I struggled, and still do, with sleeping and anxiety. My daughter and partner were busy with school and work so I had to find something to do – a way to fill my days.

I do one radio show a week and early on, they rang me. I remember thinking, please don't take that away from me too! But they actually wanted to extend my show from 3 to 4 hours to help juggle broadcasting logistics.

And then I started volunteering. I supported my local food bank a day a week. A lot of their usual volunteers are quite elderly and were shielding, so they needed the help. It was great.

But my favourite thing, I joined my local Community Transport Scheme and was giving people lifts to the hospital, picking up prescriptions and taking June for her haircut every Tuesday. I was given a high-vis vest, a badge and a pass to let me go to the front of the queue but more than that, I got to spend time with people.

A big part of being a comedian is listening and collecting stories. Whilst at times it was really raw and I was sometimes dealing with people really struggling with Lockdown or even grieving, it was lovely to be able to listen.

It wasn't always easy. They say about the tears of a clown; being unhappy but putting a face on. At times it was really hard to paint a smile on but I got so much more out of it than I gave. I gave time, which I had plenty of anyway and I got so, so much back.

The world is such a weird place right now. Sometimes I forget that we're in a pandemic. It can feel like we're accepting these changes to the economy and our health as the 'new normal' but I hope this isn't it. I hope it ends.

Getting back to work has been incredible. It's been liberating and it's no exaggeration to say I feel reborn. And every comedian I know, even the most weather-worn and cynical ones, feel the same. We're so grateful to be back doing what we love – performing to an audience.

> At times it was hard to paint a smile on but I gave time and got so much more back.

SIMON DANT
Wastewater Compliance Technician / West Sussex

I work for Southern Water Services who provide freshwater and also treat wastewater for thousands of households and businesses across the south including Kent, East and West Sussex, Hampshire and the Isle of Wight. It's a job that, unless you work in the water industry, you don't give a second thought to what actually happens when you flush your toilet or empty your bath or sink. It's a very interesting job but probably not everyone's choice!

I work on the wastewater side of the business. Despite the fact that I am dealing with the public's waste/excrement etc., the job I do is very interesting and every day is different. In layman's terms, at the end of the day, it's my job to make sure the crude sewage that comes into our wastewater treatment works has gone through several processes of waste removal and is compliant with the Environmental Agency's very strict guidelines before going out to rivers and watercourses as final effluent, and which in turn will not harm wildlife or the environment in any way. General daily routine tasks include checking all site plant is running correctly, unblocking pumps and sewer lines, taking spot samples throughout the sewage removal process and occasionally dealing with the public.

Despite Covid, it's a job that still needs doing! It's only really changed in terms of social distancing but most of the time we work alone anyway looking after our particular sites, unless we have to call on an electrician or fitter to fix some faulty plant. All team meetings and training courses have been cancelled and there's no gatherings of team members in mess rooms, but on the odd occasion where we have to do a two man job, we still keep our distance as best we can and wear appropriate PPE.

So mostly, our days are the same and it's pretty much business as usual. All twelve members in my team are all in and working and we keep in regular contact by phone or messaging. My manager and the company keep us fully up to date on a daily basis on new information and updates. To be honest, I'm glad I'm able to carry on working and doing my bit in these worrying times.

I'd like to think that the general public are grateful to see that we have kept a fresh supply of water running out of their taps and that they've still been able to flush the toilet and drain their sinks and baths. If we stopped doing what we do, things could be a lot worse for everyone environmentally and for their wellbeing. At the end of the day, we are all committed to 'doing the right thing' and hopefully there will be light at the end of the tunnel in the not too distant future. Until then we'll keep going and providing our service.

> We've kept a fresh supply of water running out of taps and they've still been able to flush the toilet — if we stopped doing what we do, things could be worse!

CAPTAIN SIR TOM MOORE
Charity Fundraiser / Bedfordshire

At the height of the Covid-19 pandemic in early April, a ninety-nine-year-old Second World War veteran decided to walk laps of his garden to raise money for the NHS. Despite using a walking frame, as well as recent treatment for cancer and a broken hip, he was determined to hit £1,000 by his 100th birthday at the end of the month, to give something back to the healthcare staff putting their lives on the line for all of us.

After gaining widespread media attention and capturing the hearts of the nation, he ended up raising £38.9 million for NHS Charities.

He broke two Guinness world records for the most money raised by an individual charity walk and became the oldest artist to reach the top spot of BBC Radio 1's Official Chart with his rendition of 'You'll Never Walk Alone', in collaboration with Michael Ball and The NHS Voices of Care Choir. He was also immortalised with a special Royal Mail postmark used on all stamped post during his birthday week.

He was given the honorary title of Colonel on his 100th birthday, becoming Captain Sir Thomas Moore and was given the Freedom of the City of London in the first ceremony to be conducted virtually.

He has since set up The Captain Tom Foundation, fundraising and supporting other causes close to his heart including combating loneliness, supporting people facing bereavement, championing education and equality, and supporting friends overseas.

A modest, decent, and charming man with a can-do attitude, a twinkle in his eye, and an insatiable curiosity and appetite for life, he has become a national treasure and a national hero, but sees himself as anything but. He only wanted to help other people – and yet he has inspired a nation to believe anything is possible by reminding us all it is never, ever too late.

The Captain Tom Foundation

The NHS entered something where they were putting themselves in danger and they did that for the good of the people. They are doing a marvellous, marvellous job.

I never dreamt that this could happen. The overwhelming generosity of people, during a period of darkness, has shown the resilience and caring people are capable of during a time when there was anguish and instability. I remain humbled by the love and gratitude that I have received from the British public and this honour is something that I will truly value for the rest of my life.

But I'm not done yet, not by a long chalk. We have to keep going. After all that we have achieved over the last few months, and with the world still in recovery, it made sense to us to create a legacy. To raise money and push towards our vision of a more hopeful world. So, together with my family, we have created The Captain Tom Foundation. Now we can all stand shoulder to shoulder to make sure "tomorrow will be a good day".

Captain Sir Tom Moore

> 66
>
> Captain Tom's fantastic fundraising inspired the whole country. He provided us with a beacon of light through the fog of Coronavirus. He's a true national treasure.
>
> *Boris Johnson / Prime Minister*

DR CAREY LUNAN MBE
GP / Edinburgh

I'm a GP at the Craigmillar Medical Group in Edinburgh, part of a large team at a very busy general practice, working in one of the most socio-economically deprived areas in Scotland. We are a close team, and are passionate about looking after some of the most vulnerable people in society.

Within a very short space of time, we had to radically change the way that we delivered healthcare – moving from mostly face-to-face appointments to telephone or videolinks to try and minimise footfall into practices and reduce the spread of Covid-19. This took a lot of getting used to, both for the team and for the patients. We also had to change the way that the practice was laid out, with one-way systems, 2 metre distancing in waiting rooms, empty rooms to make cleaning between patients easier, and us all wearing PPE to keep everyone safe.

It felt strange. We all understood it was necessary for infection control, but a big part of being a GP is the relationships that we build up with our patients over time, and it is harder to 'connect' with people over the telephone or video, especially if they are anxious or frightened, or embarrassed.

We had the technical challenges of getting new video software installed, and then getting confident in its use. We also worried about digital exclusion for those that can't access our services because of poverty, sensory problems or having English as a second language (three-way translated appointments over the phone are very challenging!).

We were also all aware that patients weren't always contacting us as they normally would at the start of the pandemic, either because they were frightened about the risk of Covid-19, or were worried about overwhelming the service, or simply didn't know that we were still 'open' so we had to work hard to overcome this and reassure people that we still wanted and needed to hear from them if they had a concern about their health.

Over the last few weeks, workload in the practice has increased, back to normal levels. We have a backlog of work to catch up on, and everything takes longer because of the PPE and the distancing and cleaning. We're all pretty exhausted too!

But there were also some positives. Early on, we recognised the importance of coming together every day, as a team for a 'huddle' and providing a bit of peer support. The need for us to work in different ways also allowed us to be more innovative too. We made a little video tour of the building to help explain how things would feel if patients needed to come in for a face-to-face appointment. One of our mental health nurses also made some Vlogs of simple wellbeing techniques and our patients really appreciated seeing a face, and hearing a voice that they knew, with techniques to help them when they were struggling.

At the start of the pandemic, there was a huge focus on proactively contacting patients with the highest medical needs. Some of these conversations were very humbling and gave us deeper insight into the difficulties people face in their day to day lives, made worse by Covid-19. But we also became aware that some of our patients with the greatest social needs, whom we usually have frequent contact with, had not been in touch. Our care coordinator team set out to contact the people we were most concerned about. Around 80% of the people that we contacted in this way ended up being referred on for extra support.

Knowing that we can help people who are frightened, unwell and vulnerable is a real privilege, and it reminds me of how lucky I am to have my health, and a job that I find so rewarding. Having great colleagues makes all the difference, so even the darkest, hardest days are possible. My husband, who is also a GP, has been an amazing support, and we try to have as much Covid-free time as possible when we are not at work. We have bans on technology, play music and go for stomps on the beach. I am also lucky that John loves to cook and that I love to eat. Win, win.

To be honest, getting the Honours was quite overwhelming and very unexpected! I accepted it on behalf of all GPs and their teams across Scotland. Much of the amazing work that they do is hidden, unrecognised, unreported. I have always been proud to be a GP, but never more so than now.

> I have always been proud to be a GP, but never more so than now.

We stood on our doorsteps and clapped (and banged saucepans and honked horns) every Thursday night at 8 p.m., to show our appreciation for the NHS and key workers ...

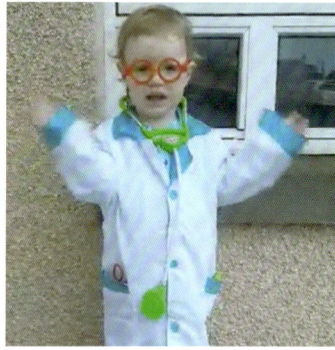

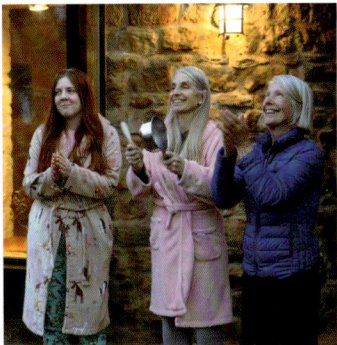

COSTA DRIVE-THRU BLOOD CLINIC

During the pandemic, Costa became home to the UK's first drive-thru blood test clinic to help us reduce the risks whilst we carried out routine blood tests.

We carry out a lot of regular blood tests on a lot of people – for example, those on Warfarin or with diabetes – and we couldn't stop doing this because of Covid. However we were concerned about how to best do this whilst following Lockdown and social distancing rules and wanted to reduce the risks as much as we could at this difficult time.

We were going to set up a gazebo outside the practice as a kind of drive through facility but then our advanced nurse practitioner and partner Tracey Hembrough came up with a genius plan. She said, "why not use an actual drive-thru instead".

So we contacted Charyln, the manager of the Costa Coffee Penzance Drive-Thru – which is the busiest in Cornwall but had closed for the time being – who said she was happy to help and got the full support of her regional manager.

We had a test run when the manager and assistant manager opened up and turned off the alarms before our nursing staff arrived, kitted out in face masks. More than 50 patients drove up, gave their details, stuck out their hand and had their pin prick blood test done. It was a fleeting contact at arm's length that meant we will still able to continue these important tests.

We'll be doing this twice a week, testing patients from our three practices and also rolling it out to other GP surgeries in Penwith.

But it got even more unusual too, with Cornish Pirate's rugby players volunteering as security to manage the queues and ensure driver's didn't turn up for a drive-thru coffee! We had big queues at the St Clare Pharmacy and after waiting an hour, some people have been a bit 'teasey' with staff. Simon, the Pirate's physio, offered to help and some of the players have been marshalling the queues whilst wearing security vests. Everyone queues nicely now!

Dr Matthew Boulter / St Clare Medical Centre

> "
> *Costa helped us set up the UK's first drive-thru blood test clinic so we could continue these important tests.*

After temporarily closing our Costa Coffee Penzance Drive-Thru, we were delighted that it could be used to support the local NHS Trusts in Cornwall, allowing them to use the drive-thru lane as a blood test centre. By using the drive-thru lane, we were able to help make sure social distancing measures were being adhered to, while ensuring patients could continue to receive their regular check-ups.

Costa Coffee

"Kindness is more important than wisdom, and the recognition of this is the beginning of wisdom."

THEODORE ISAAC RUBIN

KIND 20
FEST 20

#KINDFEST2020

A not-for-profit virtual festival, #Kindfest2020 is part of the kindness revolution – a global movement united against the rise of toxic and polarizing tribalism in a growing and supportive global community championing empathy and kindness.

Hosted by Teamkind, it's bringing together some of the world's leading thinkers with inspirational agents of kindness – including Captain Sir Tom Moore – in a worldwide online festival to discuss personal, professional and political kindness.

Offering practical solutions to creating kinder lives, workplaces, and communities, and putting kindness at the core of building back a better and fairer post pandemic world, the Festival is organised into themed tents:

Tent 1 Kinder Lives: Inspiring ideas for how to lead a kinder life; Tent 2 Kindness at Work: An exploration of kindness in leadership and business; Tent 3 Thinking Kindness: All the latest research and thinking on kindness; Tent 4 Kinder Politics: Exploration on bringing people together and de-toxifying political debate; Tent 5 Kinder Youth: Kindness and young people's mental health.

Each tent is curated by an expert in that field with speakers including AC Grayling, Philosopher; Alice Roberts, TV presenter and mentor; Matt Johnson, TV presenter; Prof Paul Gilbert,

Mind Ambassador and founder of The Compassionate Mind Foundation; Dr Radha Modgil, GP, writer and broadcaster and Giles Paley-Phillips and Julia Bradbury from the podcast 'A Little Bit of Positive'.

"The festival will help people discover the latest psychological, health, business management and economic research on kindness. They'll hear about the profound impact it can have on health, wellbeing, diversity and inclusion, creativity, innovation, performance, profits, and growth.

"It is essential to explore new ways of working together right now. We need to spread kindness and support people who are struggling – be they our children, loved ones, colleagues or strangers. Kindfest2020 is a chance to come together, recharge our batteries and stock up our kindness reserves."

Susie Hills / Kindfest Founder and Kinder Lives Curator

> We need to spread kindness and support people who are struggling. KindFest2020 is a chance to stock up on our kindness reserves.

RAJ KOHLI
Borough Commander / Camden & Islington Police

I wanted to be a police officer since I was 4 or 5 years old, influenced by the police box of Dr Who, the police officers of Z Cars and a police uniform my mum bought me! There is also a strong sense of service (Seva) in my religion so serving the public was always something I was going to do, following in the footsteps of two uncles who were officers in the Indian Army.

The beauty of being a police officer means there is no normal day. As a Chief Superintendent, though, it is more like running a business, making sure everything is going to plan and making sure officers and staff feel well supported and well led. I am in charge of 1,000 or so people and 5 police stations and I am responsible for making the lives of the people of Camden and Islington as good as possible. Having just typed that, I now realise what a privileged and responsible role I am in – kind of scary…

Since Covid, I've been working from home more to observe the Lockdown rules. It tends to mean that my day is longer – I usually work 10/11 hours a day anyway but I can sometimes be on my laptop until after midnight. I have been getting more comfortable using conference calls and usually have several video conference calls a day – not easy when I have two noisy and playful Labradors knocking around the house. As a people person, I really miss being in the same room as my colleagues though.

Crime has gone down although drug dealers seem to think they are key workers undergoing essential journeys! Managing Lockdown regulations is hard because we do understand and sympathise with the situation we all find ourselves in. It is much easier to police crimes like burglary, robbery etc. because the public rightly expect us to do so, but some of the same public find it difficult when police advise them about the regulations.

But there's also been lots of good too – organisations like the Queen's Crescent Community Association serving free food to the local community, to soup kitchens for the homeless and the 79-year-old woman who sent me a cheque for £50 asking me to buy some things for the officers – the list goes on and makes me very proud of how all our communities have knitted together.

My son Arjun (also a police officer) and I had captured the first photo of us together whilst operationally on duty at the same time. Knowing that we were both on duty at the same time, keeping the people of London safe alongside all my other colleagues and other key workers made me very proud. I shared the photo on social media and got overwhelming messages of support, likes and retweets. It almost went viral … well, not really but it was shared a lot and the messages I got from complete strangers really landed with me.

I am really proud - proud of what my colleagues do every day and even more so coming into work during these uncertain times and delivering high level policing every day is simply amazing. They are ordinary people doing extraordinary things, they are heroes without capes, they are the ones running towards things as others run away.

> Despite Covid, we are catching the people doing the bad things and protecting the people doing the good things.

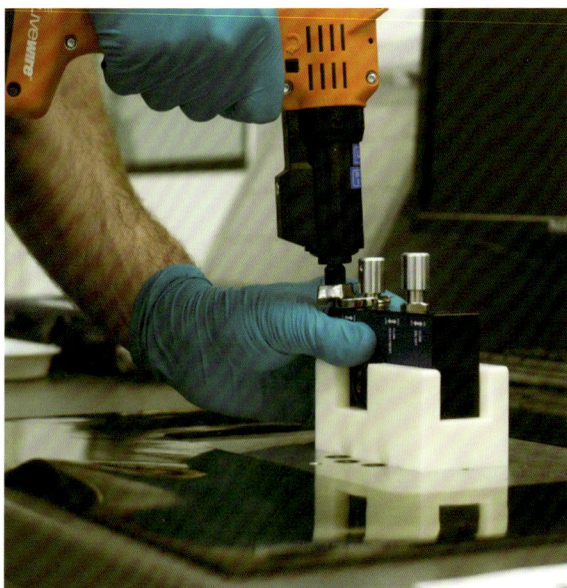

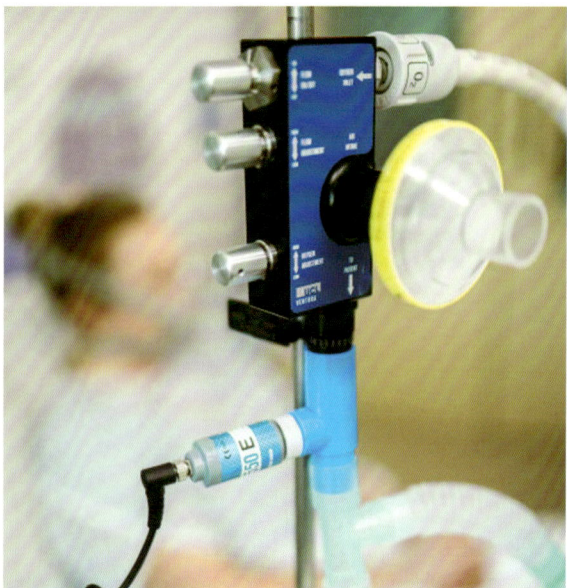

PROJECT PITLANE

Galvanised by the British Government's call for ventilators, F1's response, requiring teams to dismiss both secrecy and enmity, might have seemed unlikely. Yet just two days after the Australian Grand Prix was cancelled in March, the chief technology officer of Innovate UK – a publicly funded agency promoting research and development – called our chief technical officer to discuss how the sport might adapt to meet the needs of the NHS.

Three days later, a virtual meeting with the seven teams based in the UK (Aston Martin Red Bull Racing, BWT Racing Point F1 Team, Haas F1 Team, McLaren F1 Team, Mercedes-AMG Petronas F1 Team, Renault DP World F1 Team, ROKiT Williams Racing) was held and 'Project Pitlane', a collective effort to manufacture and deliver respiratory devices to support the national need, was put in motion.

The project aimed to pool the resources and capabilities of its member teams to greatest effect. F1's strengths are pace, teamwork and the ability to rapidly design and manufacture prototypes and complex systems in tight timelines. We are also very good at competitive analysis, looking at a complex system, understanding how to reverse-engineer it and make it.

Daily virtual meetings began to harness these skills at every UK-based team, co-ordinating with clinicians – with feedback on the effects of Covid-19 providing a constant reminder of how important the work was.

It has been remarkably effective. Within ten days the continuous positive airway pressure device (CPAP) had been reverse-engineered, designed, tested and approved. A month later, 10,000 of them had been built and shipped.

The Mercedes AMG High Performance Powertrains technology centre in Brixworth – the facility where the F1 team's highly successful power units are developed and built – was building 1,000 devices per day. The 40 machines that would normally produce F1 pistons and turbochargers were being used for production of the CPAP devices, and the entire Brixworth facility was repurposed to meet this demand.

The team also made the designs required to make the device available for manufacturers to download, in the hope that making this information widely available may help the global response to the crisis by enabling healthcare systems around the world to provide respiratory support for patients with the virus.

When it mattered, our sport delivered a triumph of camaraderie over competitive instinct and the seven teams remain ready to support in other areas requiring rapid, innovative technology responses to the unique challenges posed by the Covid-19 pandemic.

> *There was absolutely no competition, it was pure collaboration. And now we have staff members more proud of the fact they've made something that's helping Covid patients than they are of winning races.*
>
> **Andy Cowell / Managing Director, Mercedes AMG High Performance Powertrains**

"We brought highly competitive teams used to fighting each other day-in, day-out together, but there were no egos. There was no them and us. It was a truly collective effort and while rivalries will begin anew and the politicking continues, for now Project Pitlane should be lauded as the time F1 put it all aside and did the right thing. It was fantastic to see."

Mark Gillian / Innovate UK

SAM GALLAGHER BEM
Nursing Home Manager / West Suffolk

I'm the Home Manager at Brandon Park Nursing Home. I'm responsible for 65 staff and the day-to-day running of the home but I'm also a registered nurse so have a big involvement clinically as well. We care for residents with quite complex medical needs and have developed a really good reputation for our dementia care. Obviously we also manage end of life too – most of our residents don't go home.

We spent January trying to pre-empt what might happen and make plans but there's no way we could really have known the extent of just what was coming.

When we went into Lockdown at the start of April, we literally went into Lockdown. I'd had a bag packed ready and when I heard on the Sunday that we had two residents who were very ill, I picked it up and off I went. The whole team was amazing. They couldn't see family either as they had to isolate in order to able to come into work. We've got some residents who have been here for a long time and we wanted to look after them.

Residents had to isolate in their rooms so they weren't seeing loved ones or each other. We had to stop all family visits which was just awful. We did have people coming to see their loved ones through the windows, which was lovely but also really sad.

From a nursing point of view, we had to do more as we've had no GPs in here since April. They've been amazing over Zoom and have done everything they can remotely to help avoid us having to take residents to hospital. We've had to triage people for them and we've had to administer more medications.

In amongst all this, since July, we've had builders working on an extension to a separate dementia care unit to help us continue to expand our service. We had no gas for 2 days, someone got stuck in the lift and then my key snapped in the door – so we've been dealing with the normal day to day issues too.

We were really well supported from behind the scenes. The wider team had been preparing for this since January so the logistics were all in hand and we had all the PPE we needed. We had a volunteer driver who got us anything else we needed and we also had so many gifts. A farmer would drop this off for us, families would drop that off, my mum baked cakes. It really lifted us all.

The messages were changing every day which made things really hard and made you wonder "what if I'd done this earlier, or that later, or just gone with my own judgement". It was worse when we were then portrayed in a bad light by some. We'd worked so hard so that wasn't a nice thing at all.

Losing residents to Covid was horrendous. Normally we've got time; time to prepare ourselves and the families and time for the bereavement process. But people were getting so sick, so quickly and then we couldn't even say goodbye like we usually would.

I did make the decision to let one family member sit with each resident at end of life, just for half an hour and with full PPE precautions. I felt the benefit outweighed the well-managed risk and it made such a difference to them both.

We couldn't attend the funerals so we'd have a little gathering outside as they left instead and our housekeeper, who's in the Salvation Army band, would play them off. We've lost some real characters and the void is still there – they were our family. We tried to commemorate everyone by making a display with a butterfly on it for every resident we lost.

What made it worth it? Our residents. They agreed with what we'd done and understood. They'd seen the news and knew that we were doing our best to keep them safe. And the clapping on a Thursday. When I opened the door and we all heard that – just wow. It also helped to remember to be grateful; that others were going through worse.

I'm flattered about the Honours but it's not why I did it. I did it because I'm a nurse and a person. But it's boosted the whole home and it's for all of them. We've also been shortlisted for our teamwork in the Great British Care Awards and the National Care Awards which is amazing.

> We wanted to look after them.
> I did it because I'm a nurse
> and a person.

Kindness is the thread that knits each of us together to make a strong fabric of society.

// DR RADHA MODGIL

LIZ MCLEAN BEM
Co-op Store Manager / Isle of Arran

I'm the store manager at Brodick and Invercloy Co-ops – AKA Big Co and Wee Co! Every normal day's the same – just a different kind of chaotic! It begins around 4.30 a.m. making sure the orders are right, taking into consideration boat and weather disruptions, answering queries, organising and reorganising the team, attending meetings … the list is endless.

The job changed dramatically with Covid. Our long hours became even longer; our 'pick, pack and deliver' service jumped from 30 to 450 per week; and demand for special deliveries from people on the mainland increased when they couldn't come and see their loved ones.

We had to fight our corner to maintain supply as panic buying set in on the mainland. Our Regional Manager was brilliant in helping source stock as we are a lifeline service on the island and we knew we had to pull out all the stops to get it right. Special thanks goes to Colin McCort, the Port Manager, who still managed to get our artic lorries on the boat in all weathers even when the service dropped to one boat a day. He only slightly raised his eyebrows when he had to fit 4 lorries on one weekend!

The other big change was in our cleaning and social distancing routines. We were greatly supported by other local businesses who supplied gloves, masks, hand gel and cleaning materials.

The island relies heavily on tourism, so many businesses were badly affected during the initial Lockdown. We were able to help out by offering furloughed staff a job with us. Taxi drivers became our home delivery drivers and hospitality workers became our pickers and packers. We even came up with the saying, "You Can't Get Quicker Than A Co-op Pick Pack Picker."

> We are a lifeline service on the Island and we knew we had to pull out all the stops.

A lot of the islanders became worried and frightened during Covid so we kept the banter flowing with our customers by phone calls, texts and emails. We've got quite an ageing population, so I even had to teach some customers in their 90s how to use email!

We supplied the homes with flowers and kept the medical services fed and watered. They were given sun loungers, benches and other equipment that they could use when they could sneak out for 5 minutes. A lot of this was bought with money donated by our grateful customers.

We also wanted to keep morale up on the island so I did a weekly update on social media which ended with the phrase 'Keep Safe, Keep Smiling, We're All In This Together, Go Team Arran'. We printed this on mugs which were sold to raise money to help those in need on the Island.

We did the clap for the NHS every Thursday, and enhanced it with our home delivery vans hooting their horns. We even had local pipers joining in! We also came up with new words to Dolly Parton's '9 to 5' – which included working from '5 to 9' – and the video of our performance was shared on YouTube.

I love what I do and we have been so pleased to be able to continually help people in need, working closely with the Food Bank and Social Services – so much so that the retail side of that we do has become almost secondary.

The morale of the staff was given an even bigger boost when we won the Co-op 'Team of the Year' meaning we were the best in the whole of Britain. We were all given a hamper but used these to give goodies to well-deserving individuals nominated by the community. The feel good factor was passed on when some of these were then donated on again, to the local Foodbank.

Carol, my Team Manager, and I are very lucky to have accepting hubbies who totally get it when we spend so much time at work. Being awarded the BEM is great for me, my colleagues and the whole island. And from a family point of view, I'm keeping up the family tradition as my Dad danced with the Queen when he was a soldier at Ballater and his brother and sister both got MBEs for the great work they have done. When I was asked by our CEO how I was going to celebrate, I said I was going to "have a wee swally in the hoose because oor Nicola had closed all the pubs!"

AARON LEVENTHAL
First Officer and HGV Driver / Midlands

I was a First Officer for Flybe, based in Birmingham and flying all over Europe.

My child hood dream was to fly, so I joined Aircadets at the age of 13. I funded all my own training with savings, loans and remortgaging and I finally achieved my role with Flybe in February 2019.

A usual day in the life of a pilot starts in the briefing room where all the crew meet to discuss the day ahead, such as safety, emergencies and flight planning. We would then walk out as crew to the aircraft to prepare for our passengers, then I would carry out the first officer duties and preflight check stage. The captain usually flies the first sector and I would fly back.

On the 5th March, Flybe collapsed leaving 2,500 employees redundant overnight. I will always be very grateful that I worked with Flybe – it was a privilege to work along side so many amazing people. It was really like a family. We all named it our 'Flybe family'.

It was impossible to be re-employed with other airlines as the entire aviation industry has been hugely affected. It had taken over 10 years to save up to achieve my dream and I was devastated to say the least. After the initial shock and going through all the emotions, I realised I had to take control of the situation, be proactive and devise a plan.

I am looking forward to the next chapter, whenever aviation kick starts again, but in the meantime I've put myself out there to do my share in helping our nation.

I feel very lucky to have a HGV licence that I could use to help assist in this pandemic, so I started working night shifts for an agency. We cover all the Tesco deliveries to the south of the UK on the articulated lorries. It's 12-hour shifts and I'll deliver to two or three stores on each shift.

Although all the real heroes are in our NHS and the care workers on the front line, I feel privileged to be out there as a key worker delivering the essentials and helping the nation by keeping those shelves stocked up at the stores.

The thousands of comments I have received from LinkedIn have been really lovely. I seem to have been a huge inspiration and influential to thousands of people asking me for my advice and direction in life skills. This makes me feel amazing, that I have made a difference.

I put the post up originally to show the world resilience. When you get knocked down, there is always hope and strength to get back up and fight no matter what. Just be flexible and adapt, learn a new skill and use it to help others.

> 66
>
> It had taken 10 years to achieve my dream and I was devastated, but I feel privileged to be out there as a key worker helping to keep the shelves stocked up.

4X4 RESPONSE (WALES)

4x4 Response is a UK based charity whose volunteers offer the use of their 4x4 vehicles to provide logistic support in adverse conditions, working with other Voluntary Organisations and the blue-light emergency services. All responders are required to carry out enhanced DBS checks, vehicle safety inspections and document checks as well as responder and advanced responder training including many elements such as first on scene, risk assessments, navigation and off road driving, to name a few.

I joined 4x4 as a First Responder and have worked in groups all around the country. I'm now Group Co-ordinator for South Wales, which I do alongside my day job as a Senior NCO in the RAF. I have a great team of local responders, from a retired HGV driver to a Sales & Marketing Director!

In Wales, we provide support to the Emergency Planning Officers, The Emergency Services, and other organisations when 4x4 vehicles are needed to get people, equipment, and supplies to locations in times of bad weather, poor access, or other emergency conditions where it is necessary to use access routes that a normal vehicle cannot cope with.

We initially deployed at the beginning of March to assist local community groups and local authorities with Covid-related issues. Our group was the first 4x4 Response group in the UK to take on Covid-19 tasks and, as a result, the majority of other regions have followed suit.

There was some trepidation at the initial request for our group to assist with Covid-related tasks. It was a leap into the unknown but it wasn't scary. We were well organised with clear and realistic tasks. It just felt great being able to help. We're able to help and it's important that those who can, do.

We've been there to help every day for the last 5 months, answering the phone 24 hours a day. We've covered over 17,000 miles, delivering food, prescriptions and PPE to isolated and vulnerable individuals in the area as well as all sorts of other things, from moving caravans to taking a cat to the vets!

It was weird driving around with the roads so quiet. It was almost deserted with populated areas like ghost towns in apocalyptic movies. We also had to get used to delivering our service in line with new rules, regulations and PPE.

The response from people has been so overwhelmingly positive, with a mixture of gratitude, relief, joy, and peace of mind that there was support at hand. You could see real relief on the face of many, especially the older people.

There's often surprise that there are volunteers like us, willing to help. Some people thought they had to pay us and we had one resident who, when we approached his house with a delivery of medication, shouted "Oi you, whatever you're selling we don't need it so sod off!".

The people who lived alone were so pleased to have some direct contact, and a chat at a safe distance often lifted their spirits. To listen to their concerns, fears, hopes and to reassure them was all part of the service we gave. If we could also put them in touch with various support organisations, all the better.

On one occasion a lovely elderly lady living alone broke down crying uncontrollably, saying over and over "you've saved my life", when all we were doing was quite simply handing over a bag of medicine supplies. That demonstrated the depth of despair, isolation and fear that many vulnerable people felt.

Did our response team make a difference to some peoples lives? I'd like to think we did.

James Ward / South Wales Group Co-ordinator

> *We're able to help and it's important that those who can, do.*

www.4x4response.info

KENDAL BRADLEY & BABY NELL
'Lockdown Baby' / Oldham

My partner Dan and I have been together for almost 10 years and we had our first baby girl, Nell, on 31st March 2020 at 6.56 p.m. She was 11 days overdue and weighed a healthy 7lb 7oz. She was delivered at the Royal Oldham Hospital which was planned, in the birth centre which is where I had hoped to birth in the water.

Covid-19 meant I was only allowed one birthing partner which was Dan but I would have liked the option for my mum to be there at the birth too. The hospital was a scary place – we got locked on the ward after Nell was born due to Corona patients being moved into isolation wards. We left hospital as soon as we could and were home by 4 a.m. the following morning.

Given the circumstances, my labour was actually really relaxed and went pretty much to plan. I was only in active labour for 6 hours and 45 minutes and my midwife Alison was amazing! She helped me so much without me even realising at the time. It was only looking back that Dan said how she managed to make the situation calm and help me progress without me actually realising.

The down side to bringing a baby into the world during Covid is the fact that my family cannot meet their first grandchild, great grandchild or niece. The first two weeks have been hard due to only having each other as support. We would kill for family to be able to come round and sit with Nell to get a bond with her and to help us out a little ... even if it's just washing up!!

Together, we have worked as a team and managed to settle Nell into our new home. She is currently feeding better and sleeping more. She is perfect and we wouldn't change her for the world!

Even though is it hard to not see family or friends and show her off to the world, it is for the best to keep her safe at home until these scary times have passed. It will certainly be a story to tell her when she's older but right now she's oblivious and happy with her mummy and daddy. The joy she has brought to the family through these difficult times is worth everything.

> My family haven't been able to meet their first grandchild, great grandchild or niece but even though it's hard not to see family or friends, it's for the best to keep her safe at home until these scary times have passed.

THE MARSH FAMILY
Ben, Danielle, Alfie, Thomas, Ella & Tess / Kent

I'm a senior lecturer in History at the University of Kent and my wife Danielle is a postgraduate administrator there. Covid meant I had a research fellowship and a book launch in the USA cancelled and we've both been having to work from home whilst home schooling our children.

We've always made songs and funny films with the kids as a way of sharing our lives and some fun with our families, who live some distance away, especially grandparents. We did a parody of a song from Tangled for Mother's Day that, because we'd already pulled the kids from school a week ahead of the government policy, covered the theme of Lockdown before Lockdown even happened.

Then we did 'One Day More' from Les Misérables. We worked on the lyrics together to cover some of the day-to-day changes we've all been seeing in the world: bathroom sharing, homeschooling, difficulties Skyping with Grandma, and waiting for a vaccine. To celebrate lots of birthdays we knew we'd miss, we allowed this one to be shared beyond our usual circles.

And it went viral. Very viral! Our own Facebook feed had 8 million+ views in just 48 hours. But millions more were looking at the song where it had been shared by others on different platforms including media, newspaper, YouTube versions and even celebrities' Instagram pages.

At first we were very excited and overwhelmed, and at times a bit daunted with the response that came our way, for which we were totally unprepared. Some of it was a bit stressful: international copyright permissions, liaising with news agencies, threats and opportunities right, left and centre, and running it all with no training from our own living room.

Two things kept us going though: firstly the nature of the reaction we received, including amazing messages of support and thanks from all over the world that we truly cherished; secondly the support we had from our friends and local community who rallied to give us advice, lend us internet cables and wifi hotspots and left whisky on the doorstep for me!

We are very grateful for all the positive responses we've had and that we've reached so many people who are, like us, separated from friends and family at the moment. We didn't expect any of this to happen but it's just been absolutely lovely to see the positivity and people saying this has brought a smile at a moment when it's difficult to smile.

> 66
>
> I have no football match today, how can I play when we are parted? Our grandparents are miles away, they can't work Skype, we're broken hearted.

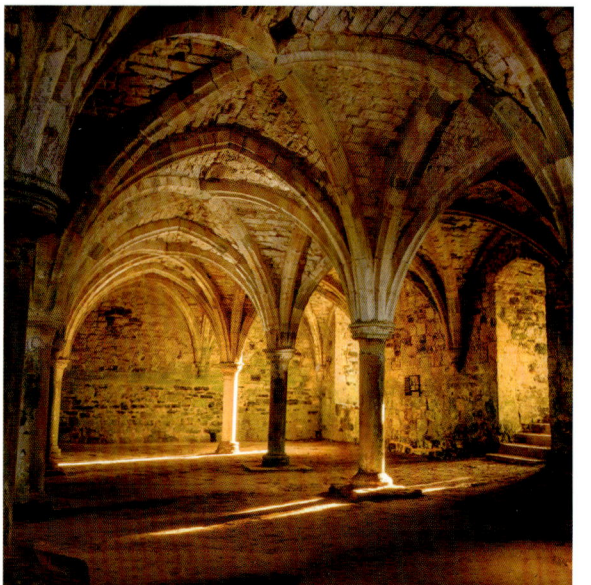

ENGLISH HERITAGE

English Heritage is a charity that cares for over 400 historic monuments, buildings and places – from the world famous prehistoric site that is Stonehenge and medieval castles such as Tintagel, to grand houses like Audley End, the Roman forts on the edge of empire at Hadrian's Wall; and even a cold war bunker. Through these properties and more, we to help bring the story of England to life for over 10 million people each year.

I'm based at Wrest Park in Bedfordshire and have responsibility for the 13 sites in my region, so a normal day is either in the office or travelling around these beautiful properties to support the site managers and ensure the best visitor experience.

In early March, we were focused on final preparations ready for 1st April, when all of our properties reopen fully after the winter. But then day-on-day the situation unfolded until we realised that we wouldn't actually be opening as usual. Around the middle of March we took the decision that we would close all sites to the public completely.

> It felt quite numb – we couldn't believe it was happening. Our sites should be full of people enjoying themselves.

Seeing the sites empty was so emotive – they should be full of people enjoying themselves. The site teams were working away as usual so our houses were immaculate and our gardens and orchards were coming into full bloom. It was all looking beautiful but there was no one there (except us!) to see it. Even travelling to the sites was surreal – the roads were almost completely empty. It all felt quite numb; we couldn't believe it was happening.

But it wasn't long before there was also a level of excitement, as we worked towards reopening. Things like PPE, Covid specific signage and an online ticketing system to support timed visits all had to be sorted out – and quite quickly. I remember walking down to the pond to go tadpole fishing with my children, with my phone tucked under my ear talking about new signs to help inform our visitors.

We felt lucky to still be working but of course, like for so many, there were pressure points. We were all juggling home schooling, home working and general anxiety about the pandemic. But the team spirit was incredible and we built a really special bond. I think it's also encouraged people to think about how we can be kinder in our connections and how we work together.

On the day we reopened the big 'eagle gates' at Wrest Park, it was so lovely to see the public flock back in. It was just wonderful to welcome families and regular visitors back and to give them the space to enjoy getting outdoors and spend time together. Our visitors, staff and volunteers have responded brilliantly to the 'new normal' so it feels very safe on site whilst still being an amazing visitor experience and we've found so many more people are taking the time to write in and say "thank you", which is really appreciated by our teams.

Emma Fernandes-Lopes / Head of Historic Properties (East)

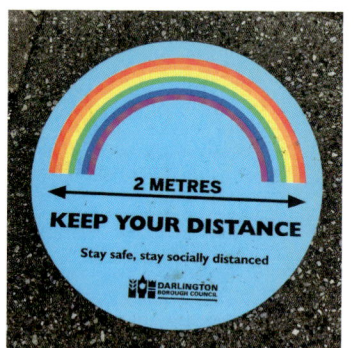

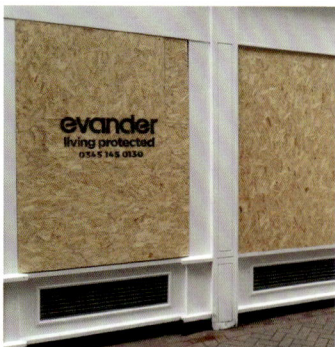

Coronavirus
This Cemetery is Closed Funeral and Cremation Acces Only Due to Government Advice

GREGGS

Please wait here until the person in front has moved forward.

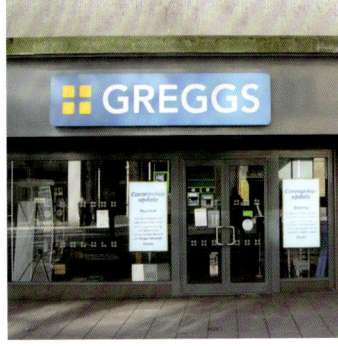

Shops and businesses closed and, although supermarkets stayed open, we queued to get in to them, had to keep our distance and shelves were stripped bare – you couldn't buy loo rolls or flour anywhere!

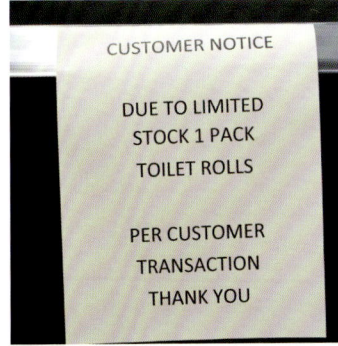

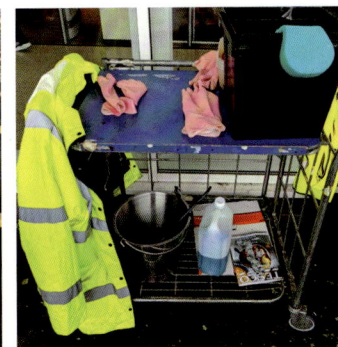

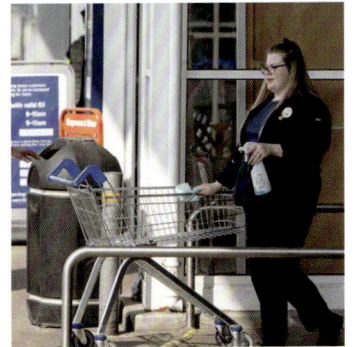

Iceland

health & beauty

CUSTOMER NOTICE

DUE TO LIMITED STOCK 1 PACK TOILET ROLLS

PER CUSTOMER TRANSACTION THANK YOU

Argos

THE BOATHOUSE

Please follow the one-way system.

2m

Area Closed
To support social distancing this area is now closed until further notice

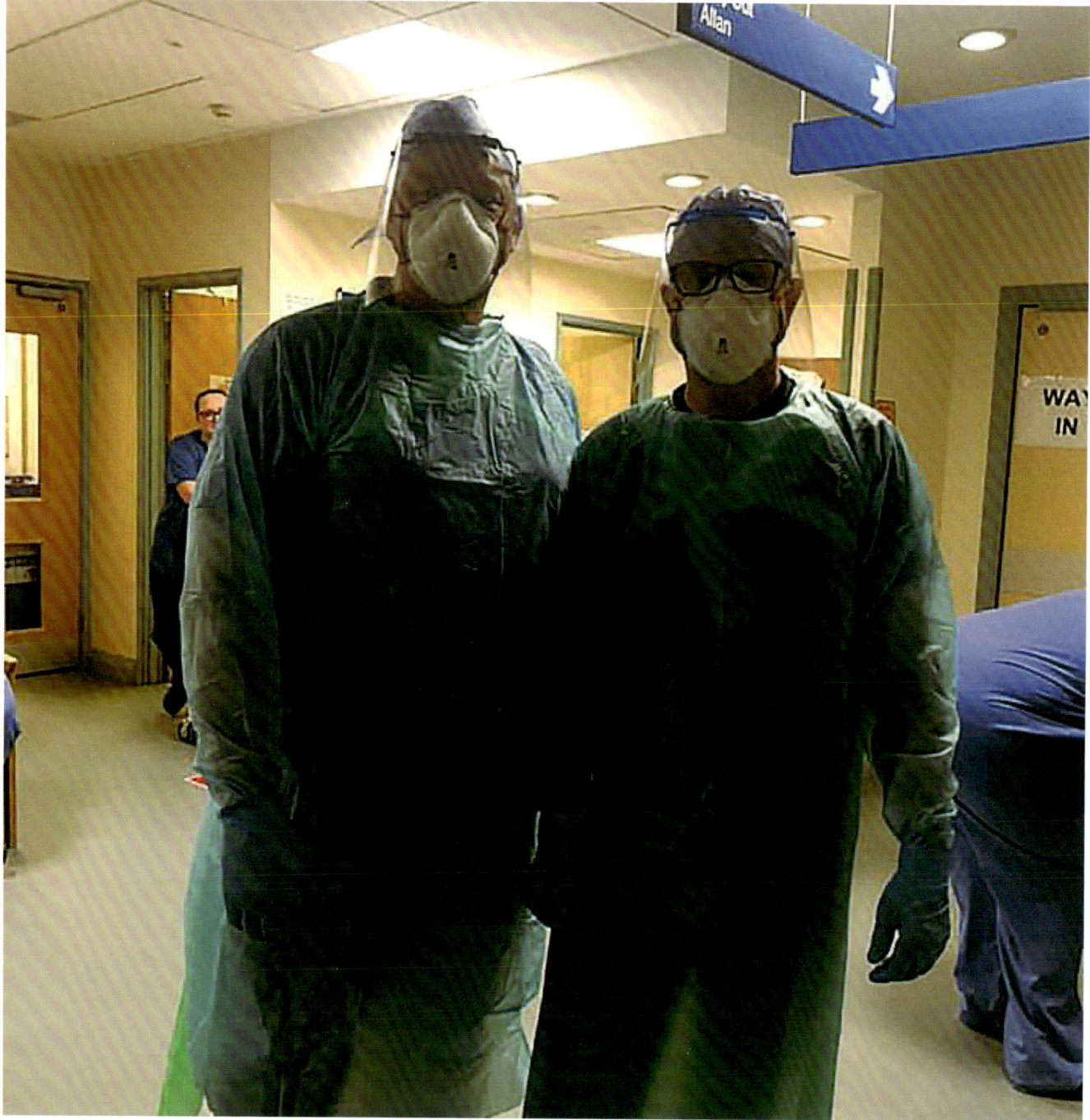

ANDREW PETTEY
Bank Nurse / Bridgend

I'm a Case Manager for HMCL Rehabilitation Services, usually working from home with fairly regular Monday-Friday hours. But I'm also a registered nurse of 26 years and have worked in ITU and Critical Care and I felt drawn to help out in the crisis. I am a man of faith and as a Christian, I felt I couldn't not do something.

I talked to my employer who was very understanding and allowed me to leave to go and help the NHS – my job is currently on hold until the crisis is over. I have a contact on the ITU at my local hospital and she made it possible for me to attend training to be upskilled ready to work on the unit.

So, I'm now working as a Bank Nurse at my local NHS trust, offering my time to work whatever the ITU requires with 12-hour shifts any time of the week, day or night. I want to be an asset to the unit and help those who are scared and fearful as I'm a positive person who doesn't feel fear from what is happening because my faith gives me a great peace and love for those around me.

I'm lucky to have a great family and support network around me as well as an allotment that helps me to switch off and unwind.

> " This is what God called me to do – I would feel ashamed if I didn't help when I know I can.

PENDLE EDUCATION TRUST

The Duke and Duchess of Cambridge spoke to children and staff from Pendle Education Trust's five academies via a video call. The call from the Duke and Duchess took place during what are traditionally the Easter holidays but this year, due to Covid-19, schools across the country have remained open for the children of key workers and vulnerable children.

Children from across the Trust had been taking part in Easter crafting activities during the holiday period and during the call showed The Duke and Duchess what they had made. Several children also showed The Duke and Duchess portraits of their key worker parents and explained why they were proud of them. Children from the Trust's academies have parents working in a variety of key worker roles, including in the NHS, the social care sector, the food manufacturing industry and in supermarkets.

In addition to showing the Duke and Duchess their Easter crafts and paintings of their family members, 9-year-old Lloyd from Casterton Primary Academy virtually presented the Duchess with an origami bunch of flowers he had made whilst 10-year-old Harris, from Castercliff Primary Academy, invited the Duke and Duchess to visit in person when the Lockdown restrictions have been lifted.

Sisters Ruby and Isobella Milligan, who attend West Craven High School, showed the Duke and Duchess a PowerPoint they had created about the Royal couple. Alicia Riding, from Colne Primet Academy, has been learning about William the Conqueror in her History lessons and asked the Duke what name he would like to be remembered by.

On the call, The Duke and Duchess also heard about the difficulties that schools, staff and children are currently facing. They also heard about the measures that Pendle Education Trust is taking to help pupils and their families, including food deliveries and mental health provision.

"It was a fantastic opportunity for our children and staff to speak to the Duke and Duchess, and share with them some of their experiences of school life over the past few weeks.

"The children really enjoyed showing off their artwork, discussing how they are looking forward to Easter and coming up with some questions to ask – they covered everything from football teams to David Attenborough!

"We're incredibly proud of how our children, and all of our staff, are dealing with the extraordinary situation we are in at the minute, and it was great that we were able to share some of the positive ways that we are helping our families with the Duke and Duchess".

Anita Ghidotti / Pendle Education Trust Chief Executive

66

Well done honestly to you and everyone who's in during this time. It must be such a relief for all the parents who are key workers to know that the normality is there for their children — they've got the structure and they've got a safe place for them to be, so really, really well done to all of you.

The Duchess of Cambridge

GYLES BRANDRETH

Writer, broadcaster, actor, Chancellor of the University of Chester and a regular on Celebrity Gogglebox, QI and Have I Got News For You

If, like me, you are over seventy, it seems that any day now you are going to be asked to 'self-isolate' for twelve weeks. It may be longer than that, of course. At this stage, nobody quite knows. Best be prepared for the long haul. What on earth are we going to do? There are only so many episodes of Frasier and Murder She Wrote that you can watch in a week.

Well, I'm not going to waste time and energy arguing about whether mandatory oldie self-isolation is the right thing to do (let's face it: nobody really knows). I'm going to use it as a unique opportunity to do all sorts of exciting and challenging things, many of which I've been meaning to do for years but somehow haven't ever found the time (or incentive) to get around to.

I'm going to start by learning a poem a week. It shouldn't be too difficult. Even an old codger like me should be able to learn two lines a day. Learn just two lines a day and in a week you can learn a complete sonnet. And with four whole months of self-isolation, you could probably manage 'The Rime of the Ancient Mariner'.

Successfully learning a poem by heart is deeply satisfying. You'll emerge from your splendid isolation with a whole repertoire of party pieces – inspiring or amusing according to taste. Poetry can make you laugh and cry. Poetry can make you think and feel. Poetry can teach you, and sustain you, and surprise you. Learning poetry by heart can, literally, transform you. And now, thanks to Coronavirus and the imminent government self-isolation edict, you have a wonderful opportunity to master a poem, or two. Or 22.

Then there was the question of how to remind people to wash their hands thoroughly and how to time that perfect twenty-second hand-wash. A couple of weeks back, the Health Secretary's first suggestion proved controversial. Matt Hancock recommended singing the National Anthem while washing your hands. Predictably, republicans objected. More surprisingly, old-school monarchists said the idea was an affront to the dignity of the Crown. Hancock's next suggestion was to get your timing right by singing 'Happy Birthday'. Twice.

At this point, the government's PR people got involved and came to me and the great Dame Judi Dench. They knew I was a poetry lover and a propagandist for the benefits of learning poetry by heart. They reckoned that Dame Judi was not only a national treasure, but also the nation's most noted Shakespearean actress.

I thought a limerick might be fun but even a full-length limerick only lasts ten seconds. Judi favoured a sonnet – either by Shakespeare or Elizabeth Browning – but you can't get through a fourteen-line sonnet in less than forty seconds.

In the end, we chose to time our twenty seconds by reciting the first verse of one of our favourite poems: 'The Owl and the Pussy-cat' by Edward Lear. We made our video in Dame Judi's kitchen and we posted it on Twitter and Instagram.

That gave me the idea to keep doing a poem a day once Lockdown started. I discovered I still had all these fabulous jumpers from the 1970s and 80s that hadn't been worn for years – and so began 'Another day, Another Jumper and Another Poem' which I posted daily on social media.

One poem that I particularly love is this one by Emily Dickinson, which I did whilst wearing my University of Chester Chancellor's jumper and dedicated to the nursing students who were volunteering to help.

> 66
>
> If I can stop one heart from breaking,
> I shall not live in vain;
> If I can ease one life the aching,
> Or cool one pain,
> Or help one fainting robin
> Unto his nest again,
> I shall not live in vain.
>
> // Emily Dickinson

ALISON MOSELEY
Retired Practice Nurse / Derbyshire

For 12 years I've been living the life of a retired person, with travel, family, friends and occasional voluntary work. When Boris Johnson announced that the UK would be 'locked down' to help combat Covid-19 virus spreading uncontrollably, I wanted to be of use somewhere for the duration of Lockdown.

Retired nurses were being asked to return to practice but I was way beyond the maximum of 3 years required since retirement, so this wasn't an option. The next best thing I thought I could offer was to work as a care assistant. I applied one day, had an interview the next and then started at the beginning of Lockdown on the 24 March, in a brand new carers uniform.

I knew that going back into any work environment would a challenge after 12 years. Although I had been in a caring profession, the relationship between working in a doctor's surgery and providing the intimate care required in a care home setting was very different. The staff I worked alongside were very patient with me, but the first few shifts still seemed to pass in a blur as I tried to get to grips with the practices and routines.

By the time I started my employment, there was already a total ban on relatives and friends visiting the home. This was also extended to services such as chiropody and therapeutic treatments, GPs and entertainment. I soon saw the difficulties this was causing the staff. On the one hand, residents found it hard to accept (or understand) that they could not have their loved ones visit and on the other, staff are reliant on visitors and outside services to compliment their work.

Another noticeable disparity for me was the contrast of being at work and away from it. In the care home there was a necessary intimate closeness between residents and staff, normal behaviour, but once away from the home, deserted streets and people actively avoiding one another was the norm.

It was about the second week of May that our Covid-free environment was compromised. There had been a number of positive cases identified amongst the residents. At that time I was in the middle of a few days off so I had a message sent updating me with this news and it felt rather strange that I would be entering into a known area with the virus. But then I thought now was the time that I may be of some real benefit to the residents and staff that I worked alongside. As with relatives, there was to be no agency staff to cover permanent staff absence when they became ill.

We were given guidance on new ways of working, keeping residents apart, closing the dining room and following the guidelines regarding personal protective equipment for care home staff. In reality the only extra equipment was a face mask, as we already wore a plastic apron and gloves when carrying out intimate care. The staff, nurses, carers, domestics and cooks took all this on with great determination and love, to do the best for the people they cared for.

As the weeks passed, most staff tested positive for the virus at some time and more residents became ill. This was a particularly low point; sick residents as well as staff off resulted in more care required with less staff to carry it out. The human cost was devastating with a third of residents dying from the virus. Mercifully, most of the sick appeared to fade away rather than display the 'classic' distressing Covid-19 symptoms.

The sad story of the virus rampaging through the care home was lessened by the fortitude and professionalism shown by the staff. I could feel slightly detached, only knowing the residents for a short time, but some of them had been cared for in the home for years by the dedicated staff. For them this was a family.

As I was leaving employment there, there were new residents being accepted and a huge amount of optimism and hope for the future running through the care home. People have asked me if I enjoyed my experience – it couldn't be enjoyable because some of it was harrowing, but I did get a great satisfaction from being with such resilient, caring and resourceful people for those four months.

> "
> I'd been retired for 12 years but felt I'd like to be of use somewhere for the duration of lockdown.

"All right," said the Gruffalo, bursting with laughter.
"You go ahead and I'll follow two metres after."

"Give me your soap and your loo rolls
And everything else on the shelf,
For I am the Rat of the Highway
And I'm taking them all for myself."

Stick Man and Lady stay home in their tree,
But they're still keeping fit with their Stick Children three.

You'd better be safe, you'd better be smart.
Stay on the broom, but stay well apart.

THE GRUFFALO & THE FAMILY TREE

Julia Donaldson and Axel Scheffler were inspired to create an extraordinary set of reimagined illustrations and verses with many of your favourite characters, from the Gruffalo to Stick Man, to help lighten the spirits of families everywhere during this time.

You can find more illustrations and verses and also special storytime broadcasts by Julia Donaldson and Friends that were filmed in Spring 2020 on The Gruffalo Facebook page.

No act of kindness,
no matter how small,
is ever wasted.

// AESOP

DEBORAH STRACHAN
Covid Survivor / Devon

I first had symptoms on March 27th, a cough, feeling hot and cold, and a sore throat. I stayed in bed most of the time, getting up for short periods of time then back to bed.

On the 30th, we rang 111 and explained the symptoms and they said leave it till the Friday and see how it goes. But by the Wednesday afternoon I had had enough and said to my husband "I can't carry on like this". By this time I couldn't even tolerate taking any more paracetamol, it just wouldn't go down and I was also having trouble stringing a sentence together.

So he phoned 111, explained my symptoms and they said to ring 999 for an ambulance. They came out, did all the checks and jokingly said "congratulations you have won a trip to hospital!".

They were very nice, took me in the ambulance, gave me oxygen. I arrived at Derriford Hospital and they took me into the suspected Covid-19 admissions part.

They put a cannula in my arm to administer paracetamol as I couldn't tolerate it orally. I was quickly sent for a chest x-ray and they took blood from the arteries which apparently tells them more about your breathing. I was tested for Covid-19, with a swab up my nose and back of my throat. The chest x-ray came back showing I had slight pneumonia as well.

I was sent up to a ward in a room of my own and, when they came to tell me I had tested positive for Covid-19, I was then moved up to the Covid-19 ward at about 3 in the morning.

I was on a lot of oxygen and antibiotics and the ICU doctors came up to see me the next morning, debating whether I needed to go to ICU because of the amount of oxygen I was on. Luckily, I missed ICU by the skin of my teeth.

The staff on the ward were lovely – even though they were all gowned up and sweltering, everybody was cheerful and very helpful, even down to the cleaners.

When I was in there, the lady in the next bed passed away in the middle of the night. It was awful.

I was in there a total of 12 days and they lowered my oxygen very gradually. On the Sunday, the doctor came around about 10 in the morning and said we will try you off the oxygen and if your oxygen stats stay steady you can go home later. They were steady and I was allowed out about 6 in the evening.

While I was in there you had to be put on portable oxygen, even to go to the bathroom so I couldn't even shower. Luckily, one of the nurses one morning washed my hair over the sink for me. If you could have seen it, well, to say it made me feel better was an understatement!

I have a husband Neal and two daughters Clare and Katie and my grandchild Emily. It does make you value your life when you realise it could have gone either way. Hats off to the NHS doing a brilliant job under very difficult circumstances.

> "
> Even though they were all gowned up and sweltering, everyone was cheerful and very helpful, even down to the cleaners.

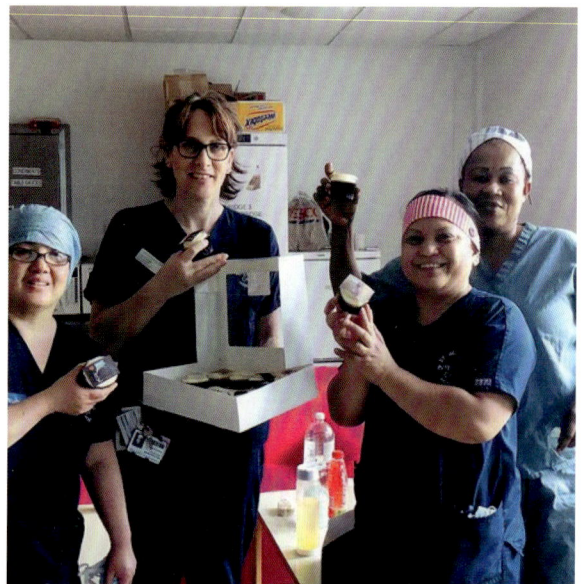

EMMA DODI
Cake & Macaron Designer / London

When Lockdown happened I realised I'd be stuck at home, with no events to bake cakes for. I am useless at doing nothing! So, I just started thinking there must be something I can do to help.

I became a volunteer for Critical NHS, a community group set up to support front line staff during the pandemic. We were delivering food into St Georges and other London hospitals – and trying to support the local shops and restaurants that were struggling by buying it all from them. We even had some celebrities helping us with the deliveries, including the actors Guy Henry and Jason Fleming and GMB's Susanna Reid.

I then thought I could also bake for the NHS front line. I wanted to give the doctors and nurses a sweet treat, but I also wanted to help put a smile on their faces and raise spirits. That's when I thought about making the cupcakes. I wanted them to be colourful and joyful and to include positive messages. A sugar rush is great but a smiley sugar rush is even better!

The reaction was incredible, from smiles to tears. The doctors and nurses from many different London hospitals couldn't believe their eyes – cupcakes with wonderful pictures and messages. It really was heartwarming and made me want to do more! As the days passed, I got authority from Charlie Mackesy, JK Rowling, Sir Quentin Blake and Julia Donaldson to use their wonderful images and words on my cupcakes. I also sent the 'toppers' to other hospitals around the country so they could use them on locally baked cakes too.

Being able to help even in such a small way – by baking, raising awareness and helping deliver meals – has been immensely rewarding. People tell me what I have been doing is incredible but in fact it is not me that is incredible, it is our NHS heroes that are. What I have got back in return outweighs what I did, tenfold.

> 66
> I started thinking there must be something I can do to help. I wanted to put a smile on their faces and raise spirits.

THE NEWMAN FAMILY
Lee, Sophie, Scarlett, Darcey & George / Worcester

Homeschooling was not something I ever thought I would do. When I overheard a teacher talking to another parent about the likelihood of the school closing and parents being expected to homeschool, I experienced a sinking feeling like no other. I was not the one to teach my children anything! I would fail them! I did a dreadful job at school. I rarely listened, did the bare minimum, just to keep the teachers off my back, and at the very earliest opportunity I jumped into the world of work without looking back. This was going to be a disaster.

The day came. There were tears as they walked out of school (especially from the youngest, who rarely shows emotions), as it dawned on them that they will not be seeing their friends or teachers for the next few weeks. If not months. I cried with them. The one thing I have learnt in my work as a grief counsellor and Samaritan is that to cry is good for the soul. Tears have healing properties.

The following day I decided to put my big girl pants on. I had a chat with a friend who was thrilled to be homeschooling. She made me realise how fun it could be, and helped me put together a timetable. As I started to explore avenues for learning, the ideas kept coming. The possibilities were limitless.

The first couple of days were rocky. They complained and whined and both needed me at the same time. I could feel the pressure inside me building and I felt like I was going to explode. I had a chat with my husband, who advised me to take the pressure off. It turned out that this was exactly what I needed to hear.

I decided to flip things around. The plan was to get the boring 'sit down and concentrate' stuff out of the way first thing then leave afternoons free to do the fun stuff.

Some of the things we have done includes preparing dinner together and baking cakes, typing up our recipes, ready to put in our very own Lockdown cookbook, researching historical milestones and painting pictures about them, writing letters and poems to stay connected to friends and family, carrying out science experiments and making dens in the garden, whilst observing the wildlife and discussing the things that grow, as well as dancing around the kitchen to classical music whilst exploring how certain music makes us feel.

Some days are better than others. The days I work, I have had to be far more forgiving of both myself and them, accepting that way less will be done. By taking the pressure off, I have allowed the girls to take the lead and this has helped immensely. I am not their teacher and they are never going to give me the respect they would offer someone in that role. I, as their mother, am their safe place. They will test the boundaries with me like no one else. Now that I am learning to accept this, it is far easier.

> " I can honestly say that this has been some of the best quality time we have ever had together. It is hard but it is worth it. The highs far outweigh the lows and I, for one, am so very grateful.

AILEEN CAUGHEY BEM
Main Grade Officer / Northern Ireland Prison Service

I've worked in the prison service for almost 22 years. A normal day would depend on where you are detailed to work. I'd usually be on a residential location doing reports on inmates' general behaviour. It's also about checking on their moods and contacting the relevant people for help if you can't.

With Covid, we had no inmates going out of the residential area. All family visits, education, workshops and church services were cancelled to limit the amount of movement within the prison. They also moved the more vulnerable to one location, to enable them to shield together. We went to limited regime and had less interaction from outside agencies and staff from other locations. Nurses were the only medical staff we had in for quite a while.

The staff and inmates adjusted very well to the changes that were being made. Social distancing worked well most of the time although there were times that you couldn't – for example, taking an inmate to hospital and being handcuffed to them.

The biggest challenge was to try and keep Covid-19 out. Staff were aware that it would be them that would bring it in, and were worrying about their loved ones but equally you had the inmates worrying about theirs. The only contact they had was by phone but when we explained to them, a lot of them understood that we had no contact with our families unless by phone either.

As with everyone in Lockdown a lot of mental health issues arose and it was trying to get things organised for the inmates to do. On Easter Sunday a few of the inmates from the upholstery workshop came and asked if it was as bad out there or was the media blowing it out of proportion; were the nurses and doctors getting it that tough and was there really a shortage of PPE. When staff explained to them how bad it was, they were shocked. They asked if they could do or give anything to help the local hospitals and nursing homes.

We got in touch with N.I Scrubs Causeway Coast and worked with them making and donating isolation gowns, scrubs, scrub bags and ear comforters to local nursing homes and our two local hospitals. When the first wave started to slow down and NI Scrubs were running out of orders, the men wanted to make more. So we started making syringe driver bags, drain bags for people that had mastectomies, facemasks for the NI Big Community Sew and transparent masks for the local deaf community.

Our prison is all about giving back to community. It felt right that at a time when the community needed help the most, the prison and inmates were still doing something. It gave the inmates pride and also helped with their mental health.

To get cards and emails thanking us all for what we had done was great but we weren't looking for recognition – we just wanted to help those key workers that needed it.

Covid has made us all realise that family are the most important thing to everyone, whether they are in prison or work in it. We have always said that we are one big family – some get on, some don't, with a few characters and jokers thrown in for good measure, but we always look out for one another when the going gets tough. This pandemic has also made me realise how sometimes we take so many things in life for granted.

When I got the email about the Honours List, I thought it was someone taking a hand out of me. I read it a couple of times before I accepted it was genuine. I felt shocked and embarrassed that I had been nominated – I only did what anyone would have done, along with my S/O and the inmates, we just wanted to help the frontline keyworkers and let them know that other keyworkers appreciated what they were doing.

When the reality had sunk in, I felt proud that someone had taken the time to nominate me. I'd told my husband Mark and my brothers but was scared to tell my Mum until the day before. She would have been that proud that she would've been telling everyone. My Dad and sister would have been so proud and happy for me if they'd still been alive. But on brighter note, it was the best 50th birthday present I could have asked for.

> 66
> It felt right that at a time when the community needed help the most, we were still doing something.

WEPA UK

WEPA UK manufactures high-quality household paper products for the UK and Ireland, supplying to many of the major retailers.

Over Lockdown we did all that we could to ensure that stock remained available, including rationalising some niche embossed patterns and focusing on larger pack sizes, which we knew were in demand, at the start of the Lockdown period.

During some weeks we had a 20-70% increase in sales, and that intensity lasted for over a month.

However, we quickly learnt a number of lessons over that initial four month period. We put our back-up production facilities into operation and quickly found a number of extra hauliers to deliver stock. With such actions, we were able to get back on track and resupply the retail chain after the first wave of panic buying.

We also consistently supported the message that consumers should behave responsibly and act on the advice provided by the supermarkets when buying.

Whilst most of our time was directed into production to meet this consumer demand, we also provided some free stock to a local charity to help support the community at the height of the Lockdown period.

> We saw a 70% increase in sales and did all that we could to ensure stock remained available.

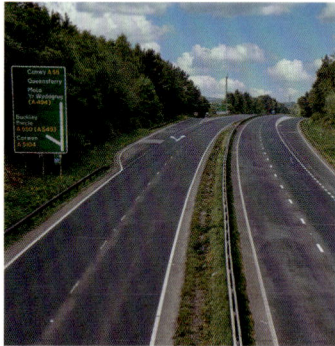

All around the country, towns, cities and iconic landmarks were deserted whilst buses, trains and motorways were empty ...

IBRAR AKRAM BEM
Service Delivery Manager / Transport for London Dial-A-Ride

Dial-a-Ride is a TfL service providing free and accessible transport for vulnerable passengers across London, to help elderly or disabled customers who have difficulty accessing mainstream transport services. In normal times, we schedule an average of 1 million trips a year. I have a team of 36 service delivery controllers who are on hand, scheduling journeys, dealing with calls from drivers and depots as well as queries from our bookings staff.

During the pandemic my role changed considerably. It became clear that not only our passengers but also vulnerable Londoners would face significant challenges getting to, or receiving basic necessities like groceries and prescriptions.

At the same time, many of our regular passengers were shielding or staying at home so we saw a significant decline in the number of requests for trips. It was clear to me that we would have an abundance of resource we could repurpose to help other organisations and the wider community.

After testing the water with food deliveries to a local Sikh temple to help feed vulnerable Londoners, I expanded this to help transport medicine deliveries, shopping parcels and PPE to hospitals including NHS Nightingale in east London. We went from being a passenger only service to a whole new way of working as we brought parcel deliveries to vulnerable Londoners.

We started this programme back in April, supporting deliveries to essential workers and the vulnerable. Through this we made 100 deliveries of PPE to different NHS hubs, which then escalated to 130 food deliveries, 350 pharmaceutical deliveries, 450 shopping parcels daily and 60 hot food parcels deliveries every day as well as 100 hot meals to NHS staff every weekend.

To be involved with what I call the 'extra-curricular work' was challenging, with its own set of hurdles to overcome. I feel that doing this was the responsible course of action to take considering the impact that coronavirus was having, especially on elderly and vulnerable Londoners, but there was a worry at the back of my mind, seeing my team come in day in, day out, dedicating themselves to the work at hand in spite of the challenging situation. At the time I saw it as my duty to help wherever required. It is only now that I reflect on the work carried out that I can look back with a sense of pride about the way it all came together.

Working for Dial-a-Ride, I am acutely aware how we have some passengers who have no family to help them. With the necessary restrictions the Lockdown placed upon us all, this situation would only have been exacerbated. I found myself imagining what it must be like for these passengers who had nowhere to turn to for help, so I saw it as my duty to help with supplies of basic necessities. By doing this, we would be also able to prevent people going out unnecessarily, which in turn could protect them from becoming infected.

The level of collaboration during this time was unprecedented. What helped me get through was keeping in mind that we can prevent vulnerable people going out, and that we could help be a part of the Government's guidelines to help stem the spread of the virus.

At home, I couldn't have asked for a better family. My family has been supportive of my role, knowing helping the vulnerable in these difficult times is the best thing one can ever do.

I am extremely happy to have been recognised with this honour, but I see it as an honour for all of my team at London Dial-a-Ride. I am so happy that we have been able to provide essential support to so many people when they have needed it most. I'm truly proud when I hear colleagues from all over TfL talk about what a great help our service has been to vulnerable members of our communities in these worrying times.

> " I am so happy that we have been able to provide essential support to so many people.

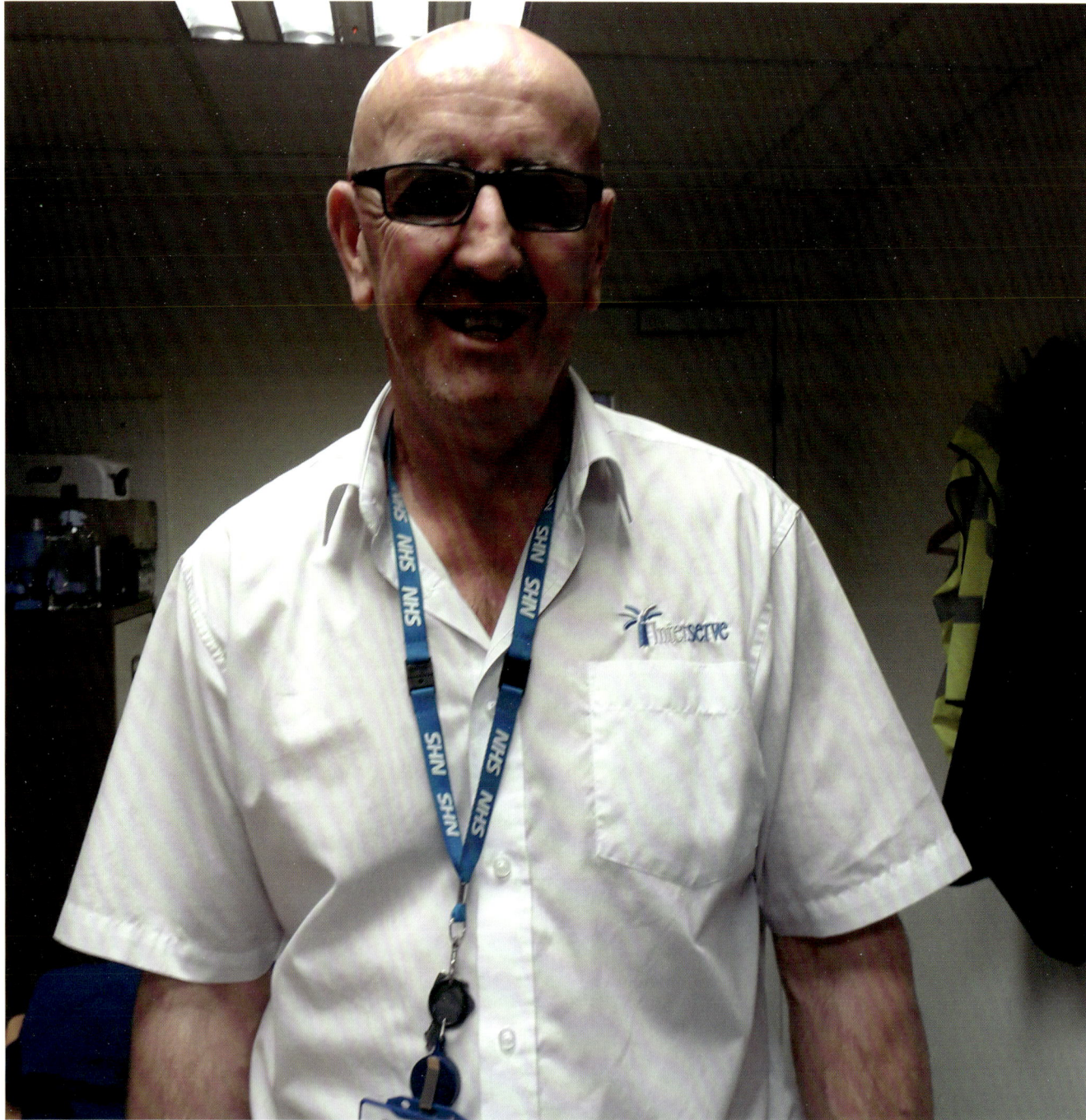

PAUL HICKS
Interserve Cleaning Supervisor / Poole

I'm a cleaning supervisor for Interserve at Poole Hospital. I've been with the company since 2017 but have worked at the hospital for 20 years, so it's a special place to me. I started as a temporary worker in 2000 and never left because I love it. I like joking with the patients, keeping spirits up and obviously cleaning to ensure the environment is in the best possible shape it can be to support people to get well and hospital staff to work safely.

There are around 200 of us working for Interserve on a facilities management contract for the Poole Hospital NHS Foundation Trust, cleaning all of the hospital's clinical and public areas, including window cleaning and grounds maintenance.

I was responsible for carrying out cleaning duties before Covid and that still required you to be mindful of highly contagious diseases, but now the absolute focus is upon health and safety, NHS guidelines and staying safe during the pandemic.

I'm responsible for a team of workers who clean public areas and wards which are used by Covid-19 patients and we all work extremely hard. When carrying out cleans of infected areas, the team wears the prescribed Personnel Protective Equipment and cleans the area thoroughly before using a machine which sprays disinfectant to kill all the germs. We also use anti-bacterial cleaning agents and use multiple methods to ensure the area is hygienic. This method gets everything.

There's an army of people working together here as a team and it's fantastic to be part of the hospital's response to Covid-19. Whether it's kitchen staff, logistics, cleaners, doctors, nurses – every single job role – we are all absolutely committed to doing the best we can and being part of a team and supporting the NHS to save lives.

> ❝
> We are all absolutely committed to doing the best we can and being part of a team and supporting the NHS to save lives – it's as straight forward as that!

NICOLA STURGEON
First Minister of Scotland

I know that all of this has been incredibly tough – and six months on it only gets tougher. But never forget that humanity has come through even bigger challenges than this one.

And though it doesn't feel like it now, this virus will pass. It won't last forever and one day, hopefully soon, we will be looking back on it, not living through it.

So though we are all struggling with this – and believe me, we are all struggling – let's pull together. Let's keep going, try to keep smiling, keep hoping and keep looking out for each other. Be strong, be kind and let's continue to act out of love and solidarity.

I will never find the words to thank all of you enough for the enormous sacrifices you have made so far. And I am sorry to be asking for more.

But a belief I hold on to and one I am asking you to keep faith with in those moments when it all feels too hard, is this: if we stick with it – and, above all, if we stick together – we will get through it.

> Be strong, be kind and let's continue to act out of love and solidarity.

JAY FLYNN MBE
Now Full Time Quiz Master / Darwen

I've run quizzes before in pubs but now my life is devoted to creating pub quizzes for the virtual channel and community that's been created during Lockdown. I've been working from home writing and researching lots of fun quizzes which means I've been learning a lot!

I wanted to create a quiz for local friends and quiz teams to keep them entertained. The event was set public by mistake and was shared far and wide – there were over 500k responses to it! Our audience peaked at 182k which broke a Guinness World Record!

The response was incredible. We inadvertently created a virtual quiz community of people that had something to look forward to twice a week, and because of that we have been able to work with some incredible charities and raisedover £750k for them.

In May, I was asked to host a one off 5 question quiz on Zoe Ball's Radio 2 Breakfast Show and it's been going ever since. It's such an honour to have a small part in the show and the team have been lovely and really encouraging. They are also quite competitive which makes it lots of fun as well!

It's an amazing feeling to be a part of all this and to read messages from people who have been isolating and had no one else but us. So to have created that and to have been a small part of helping to keep people sane during these crazy months, as well as helping to raise money for some charities at this difficult time too, is such a proud feeling.

I've become part of an incredible community and I've also been able to spend more time with my family as well which has been heart-warming.

I was humbled to receive the MBE. To be on the list alongside some incredible people is such an honour and one that I can cherish for years to come.

> 66 It's amazing to have been a small part of helping to keep people sane during these crazy months.

RANI KAUR BEM
Sainsbury's Food Service Assistant / Bedford

Usually, I work on the supermarket food counter but due to Covid-19 it was closed until further notice. Throughout the peak of the pandemic, I moved to working on the shop floor and checkout instead, although I am now back on the food counter. One of the big differences for my working day is that I now have to wear PPE such as face masks which are provided by Sainsbury's. During the start of Covid-19 the supermarket was very busy, however things feel more settled and less hectic now.

At the start of the pandemic, going to work was quite daunting as none of us had ever faced anything quite like this before. However, when the store started to add greater protection for those of us working, such as PPE and protective screens, this made me feel a lot more comfortable with the situation. Keeping a distance from colleagues and customers and wearing a mask throughout a whole shift was one of the biggest challenges and took a lot of time to get used to.

Initially, seeing emptier shelves was worrying because it made us fear whether there was going to be anything left for us to buy, by the time we were able to do our shop. However, luckily this initial panic didn't last long, and Sainsbury's introduced measures that ensured there was always enough food for everyone as well as priority shopping for our vulnerable customers.

The general public seemed very appreciative of the work that we were doing for the nation during a very difficult time. I would often get customers come to me and say thank you. This was strange at first, as it was unusual for supermarket staff to get this sort of recognition. But I think the public really appreciated that we were putting ourselves on the front line and keeping them fed throughout the pandemic.

During the pandemic I was helping to feed the nation, both at Sainsbury's and outside of work. I also delivered hot meals to shielding customers, NHS staff and other key workers outside of my Sainsbury's working hours.

Since Lockdown started, volunteers at Sri Guru Ravidass Sabha and Community Centre in Bedford had been preparing and delivering hot meals to both vulnerable people and key workers. This included individuals from the emergency services, care workers, elderly people, and families and individuals who were self-isolating. Over 110 days in Lockdown, over 18,000 hot meals were delivered! I was desperate to get involved, so I made samosas and chapatis across a number of days. I also did some fundraising for facemasks, which I ended up donating to my local hospital to provide them with PPE.

During these crazy times, being able to help people was one of the main things that kept me going. Supporting others made me feel happy, and I was proud of myself knowing I was making a difference to people. I am also very grateful for my store colleagues, manager and our head of store who always encouraged me and who helped and supported the cause.

It was a huge honour to be mentioned on the Queen's Birthday Honours list, and it was very unexpected. However, I am extremely proud of myself for this achievement. My goal was only to help people during these difficult times, therefore to get recognised for this was an unexpected but a proud honour.

> Supporting others made me feel happy — and I think the public really appreciated that we were keeping them fed.

Kindness is one of the best ways to show that love exists. Kindness always matters.

// GILES PALEY-PHILLIPS

THE #MAKEITBLUE COLLECTIVE
Event and Entertainment Professionals / UK and Worldwide

We're a collective of out of work event and entertainment professionals. We're the people that create and build many of the events you normally enjoy. A normal day for us is as varied as the people who make up our collective. We're used to working from homes, from offices, from trains and from airport lounges – anywhere that allows us to get the job done.

Wherever an event takes place, we will have been involved. We are there right from the early planning stage, through costing, designing, creating, building, editing, rehearsing and recording. There are so many kinds of public and business events, including shows, tours, conferences, exhibitions, ceremonies and sporting events…. You name it, our members will have worked on it.

With Covid, everyone's job was put on hold indefinitely. Ours was the first industry to close and will be one of the last to return – and even then it will be in an altered form. Most of the businesses in our industry will have received no revenue and many of our people will have had no work and therefore no income. With events everywhere cancelled, we lost our clients, our audiences and our livelihoods.

As people accustomed to creating events, we hated our enforced inaction and needed to motivate ourselves and our industry colleagues. We wanted to highlight the fact that so many hundreds of thousands of us are out of work… but in a positive way. So, we came up with the #LightItBlue campaign.

We used our skills and contacts to arrange for landmarks and iconic buildings to light blue on Thursday nights and it became a nationwide gesture of thanks to the NHS and other care workers for their efforts to keep us well and safe. We shared beautiful blue images on social media channels to invite more people to get involved – not only those within our own industry, but members of the wider public, who we invited to #MakeItBlue in their own way, while at home in Lockdown.

After our first five days of intensive work, we succeeded in persuading 100 locations to 'light up blue' in the UK. The campaign snowballed and over 300 buildings and landmarks joined in, across England, Scotland, Ireland and Wales.

In under 50 days, 36 countries were turning their buildings blue across six continents. They shared the same causes of healthcare support and mental health awareness. Organisationally, we had grown to six separate international collectives – in the UK, USA, Spain, Singapore, Japan and Argentina, and we had received global recognition on television, on the radio and national press.

We are so very pleased that an idea that was hatched and executed within a week became such an international success, uniting countries around the world with the same sentiment of hope and positivity in a time of crisis.

The #LightItBlue campaign peaked here in the UK at the time of the NHS' 72nd birthday. NHS England asked us to help them send a message of thanks of their own, to the British public and all those organisations that had given their support during such a challenging time. It was so gratifying for us that, having set out originally to thank the NHS, ten weeks later we came full circle in being asked by the NHS to thank the public in the same way.

> We used our skills and contacts to unite countries around the world with the same shared sentiment of hope and positivity.

NET

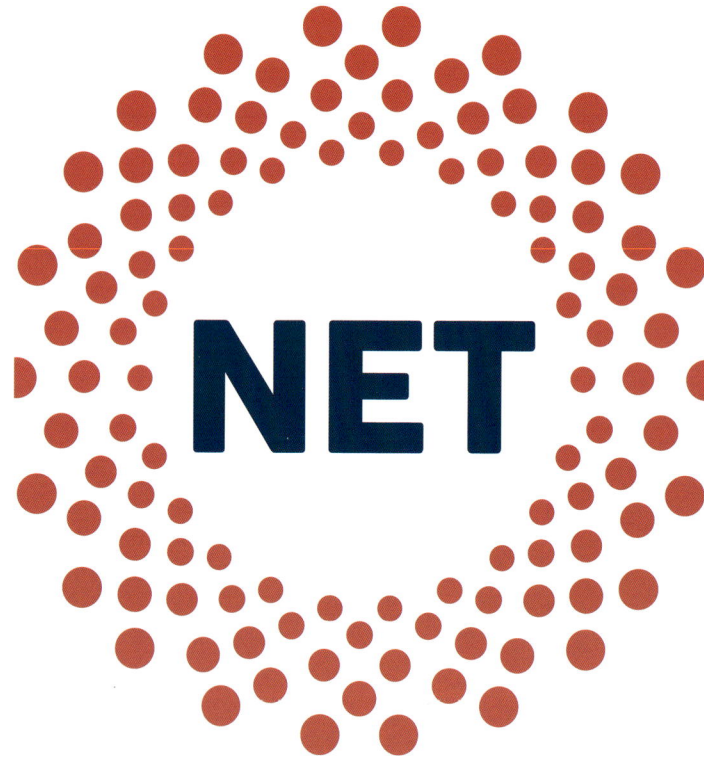

NATIONAL EMERGENCIES TRUST

THE NATIONAL EMERGENCY TRUST

The National Emergencies Trust (NET) was set up to provide the public with one trusted place to give during domestic disasters.

Victims often find it difficult to know who to turn to in the tragic aftermath of a national emergency. The Trust will be there for those victims to facilitate a single point of contact to apply for help. Financial awards can be made to victims quickly and efficiently, avoiding the bureaucracy of multiple applications. It should also help use money more effectively and minimise fraud.

Just four months after our official launch as a charity, we launched our first ever emergency appeal – the Coronavirus Appeal – on 18th March 2020 in response to the global pandemic.

Between March and September 2020, the Coronavirus Appeal raised nearly £100m, thanks to the overwhelming generosity of the public, corporates, and charitable trusts and foundations. By September, almost all of these funds had been allocated to help thousands of grassroots charities and groups across the UK to help those in urgent need in their communities.

When Lockdown started, donations to the Appeal helped to get thousands of hot meals and other essentials to those in self-isolation and shielding. They also helped to provide emergency accommodation to those in great need.

Over time, donations have enabled small charities to digitise their services so that they can still offer mental health, wellbeing and a range of other support from a safe distance.

And today, the ongoing generosity is ensuring that, as people's needs change, they can continue to receive vital help, whoever and wherever they are.

The NET team exploded in size over the Spring and Summer of 2020 – from a team of just three, to more than 180 people at the Appeal's peak. The majority of these were incredible volunteers, who donated their time during furlough or gave up personal time around their day jobs to transform donations into difference for communities all over the UK.

> Funds were allocated to help thousands of charities and groups across the UK to help those in urgent need in their communities.

THE DANCING BIN MEN
Jack Johnson, Adrian Breakwell & Henry Wright / Wolverhampton

Whilst continuing to service the city of Wolverhampton by collecting garden waste, we noticed a few things. Firstly during Lockdown the roads were much quieter, particularly with the lack of school and work bound traffic enabling us to manoeuvre our truck with greater ease and avoiding delays.

We also saw a massive increase in the volume of garden waste. Bins became much heavier, packed to capacity – with more people at home enjoying fine weather, more time was given for those gardening jobs that routinely never get completed.

We've not felt scared, we've taken as many precautions as possible. We are proud that none of our three man team have missed any days. It sometimes appeared that we were walking the streets alone with nervous residents peaking out at our movements. But it was imperative the service we provide continued – there could be no suspension of service when it comes to being there to service our city.

It was in the first weeks of Lockdown that we decided to entertain ourselves and residents with humour and dance routines. This was a difficult period, spirits were fragile and people needed a distraction. Our first notoriety came when a resident secretly filmed us running through a little routine. I guess three guys in hi-viz clothing are hard to be discreet in a cul de sac!

> ❝
> We were so proud to be able to make a difference, three humble waste operatives making a difference. We will never forget that for the rest of our lives.

Inevitably, the footage was posted online and made the local printed press and gained TV attention. An early performance from Grease proved hugely popular – my colleague Henry portraying Sandy, complete with wig, sent views soaring past one million in one day. It has since topped eight million.

The popularity of the videos became the talk of the town and social media. The more our spontaneous dances popped up around the city, the more the clamour from the public to catch the now entitled 'Dancing Bin Men'.

The appreciation shown by the public was immense. Gifts were left on bins alongside lovely messages of thanks and hope. Children's excited faces would appear in windows or people would rush to wave from a distance. Their reaction truly moved us and warmed our hearts. We were also able to raise a substantial amount for a local hospice who we had read were suffering with the effects of coping with patients of the virus and getting sufficient PPE. We were so proud to be able to make a small difference, three humble waste operatives making a difference.

Our team became stronger and although tougher days continued, a creative spark between us would then lift and motivate us to continue to dance. The social media attention had truly reached around the world and we were deluged with good will messages. People also posted videos of themselves dancing around their own bins, from Australia to the USA. Who would have believed these three guys could create a following of such supportive people and have such a positive effect on our society.

One particular highlight was when we learned we had been immortalised in LEGO brick at Legoland Windsor, to celebrate heroes of the pandemic, alongside our wonderful NHS, Sir Tom Moore and Joe Wicks. We were honoured.

We have all privately dealt with longing for normality to resume. Two amongst us have been separated from children, another taking extra care as he's living with a vulnerable parent. But through it all we've given our best and represented our city on the world stage. We will never forget that for the rest of our lives.

GOVIA THAMESLINK

Govia Thameslink Railway (GTR) unveiled three rebranded trains paying homage to NHS staff fighting Coronavirus across the UK, one each for its Thameslink, Great Northern and Southern services.

The rebranded NHS and Key Worker trains echo GTR's 'We're With You' promise and illustrate our heartfelt support and gratitude to NHS staff and the 200,000 key workers who rely on GTR's rail routes each week.

The Thameslink train, which is now running across the extensive Thameslink network, taking in locations such as Cambridge, Peterborough and Brighton, stopped at London Bridge on Thursday last week for rail staff to applaud representatives from nearby Guy's Hospital as part of the nation's 'Clap for Our Carers'.

The Thameslink Class 700 train is unit number 700111 – selected to show thanks for the tireless efforts of the NHS's 111 advice line, with the Southern Railway unit number 377111 also celebrating the NHS service. The Great Northern train is unit 717011 (as there are only 25 in the fleet!).

The initiative was part-funded by Porterbrook Rail and Cross London Trains, with the new train liveries designed, created and installed in less than a week by the team from Aura Brand Solutions in close collaboration with the team at GTR.

"We are proud to be supporting the NHS, social care and emergency services during this crisis. We hope that our NHS and Key Worker trains show how grateful we are to those working so very hard to keep people safe and beat this virus.

"There are more than 50 hospitals across our network and our trains carry more than 200,000 key workers each week. The team at GTR appreciates each and every one of them.

"I am also really proud of our teams, key staff themselves, who have worked so hard to support this project. Everyone wants to do their bit to show their appreciation for the NHS and carers."

Steve White / Chief Operating Officer

> Our trains carry more than 200,000 key workers every week and we appreciate each and every one of them.

AGGREKO

In response to growing demand for enhanced testing for Covid-19, temporary testing sites were being stationed across the country – in major retailer car parks through to unused theme park facilities. As the number of temporary testing sites increased, so too did the need for access to reliable, modular power, particularly as many of these sites will not have had easy connections to mains electricity.

To support the set up of these testing sites, Aggreko offered the UK government the use of its available fleet of small canopy generators – up to 1,300 units – which provide flexible, modular power to temporary venues.

As with most of Aggreko's products, these generators can be remotely monitored without the need for an engineer to be physically present. This design feature is advantageous during this time of social distancing, as it will help limit the number of people physically present at designated testing sites.

Aggreko is ready to help the Covid-19 relief effort in any way that we can and we are already supporting the healthcare, pharmaceutical and food & beverage industries. The need for more Covid-19 testing sites across the country is clear, and our generators can be deployed very rapidly to ensure consistent and stable power to temporary venues.

If we can be of service, we are ready and willing to help. As many of these units had been earmarked for outdoor events, such as Glastonbury, that have largely been cancelled or postponed, we are offering them pro-bono. All that's needed is fuel and freight costs to start providing power.

Chris Rason / Managing Director at Aggreko Northern Europe

As a power provider, we're immensely proud of our team who are providing essential services around the world to ensure society can continue to function throughout this pandemic. We're providing our key workers with all the support we can to ensure their safety is protected as they work tirelessly to deliver much-needed energy to communities and crucial industries.

At Aggreko, we've adapted to find new, safe ways to deliver vital power supplies to our customers when they need it most. This has ranged from ensuring that vital services have been able to run without interruption, to providing power and temperature control solutions to facilities supporting the front-line response, such as temporary hospitals. A heartfelt thank you from me to each and every member of the Aggreko team. Without their dedication and determination, this simply couldn't have happened.

These are unprecedented times and, as a global community, it is absolutely vital that we work together to support the effort to combat the virus. We will do everything we can to support our people, customers, partners and the communities in which we operate through this particularly challenging time.

Chris Weston / CEO

> If we can be of service, we are ready and willing to help.

Thank you to our shelf stackin' green grocin' meal preppin' heroes.

NHS
NOBODY DOES IT BETTER

THANK YOU NHS

#Thankyou NHS

YOU ARE THE REAL HEROES
NHS
THANK YOU!

'Thank you to our croc wearin' patient carin' stethoscope slingin' ward cleanin' phone answerin' street sweepin' bin collectin' letter postin' green grocin' prescription fillin' shelf stackin' shop runnin' passenger movin' scooter ridin' lorry drivin' loo roll deliverin' heroes.

THANK YOU

CROWN PAINTS

THANK YOU NHS

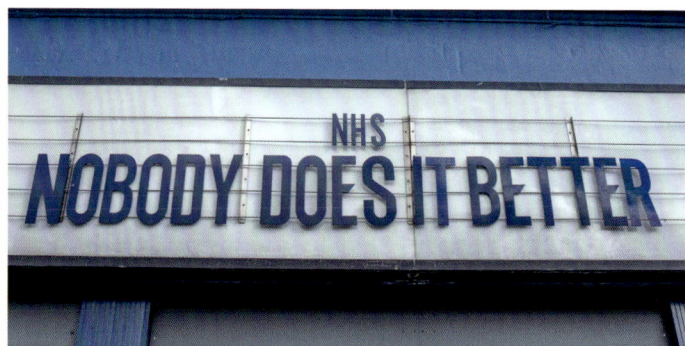

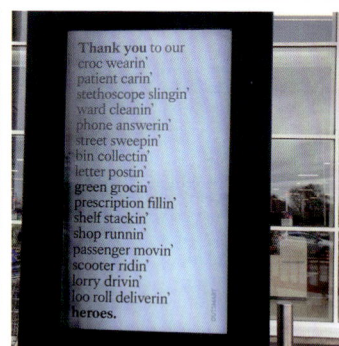

Messages of support and appreciation for the NHS were printed on banners, cut into grass and even sprayed on roads ...

THANK YOU

NHS

THANK YOU NHS & KEY WORKERS

NHS

THANK YOU NHS AND ALL KEY WORKERS

THE WATFORD COMMUNITY REALLY APPRECIATE YOU

Thank you NHS AND TO ALL OUR CARERS AND ESSENTIAL WORKERS
mfg
unleaded 95
E5

E5
95 Octane
unleaded

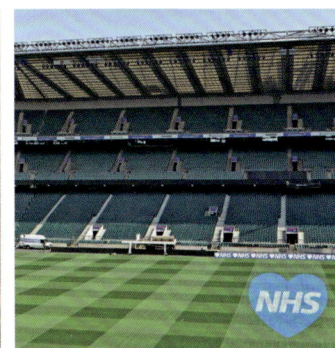

GREG DOUGHTY BEM
Traffic Officer Highways England / Blackpool

I'm a Traffic Officer for Highways England, patrolling a given route to see what is going on and deal with any incident that presents itself, from debris in the lanes and pedestrians on the network, to collisions or disruption of normal traffic flow. Our Regional Operation Centres will also deploy us to any specific incidents along with Motorway Police units and other Emergency Services.

Before Covid, as long as we were trained for it, we could find ourselves working either single-crewed or as a double crew. Now, to comply with social distancing, all Traffic Officers work as a single manned patrol. Officers who were not single crew trained, operated as a normal double crew but in separate vehicles, so some Call Signs come as two vehicles together.

Booking on and off shift had to be reworked, so that the numbers of Traffic Officers mingling during shift change was kept to a minimum. This meant the banter that normally took place almost stopped and we saw less of our colleagues on other teams.

Despite the reduction in traffic on the motorway during Lockdown and the reduction in certain types of incidents, there were still the fair share of incidents to attend but it was odd seeing the roads so empty. The sounds that we become accustomed to on the network are often the triggers for the sixth sense that we develop over the years, so when all of a sudden we don't hear those familiar sounds, which are often a warning, it changes the dynamics somewhat.

Outside of work, I am a licensed Lay Minister in the Church of England. For the past 10 years, I have worked with several projects in Blackpool, focusing on people that are homeless, below the poverty line and/or struggling with chaotic addictions.

During Lockdown, all the rough sleepers and other homeless, were placed into local hotels or B&Bs. I, along with others, put together a team that worked together with other agencies and charities to provide and distribute a cooked breakfast, a packed lunch and a cooked evening meal for individuals in this temporary accommodation. We also coordinated the delivery of other health and welfare products at the same time. Over 30,000 meals were prepared and delivered during Lockdown.

Why did I do this? Because, as a Christian, we are called to help those who are less fortunate than ourselves or that need help to get through a particular stage of their life. It may sound like a bit of a cliché, but it had to be done and someone needed to do it. It's no good preaching it, if we don't get up and do it.

The community that we served were, in the main, grateful and appreciated what was being done for them. Most of the people were individuals that we know and have worked with for a while, so they get what we're trying to do.

Providing for the people that we do, always fills me with mixed feelings and during this time that was no different. My wife, Catherine, and I have driven home from an outreach session, sometimes in floods of tears because of certain situation, or sometimes roaring with laughter.

Like everyone else who has been affected by this situation, there are some things that are really difficult. As Grandparents, we have missed the contact with our grandchildren, but enjoy the regular phone contact with our sons. It has been good to experience people encouraging each other and looking out for one another and it's been great seeing the innovative ways that people have come up with to replace some of the things that we can't do at the moment. Personally, my IT skills, although still not brilliant, have improved no end!

Obviously, it was a great honour to be given the award from the Queen. It was very much a surprise but whilst it really is great to get it, we must never forget that I was part of a team and there are many others, not mentioned, that I received this award on behalf of.

> " We are called to help those who are less fortunate than ourselves. It's no good preaching if we don't get up and do it.

YUNUS DUDHWALA
Head of Chaplaincy, Barts Health NHS Trust / London

Chaplains have always been here to support patients and staff in times of loss, but we are now having to work differently, making sure we are resilient and ensuring we have our own self-support so we can adapt and help those in need.

Ordinarily, we would receive referrals from palliative care, ITU or wards and we would have a list of patients to go and see. We may also have some wards allocated to us and we would go to see the patients and staff on those wards to provide support. We usually hold prayers and services during the day too.

Covid-19 really changed the intensity of our work, as well as adding a changing picture, daily. Services had to be postponed, our prayer rooms closed, we aren't able to visit wards as regularly and we have to wait for referrals rather than proactively visit the wards. I was also called upon to help the new Nightingale Hospital set up its Chaplaincy and Bereavement Services.

As cases started to grow in the hospitals I worked at, and death rates grew, I was liaising with bereavement offices, funeral directors, and cemeteries on a much more regular basis. Funeral processes were also constantly changing.

In London, initially for the first few weeks of the pandemic, there was only one Muslim cemetery that was accepting Covid-19 deceased and they were the only ones doing the washing and shrouding (an important part of the Muslim funeral rituals). I liaised with other funeral directors, helped them to be trained and helped create the guidance on washing and handling deceased within the Muslim community, to decrease the burden on this one cemetery.

There were also some false rumours being spread about the pandemic, especially on Muslim social media sites, that I would then respond to through messages and videos.

Whilst the Nightingale team and services were being set up, I would help advise families and, wherever they needed support, would help arrange video calls to families as slowly but surely, visiting to the hospitals had been stopped.

Our communication methods with families and patients have also had to change and I've found the 'distance' difficult. We either have to be wearing PPE if we are speaking face-to-face or we provide virtual communication via the use of tablets. This has been really sad – especially for end of life calls – as it isn't as personal as face-to-face, but it has enabled us to talk to over thirty family members at a time both in the UK and abroad to provide invaluable support. My heart goes out to those who are not able to attend the funerals of loved ones. We've helped them look at how they can use technology to help with this and we can provide comfort and support.

The intensity has been challenging – seeing and hearing about the number of people dying and then the new and different arrangements for the funerals. I have seen some traumatising things in my line of work and we are, as with everyone else on the frontline, anxious about our own safety when we leave our homes to care for patients, staff and families. Many of us continue to struggle with these fears and I'm grateful for my faith which enables me to continue to engage and to hold everyone involved in my prayers. My family have also been a huge support for me, and colleagues are always there when you need them.

It's all about being there for people whenever they need support at the most neediest and vulnerable times of their lives. This pandemic will live with the world for a long time and we need to support each other to try and cope in these times of loss.

> I have seen some traumatising things in my line of work but it's all about being there for people at the most vulnerable time of their lives – we need to support each other.

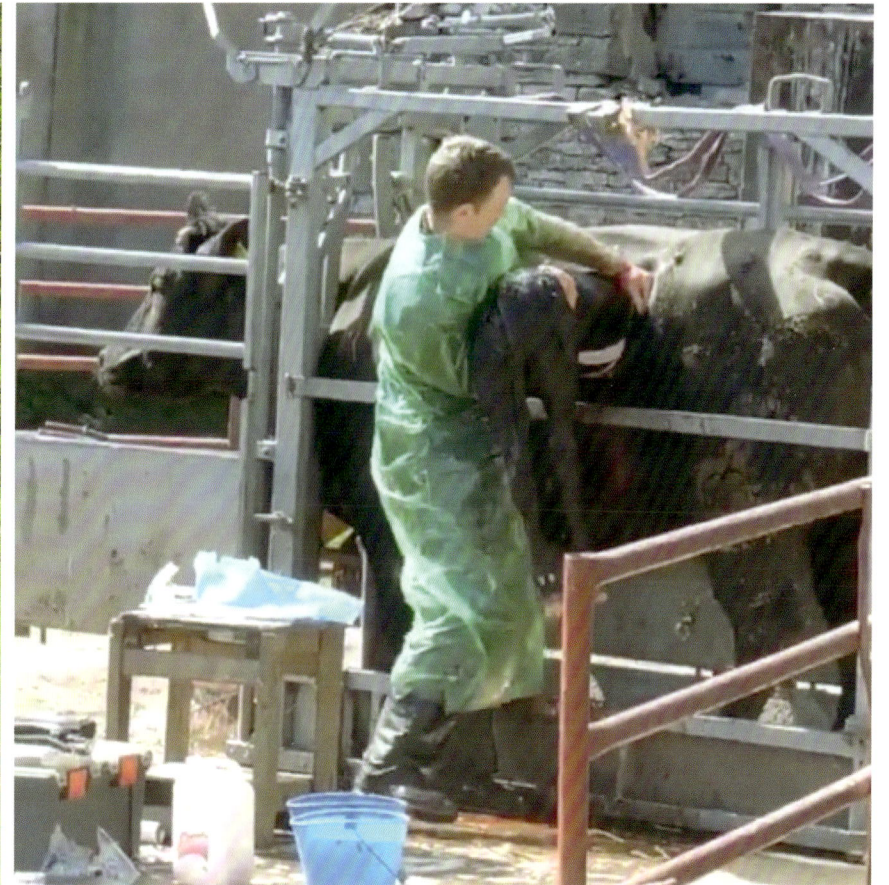

RACHEL MARSTON
Farmer / Cumbria

I live on a hill farm in the stunning Eden Valley with my husband Andrew and three girls: Catherine, Abigail and Olivia. The farm belongs to Andrew's parents, Donald & Christine, who both live and work on the farm as well.

I was born on a farm so it's in my blood and all I have ever wanted to do from a very young age. Andrew and I have been together since I was 13 so we have grown up together and share the same passion for farming and good quality livestock.

In 2011, we were very privileged to host BBC 2 Lambing Live with Kate Humble and Adam Henson. After the program, we received many letters from all around the world, which made us realise that the general public are interested in what we do. To cut a long story short, we restored an old redundant farm building into a holiday cottage so that people could come and join us down at the farm and experience life on a working farm as part of their holiday. The cottage is usually a hive of activity especially in March and April due to the lambing season and this year was to be no different but we have had to cancel all bookings so the farm seems to have been rather quiet.

However, animals don't stop giving birth just because the world is in turmoil – so with over 1,000 sheep to lamb and a few cows to calve, we knew that when Lockdown started that we definitely wouldn't be bored!

We've worked around the clock for the last two months. My day would start at 5 a.m. and finish around 11 p.m. Andrew would rise slightly later and finish a bit earlier but he would also get up in the night to check the sheep lambing inside. Catherine, who is working on the farm, put in shifts from 9 a.m.-10 p.m. but would also get up at 12.30 a.m. to check the sheep.

We had a batch of eight cows to calve, and having a C-section is not uncommon on our farm, so we had already discussed with our vets what we would do if this was needed and how we could incorporate social distancing as we always assist the vet with lifting the calf out. It was decided to do the C-section outside and place a pile of straw about 4 metres away from the cow for the calf to be placed. The vet, Richard Spooner, had done one on his own before so was happy to do this but we were stood at a safe distance kitted up with gloves, gown and facemask in case we needed to rush in at the last minute. Our vet is very capable and the section couldn't have gone any better. The calf was up and sucking from its mum within a couple of hours both are outside now enjoying the beautiful weather.

Lambing time has acted as a very good distraction for us but Covid- 19 has never really been far from our thoughts. The amazing weather has definitely helped in our job and made it less stressful. Having the kids at home has been really helpful and kept our moral up but also knowing that we were all safe. Getting food has been an issue – the shops around here had limited food and you couldn't get any deliveries so there is great excitement when we do get food in the household and many an argument if someone has had one more slice of bread than anyone else!

You can learn a lot from watching animals and one day, as I was checking the sheep outside, you could see the rain coming in from across the hillside and all of the sheep ran to the stonewalls for shelter. It made me think this is exactly what we need to do.

> Animals don't stop giving birth just because the world is in turmoil!

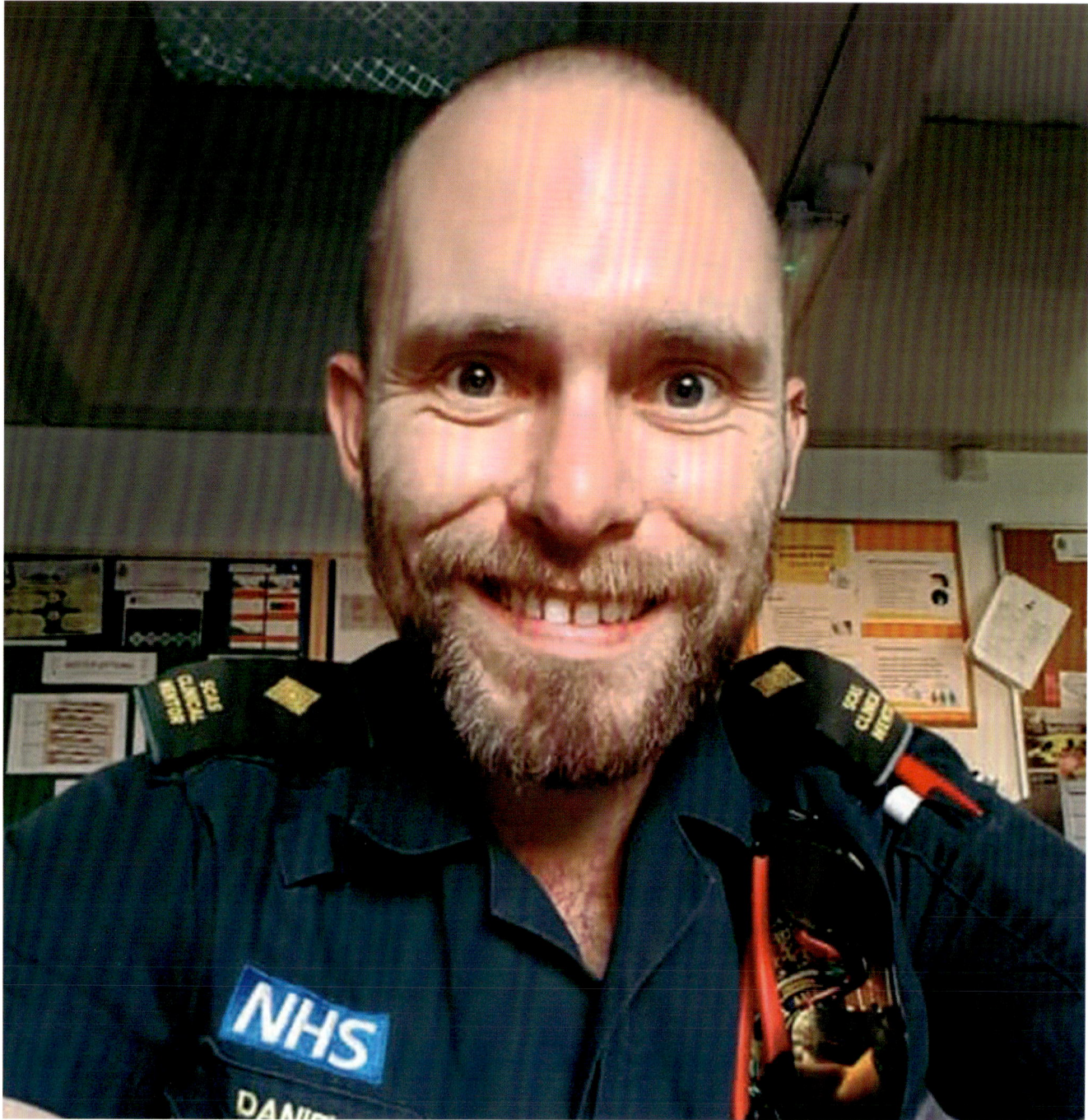

DANIEL MELLISH
Paramedic / Hampshire

It has always been my dream to be a paramedic. I have always wanted to help people and I feel proud to be a part of the NHS.

At the station I am at, I work a 10 hour shift and we have a shift pattern of 5 on / 4 off. Within that shift, I respond to various category calls sent to us from control dispatch. This can be anything from a social welfare call, to a road traffic collision or a cardiac arrest. Every day is different.

With Covid-19, we are still working the same shift patterns, however all training and meetings have been postponed. We have to wear PPE to every job, and we are also having to make some very difficult decisions regarding patient care. I have also had to shave my beard off, which has been my normal look for the past 16 years.

I feel as though I am just still carrying out the job that I love. I carry on throughout the current situation because it is my job and people need help. I am so proud to be part of the front line.

The support the public have shown to the NHS has been amazing and I hope that the appreciation will continue to remain. Thank you to everyone for showing the support to the NHS and essential workers in these times.

My wife is my rock, she supports me when I get home. She is a paediatric nurse, so we are there for each other. My colleagues are my extended family. I think to be in the medical profession you need to have a certain personality, and to get through these times we have to be there for one another.

“
The support the public have shown the NHS has been amazing. I am so proud to be part of the front line.

CHRIS SKAIFE
Ravenmaster & Yeoman Warder / Tower of London

As Ravenmaster and a Yeoman Warder, otherwise known as a 'Beefeater', I live and work at the Tower of London. Usually, it's a very social place to be. On a normal day we'll have around 6,000 members of the public visiting but it can be anything up to 17,000 during peak periods in the year. We'll be busy telling stories to visitors about the Tower of London's thousand-year-old history.

That all changed massively with Covid. In the weeks leading up to Lockdown, we noticed a drop-off in visitors. At that point, they were allowed to visit but there was virtually no-one here. In line with the Government guidelines, the Tower of London was closed to visitors completely from the evening of Friday 20 March 2020.

I've worked at the Tower for over 16 years and on the busiest days, I've often wished for a brief moment of quiet and solitude. I got that – and more – but after 2 weeks, I was desperate to see visitors again.

This is an iconic site that's meant to be full of people learning and discovering history. It was really strange to go from as many as 17,000 visitors a day to none in the space of a few weeks. You could say it was a key moment in the Tower's history – at no time was it this empty. Even in the war, it was a garrison for soldiers.

The Tower is home to a small community of people who live and work at this famous landmark and for us, with the Lockdown restrictions, it sometimes began to feel like the prison it used to be. And of course, the Tower's income was massively affected. The Tower of London is managed by independent charity Historic Royal Palaces and we rely on the support of visitors as a valuable source of income.

But some things still had to carry on … We didn't have our maintenance and gardening teams so we all had to keep everything going and keep it all clean.

I also had to keep looking after the ravens. They're in their own little world a lot of the time so I don't think they missed the crowds too much but they do need engagement (and food!) to make sure they stay around. It's said that the kingdom and the Tower of London will fall if the six resident ravens ever leave the fortress. There are eight ravens at the Tower today — the required six, plus two spare!

> 66
> Usually it's a very social place to be – at no time in the Tower's history has it ever been this empty.

If you smile at someone maybe they'll smile back, and it's just the same with kindness;
if you show some kindness to people then maybe you'll get a little bit in return.
It is important that we show kindness to a lot of people because they are so short of kindness.

// CAPTAIN SIR TOM MOORE

DEBS DAVIS
NSPCC Childline Service Manager / Wales

For many young people, the difficult circumstances they were already facing, including abuse, domestic violence and difficult family relationships, were exacerbated during Lockdown, leaving them feeling alone and trapped.

But at the NSPCC we made sure we were still there for them, with direct services as well as our free Childline helpline and website.

Coronavirus was first mentioned by a child contacting Childline in January and, in the five months that followed, our volunteer Childline counsellors provided almost 7,000 counselling sessions to children and young people from across the UK and Channel Islands who got in touch with a concern relating to Covid-19.

Between the start of the national Lockdown in March and 10th May, Childline delivered over 2,000 counselling sessions every week to children concerned about their mental health and emotional wellbeing – totalling nearly 17,000 over 7 weeks. This included worries about self-harm and suicidal thoughts and feelings.

Our volunteers at Childline have been unwavering in their support. We were surprised with lovely messages of support from a number of Welsh Rugby stars, singer Lucie Jones and even a special rendition of Jess Glynne's 'I'll be there' by the Only Men Aloud choir – all to thank us for our resilience during Lockdown and for enabling the charity to still be there for children.

Our charity has had to adapt the way in which we work, so that we can offer our services virtually to children, young people and their families at a time when schools were closed, families were struggling to adapt to Lockdown and vulnerable children were at even more risk.

Throughout, our selfless volunteers and fundraisers have continued to get behind us, often in innovative ways to complete fundraising challenges as part of a virtual team whilst in Lockdown. That's been vital as we rely on public support for 90% of our income to make sure we can continue to be there for children and young people.

We looked into the risks children might be facing and why they might intensify during the pandemic, including the increase in stressors to parents and caregivers, the increase in child and young person vulnerability and the reduction in normal protective services; and we then recommended a national and local response for Government and statutory agencies.

As a result, we also expanded the services that we offer to children, young people, parents, caregivers and schools, to include specific coronavirus advice such as how to talk to children about the pandemic, coping with tantrums and family tensions and working from home whilst home-schooling as well as return to school support.

Before the pandemic, our NSPCC Schools Service delivered its free 'Speak Out.Stay Safe' assembly face-to-face, in more than 90% of all primary schools across the UK. In 2019/20, they visited nearly 7,000 schools, delivering workshops to almost 1.6 million children before Lockdown was imposed. We're not able to deliver the assemblies in person at the moment, so instead we've made a 30-minute online assembly with the help of Ant & Dec that is available to all primary schools in the UK and Channel Islands, helping children understand how to recognise different forms of abuse, and how to speak out if they need to. As well as this, it also focuses on some of the additional worries that children are experiencing due to the Covid-19 pandemic.

> " We've had to adapt the way we work so that we can offer our services virtually and still be there for vulnerable children.

STURMINSTER NEWTON FLOUR MILL

The mill was last a commercial enterprise between the 1920s and 1970s – back then it was a Feed Mill, producing animal feed. It stopped commercial production in the 70s but during the 80s was run on an ad-hoc basis to produce animal feed and some flour.

In the 1990s, the Sturminster Newton Museum Society took responsibility for the running of the building as a means of producing funds to keep the town museum going. The mill was opened to the public 4 days a week and although some flour was produced as a result of demonstrating the machinery, initially it was not allowed to be sold.

In 2014 we sought permission to sell the flour and – after inspections and following recommendations – we got approval to sell to the flour to visitors. It was never intended to be a high-powered commercial venture, we just thought that a natural conclusion to a trip to a mill would be to buy a bag of flour. We usually produce and sell about a ton of grain per season.

We were due to reopen after the winter but soon realised it would not be possible bearing in mind the vast majority of our volunteers were in the 'vulnerable' bracket and it would be difficult to comply with the social distancing. So we made the decision quite early not to open the mill and closed the museum.

We were extremely disappointed – it was going to be a big year for us. We had several events organised to increase visitor numbers and to fit in with aspects of our application for a lottery grant. We need £500,000 to maintain the mill and we had to show that we could widen the audience and raise the profile of the mill.

But the grain had already been purchased along with stock for the shop so the millers decided that, rather than leave the grain in the store, they would see if it could be put to its intended purpose because they knew there was a shortage locally. The millers worked out how the task could be done safely observing the distancing and then the grain that would have lasted our summer for demonstration purposes was winnowed, milled and bagged up in a very short time.

Most of the flour went to two local businesses – a local baker and a local independent supermarket. We were especially pleased because we knew that both were operating extra services to help people that were unable to go out to shop.

The bags of flour were delivered in the back of the miller's own car to the supermarket and dropped off to the bakery en route.

The reaction has been incredibly positive – the businesses were really pleased that we could contribute to their efforts and help supply their customers. Beyond that, the mill is suddenly being talked about, which is great. We have had contacts from literally from New Zealand, Australia, Canada and the States. It is a weird feeling that from being initially shut down by Covid-19, the mill has had its profile raised and bought to the attention of so many people as the result of a dire situation.

Once this is over, the mill will revert to its role as a historic, atmospheric, working museum.

> " There was a shortage locally so, instead of leaving the grain in the store, we put it to its intended purpose.

SALLY BURGESS
Project Wingman Volunteer / Edgbaston

I was Senior Cabin Crew for Flybe, based out of Birmingham Airport. I worked for Flybe for 15 years and when they went into administration in March, I lost the job I loved. I thought I'd hung up my purple uniform for good.

Then I heard of Project Wingman – a volunteering programme set up by airline captains Emma Henderson and Dave Fielding. Bringing together grounded aircrew from multiple airlines, the programme sets up first class lounges in hospitals to give staff a morale boost and support their wellbeing.

I jumped at the chance to put my uniform back on and joined the Project Wingman team at the Queen Elizabeth Hospital in Edgbaston.

By simply giving NHS staff a cup of tea, biscuits and a friendly smile plus a safe and welcoming space to unwind during their breaks, we helped them to feel appreciated and valued. Project Wingman has also been a saviour for myself and many other crew – some are also under threat of loosing their jobs but volunteering has enabled us to support each other as well as looking after our wonderful NHS.

In May 2020, Project Wingman became a registered charity with bases in over 50 hospitals and around 5,000 volunteers putting smiles on the faces of NHS workers every day across the country.

> We are united by wings and I am proud to have helped others at such a difficult time.

IAN BROUDIE
The Lightning Seeds / London

It was an exciting start to the year. We were doing our first tour in about 6 years, to celebrate the 25th anniversary of the 'Jollification' album. We'd been working towards it for about 8 months with a huge amount going on behind the scenes and a massive set build in production. It was a big moment for everyone involved and I was feeling more engaged with my work than I had for a long time. We also had a lot of other appearances planned so it was going to be the busiest year we'd had for a while and there was a great buzz.

We got to the second night of the tour and everything was stopped.

Immediately, there was a lot of work to do. Unpicking arrangements for the tour and other events we should have been at. We should have been playing Glastonbury, Isle of Wight and lots of other festivals. Unarranging everything meant we were still busy but it all had a negative feel about it now.

We were so disappointed for our fans so we quite quickly rescheduled for next year. Some people said we should have rescheduled it for earlier than we did but now, who knows when it's going to be ok to perform like that again and whether we might have to postpone the gigs yet again. I really hope not but you've got to do what's safe.

I watched my tour figures go from 'sold out' to 'not sold out' and then back towards 'sold out' when we rescheduled. That's never happened before and it was a really funny feeling.

We also agreed to do a load of the drive-in concerts that were popping up. We wanted to be able to give something to our fans even if it wasn't what we'd originally planned. We got everything arranged but then these got cancelled too due to local Lockdowns, so we had to unarrange those as well. It's been a strange situation.

I live in the middle of London so I've not really been out of the house much. All the things I love doing – playing live music, going to see live music, working with bands – I couldn't do any of it. As for many, it's been a real shock to the system. Early on I did some listening parties and radio interviews from home to try and keep in touch and just to share some music with other people but I'm not really comfortable performing online or down phone lines so I found that quite difficult.

I tried to use the opportunity to do a lot of writing but my concentration wasn't always there. I kept thinking of the film 'Groundhog Day'. By the end of it, he'd taught himself all sorts of new things. I kept thinking I should do an Open University course or learn to bake bread or something but it never happened. Fiddling on the guitar made hours go by though!

One good thing all this did do was make me realise that all my life I've had an obsessive focus on music and maybe I need to rethink that a little. I was stuck down here in London and lots of the people I care about most and really wanted to see were up in Liverpool – it's made me understand my priorities.

> "
> All the things I love doing – playing and going to live music – I couldn't do any of it. But it has made me rethink and understand my priorities.

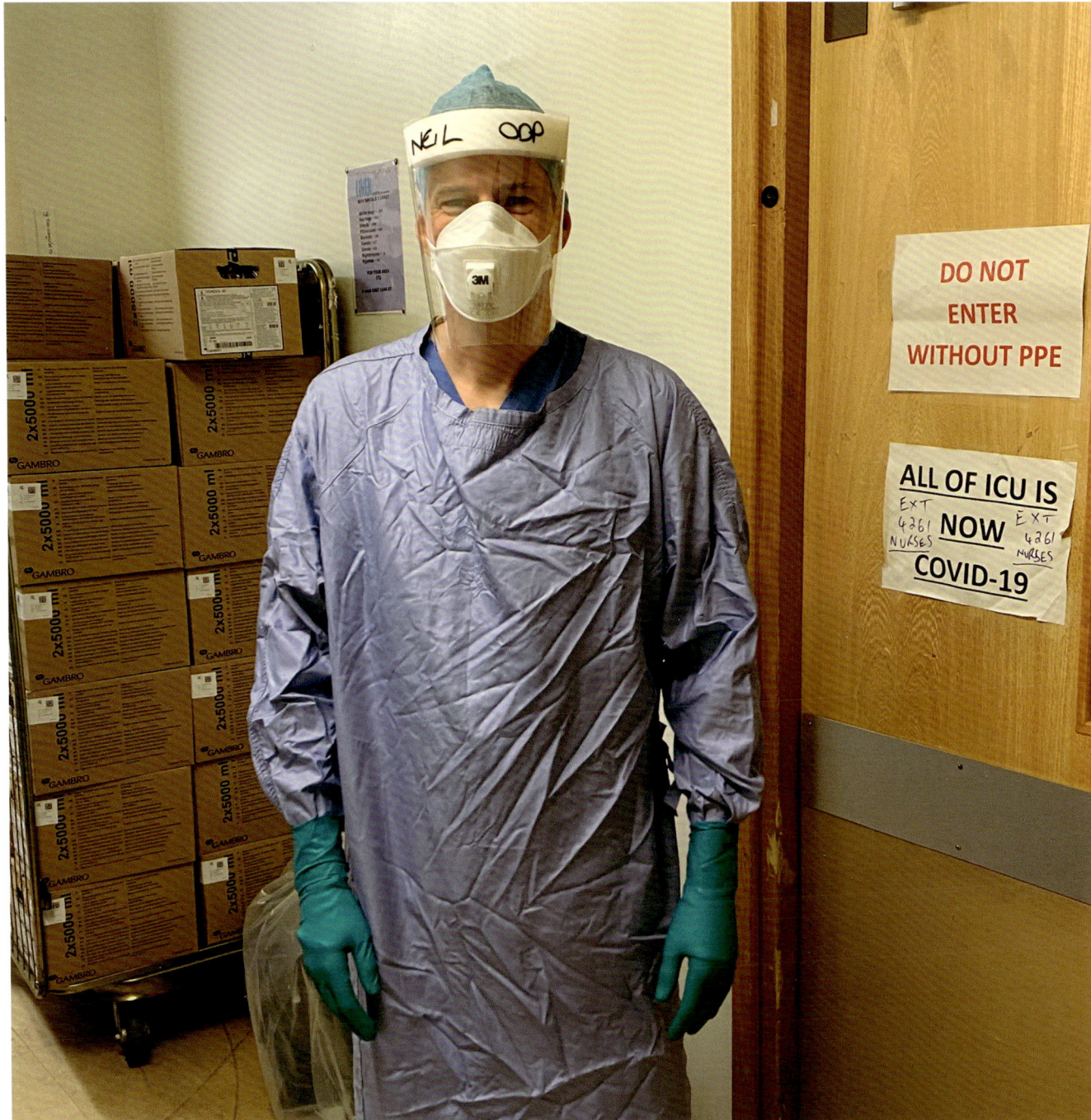

NEIL MALLIN
Operating Department Practitioner / Warwickshire

I'm an Operating Department Practitioner, working in Theatres at Warwick Hospital. I was looking for a change of career from IT Support and had always fancied doing something totally different when I looked on the NHS jobs website and came across ODP. I'd never heard of it before but it was the best decision I made to change career.

My day usually consists of setting up the Anaesthetic Room to prepare for whatever operations are taking place that day. I then assist the Anaesthetist with putting the patient to sleep, inserting and securing the airway, positioning the patient, looking after them throughout the surgery and then waking them up after.

Since Covid, all elective operations have been stopped so I have been redeployed to work in the ITU. This is because they are expecting ITU to reach capacity and that they will have to use theatres as an extended ITU. They are training up theatre staff to do the ITU nurse role as they will not have enough trained ITU nurses so my role has changed massively and I am now doing the role of an ITU nurse.

> I'm just doing what anyone in my position would do – step up and help in any way I could. I would much rather be doing this than sitting at home doing nothing.

I'm currently working nights, caring for critically ill Covid-19 patients. I help evaluate and monitor the patients progress, identify sudden or subtle changes in their condition and respond accordingly. I help deliver their treatment and take care of their hygiene needs.

It's definitely scary, although I'm feeling a lot more relaxed the longer I'm working there. It's a totally different environment with different equipment. Patients are mostly very sick with totally different care needs as compared to patients who come to theatre. What the ITU nurses do is just amazing.

It's also really tiring. I'm doing longer shifts than normal and working nights, which takes some getting used to. Also, wearing full PPE during the shift gets very warm and the FFP3 face masks really hurt your face. Because of this, we're having to take more breaks than usual and therefore using up even more of the dwindling stocks of PPE.

Having my fiancée Emma at home during these times helps massively. If I had to come back to an empty house it would be very hard – not only for company and someone to chat to and have a laugh with, but also help with preparing food and household chores while I'm doing the long shifts. We've had to cancel our wedding but she's kept us both positive and upbeat and really looked after me.

Why do I do it? Because it's my job! I'm very grateful to have a job at the moment and to be able to help. It just happens that my line of work is really needed during this crisis so I'm just doing what anyone in my position would do, step up and help in any way I could. I would much rather be doing this than sitting at home doing nothing. I love my job and working for the NHS and the support off everyone towards the NHS has been amazing.

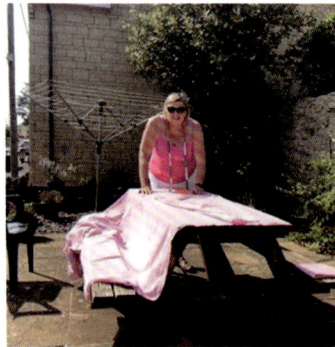

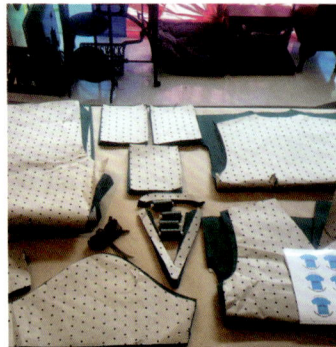

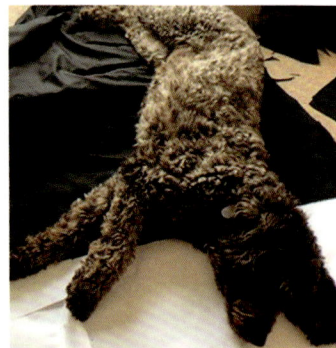

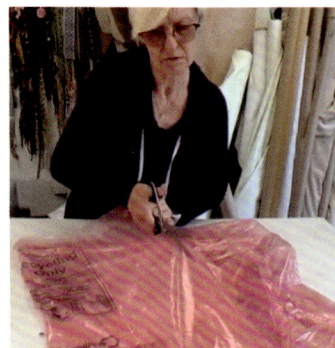

When PPE was in short supply, an army of 'makers' rallied together and made millions of masks, visors and scrubs for NHS workers ...

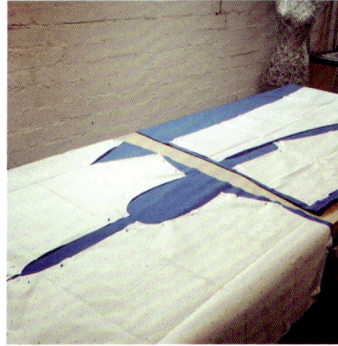

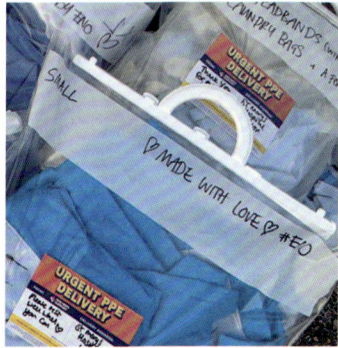

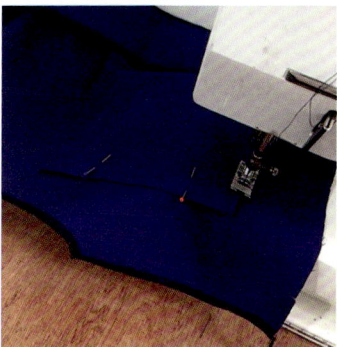

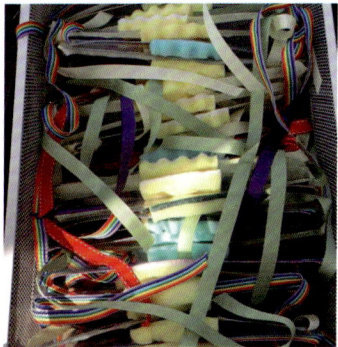

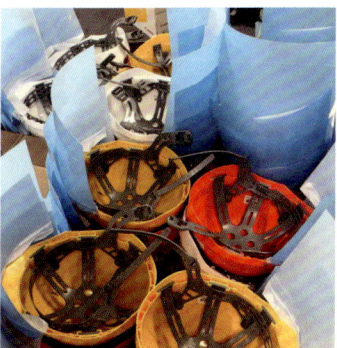

GG HOSPITALITY

GG Hospitality is a hospitality management company co-owned by Gary Neville, Ryan Giggs and Singaporean businessman Peter Lim. We manage Hotel Football which is just across the road from Manchester United's Old Trafford Stadium and is owned by the 'Class of 92' teammates, as well as the Stock Exchange Hotel, based in the original 1900s Manchester Stock Exchange building.

With the situation caused by the Covid-19 virus, we felt that we had to temporarily close these two hotels in order to ensure that the health and welfare of our team members, as well as that of our guests, was safeguarded to the best of our ability. We worked with our team to put together a package for the coming months, so that we didn't make any member of staff redundant or put anyone on unpaid leave.

Following discussions with Manchester University NHS Foundation Trust, we also then offered to accommodate their healthcare workers and medical professionals free of charge at these hotels, providing them with a comfortable place to stay in the city centre and near to work during these challenging times.

We're living in unprecedented times and we've taken these decisions in the most responsible way possible and in a way that supports our team whilst also extending further support to the wider community.

Winston Zahra / CEO

A key consideration in our plans was to try and support the wider community and more specifically our local NHS hospitals. By offering both of our hotels without cost to the health service, we hope it gives some support to the healthcare professionals in a time when they need it.

We will reopen to the public once the situation is declared safe and in the meantime we will do our utmost to ensure our team are looked after and to help the wider community where possible. These are not easy times but we are confident we will come out on the other end stronger as a company and a community.

Gary Neville

> A huge thank you to Gary and the team for this incredible gesture. It will give a real boost to our hard-working NHS staff who are working around the clock to provide care for the communities we serve.
>
> *Gill Heaton / Group Deputy CEO at Manchester University NHS Foundation Trust*

STUART FEARN MBE
Head of Customer Contact / Newcastle Building Society

Pre-Covid, a normal day was helping people to save and invest whilst helping others to fund their dream purchase of their home. Working from head office, surrounded by colleagues and getting out and about across the North visiting branches and meeting community contacts. I lead a great team of 200 people across 31 locations.

The Society has a stated purpose that could be considered a fixation of mine: "connecting communities with a better financial future". This focuses us on those around us, whether customers or not, and as a result we see an awful lot of great things taking place, from the community groups we support financially to the rooms we provide for free in our branches or the volunteering and support of those in need that takes place every day.

Since Covid, the greatest challenge has been the stop on moving around. However with the use of Teams, Zoom, Google and all those other great video tools, things are immediate and contact is possible, just through a screen.

In terms of work I can truly say I have never been as busy, keeping our locations, colleagues and customers Covid safe. It is a new job in itself that changes daily. We have to keep on top of it and sometimes double check we've got it right – it can be confusing!

The significant majority of colleagues needed to be here as an 'essential service'. Access to cash is really important for many of our customers. My team maintained an almost flawless performance delivered at the highest standard through this, often when concerned and frightened themselves.

We did receive a significant level of calls around mortgages and from concerned customers worried about, "what next?". Positively, we were one of the first out there immediately providing the assurance and support required. Again it was one of those moments that the teams all pulled together to support one another and the worried customers. How did I feel? I felt proud! Proud that there were no second thoughts, proud that it was simple … let's make this happen, let's help our customers get peace of mind.

It was clear early on that this was one of those moments in life that will (hopefully) never repeat itself. We weren't ready for it and most lived in some form of shock for months. With some other photographer friends, we made a plan to help capture the moment for many, on their doorstep, through their window and all socially distanced. In return and where possible, they gave a donation to the foodbanks who were struggling and needed support. I photographed hundreds of people and filled shopping trolley after trolley with food for the foodbanks. It felt amazing!

I also got involved in a couple of other wonderful projects – an online portal to help direct people to some of the struggling high street businesses in North Tyneside and also bringing the 'On Hand' volunteering app to the North East.

Personally, I have watched my family thrive. My now 10-year-old has learnt so much and has really advanced digitally. My wife has supported us throughout, held a full time job, home schooled and put up with me at home. My middle daughter gave birth quite dramatically. She was blue-lighted from York to hospital in Hull, about to deliver baby Bobby at 23 weeks. He held in, was delivered a few weeks later and is now 6lb and healthy – a miracle amongst all of this chaos.

I was shocked to get on the Honours List. It's not something I could ever have considered. I honestly feel that I'm fortunate because I work with and know so many great people doing such great things. This couldn't have happened without them and it is for them all.

> " I felt proud – proud that there were no second thoughts, proud that it was simple. Let's make this happen – let's help our customers get peace of mind.

BOB JESSHOP
Open Micsolate / Batcombe

Picking up my guitar and singing always cheers me up. With the need to stay at home, I had a chance to play more but knew I'd miss playing at the open mic in my local, The Three Horseshoes, which is brilliantly run by Frank and Lisa.

So I thought I'd start a little Facebook group for a few people to post a tune or two.

Well it all went a bit mad from there – 200 hundred participants in a day blew me away! Then more than a thousand members in a week. Less than two weeks later, it was over 2,500 members and 30,000 posts, comments and responses. There's now a team of admins who all work really hard to support the group and our members.

People have sung, played, joked and read poems. Some have been really brave and posted their performance in public for the first time. And many have mentioned it's been helping them get through being stuck indoors in the early stages of Lockdown.

Any style, any standard is what we say. If it makes you happy to sing, why not share it – you probably won't be the best or the worst so, if you fancy it, go for it. Equally, if you just like to listen, that's great too.

We've enjoyed listening to so much fantastic music and if it's made a few people a bit happier, I'm delighted. The comments and feedback have fostered an unbelievably positive and encouraging atmosphere and a wonderful online community who support and look out for each other.

At last count, we have almost 7,000 members from over 30 counties. Music unites us. Music is the glue.

> Playing, singing and gigging has been central to my life for years now. At the time of the lock down there was no little anxiety that it could be months before any of us could play together again but Bob's Open Micsolate page relieved that anxiety. And let's face it, us musos are tarts for an audience. This has given us a chance to feed the ego and stay sane. It's been a delight.
>
> *Andy Barrett*

BHAGTI PATEL
Paralegal and Volunteer / Kent

I'm a paralegal and, pre-Lockdown, my workday mornings began with me running to catch the overground train, seeing all the familiar faces of my commuting 'family'. Depending on how delayed my train was, I would alternate between walking and taking the tube for the second leg of my journey.

I would sit in a pod of six desks surrounded by a lovely team of paralegals and the rest of the team dotted around close by. It is that social aspect that I have missed over Lockdown – Zoom meetings and telephone calls can't replace those moments!

Sitting at my office desk was very quickly replaced with sitting on my bed with my laptop, curtains shut to prevent the glare of the summer sun reflecting on my laptop screen and turning me into a shadow on the several Zoom calls that had suddenly become my main form of professional interaction.

Having that distinction between work and home was more difficult that I thought it would be. Once I'm in my 'zone' it's difficult for me to pull myself away from my work. When you're in the office you have to stop working at some point to commute back home but at home the 'five more minutes' very quickly turns into several hours.

It's amazing how much time is saved when you don't have to commute to work though. I've had more time to spend catching up with family and friends and to explore and engage in different hobbies. I've had the chance to take advantage of the warm weather and have done a lot of gardening. With my cousins, I put together a greenhouse in which I now have all sorts growing!

I was furloughed in May but then started volunteering with the National Emergencies Trust. My role with NET was a lot more fast-paced than my 'normal' job. I had a lot more responsibility and, as it is a much smaller organisation, there is a lot more internal communication which was great especially during Lockdown as it very quickly made me feel like part of the team.

I have learned a lot about grant giving and the amount of work, thought and effort that all the different individuals across charities and other organisations put into planning, presenting and assessing grant proposals. It's amazing how quickly we all came together to try to help individuals in the UK during this difficult and uncertain time and it just goes to show that where there is a will, there is a way.

The uncertainty about the virus, about work, about how our lives will be impacted – this was most challenging before the Lockdown was in place. I know others who have felt differently, but the safety of having more control over my environment and who I was exposed to, provided a bit of comfort.

I wanted to do as much as I could to help. At our weekly meetings, the team would share stories of the beneficiaries we were helping. Hearing about the difference our work was making, such as putting food on the table of thousands of families every week, motivated me to put in as much effort as I could so that our efforts to provide emergency relief could reach and help even more people.

> "It's amazing how quickly we all came together to try to help. It just goes to show where there's a will, there's a way.

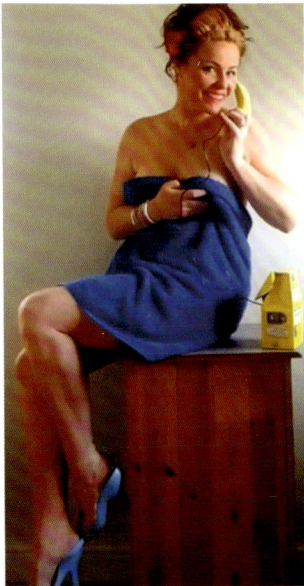

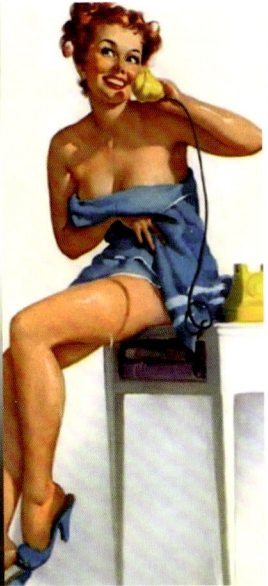

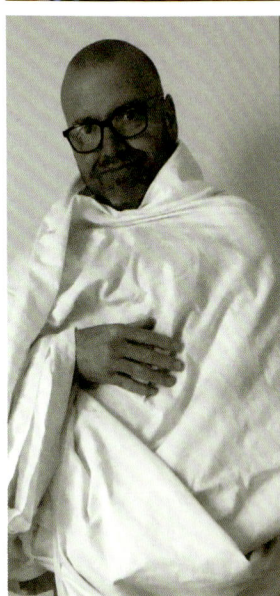

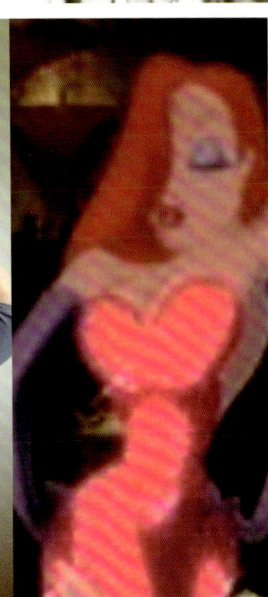

KATIE RICHARDS & JAMES WILKINSON
Couple Separated By Lockdown / Newquay

We've been together for 19 years – with a 16 year break! We first dated back in 2000/2001 but we parted ways and both went off and had new relationships. I got married and had a son called Eddie. James and his ex-partner had a daughter, Lyra. We lost touch and hadn't spoken for about 7 or 8 years and then in July 2018, we bumped into each other at a festival. We spent the weekend together and the rest is history!

We're not together right now because we live separately and need to stay that way over Lockdown so that James can continue to see his daughter. I'm considered high risk due to an auto-immune disease, so I'm following government shielding guidelines. Right now it's early days but it feels pretty strange, and July certainly seems a long way off. But I figure we survived 16 years apart so we can manage 12 weeks!

We are both quite creative. He is the artistic one whereas I'm is more of a mess maker under the guise of creativity. I'm not sure who made the first recreation suggestion but now it's a daily challenge. We send each other an image and have to recreate it within 24 hours using just what we have to hand. I'm a hoarder and James is a minimalist but so far he has done pretty well with all his challenges!

We share the images on our Facebook and social media and friends and family are loving it! I think they're getting keen to throw in some suggestions of their own and with eighty something days to go I reckon we may have to call on their ideas sometime soon!

I love the reveal when he sends me his photo. I never know how he's going to interpret the challenge or when I'm going to get the photo and it brightens up my day for sure.

Katie

Katie and I bumped into each other at a Port Eliot Festival after 18 years apart. I was wearing a tutu and a foxtail so obviously very attractive! One thing led to another and we got back together. I guess destiny stepped in.

I live close to my daughter Lyra who I co-parent and I have her roughly 50% of the time. As long as myself and my ex-partner, who also lives alone, have no contact with anyone else we can continue to co-parent her. I'm a very committed daddy, and it's important to me for her to know I'm close, more so than ever right now. Katie has to be shielded due to underlying health conditions so I can't have any contact with her for 12 weeks.

It's not ideal, but other people have it a lot worse and it's protecting lives, which is what's important right now, whether it's friends or strangers. We've got to think of others, not ourselves right now. We've got this, and we're just trying to send some positive vibes.

Basically, we send each other a picture or character and you have to dress up as them using stuff in your house. Katie has a more impressive wardrobe whereas I've a wig and lots of random stuff. It's got some great reactions if I'm honest and I'm more than happy to make an idiot out of myself to make someone else smile. I don't think Jason Momoa is under any threat from my Aqua Man! It's making people smile and right now, I think that's nice. I'm more than aware it's not going to change the world but I'm quite a happy, smiley positive person and if it cheers someone up, then hey that's nice.

I'd like to say thanks to all the key workers and the NHS. We're grateful beyond all belief, they are unbelievable. And lots of love to all those out there on their own right now – it's not easy. Stay safe everyone, it's cool to be kind, smile it can change someone's day, oh and please wash your hands.

James

> " We've got to think of others, not ourselves right now. We're just trying to send some positive vibes.

DON'T QUIT

When things go wrong as they sometimes will,
When the road you're trudging seems all up hill,
When the funds are low and the debts are high
And you want to smile, but you have to sigh,
When care is pressing you down a bit,
Rest if you must, but don't you quit.

Life is strange with its twists and turns
As every one of us sometimes learns
And many a failure comes about
When he might have won had he stuck it out;
Don't give up though the pace seems slow —
You may succeed with another blow.

Success is failure turned inside out —
The silver tint of the clouds of doubt,
And you never can tell just how close you are,
It may be near when it seems so far;
So stick to the fight when you're hardest hit —
It's when things seem worst that you must not quit.

// WRITTEN BY JOHN GREENLEAF WHITTIER
READ FOR THE BBC BY IDRIS ELBA

NHS CARE PACKAGES
Amy Jackson & Laura Tinald / West Sussex & Birmingham

I'm a self-employed costume designer and whilst everyday is usually different, my work is pretty constant. Depending what phase of the project I'm in, I could be drawing designs, visiting costume makers, buying fabric or going to fittings.

With Covid, the live entertainment industry has completely vanished so I don't have any costume design work at all now. Somehow though, I've never been so busy.

I came up with the idea of making care packages for the NHS staff after seeing the pressure marks, bruises and sore skin they were suffering from all the extra PPE they have to wear. I decided to make maybe perhaps 50 packs for nurses locally and asked a friend of mine, who is a specialist hospice nurse, if this would be wanted or of any use. He said they'd all love it. He came back with a long list of wards in the hospital and other places, like St.Wilfrids Hospice, that were all affected by this too.

I needed to make at least 300 packs just to cover the hospice staff, my local ICU ward and Covid ward. So I started to call skincare and chocolate companies, asking them to donate their products to these packs.

I asked Sally from Sweet Theatre Ltd if she would send some of her chocolate bars and she very kindly sent me several boxes. When I said I was attempting to make several hundred packs, she came up with the idea of making a special NHS chocolate bar, which Laura designed a beautiful illustration for.

For me the packs had to be more than just practical help. I wanted to include products like lip balm and hand cream, and also some more luxurious products for them to take home and relax with – stress relief and sleep aids, as well as chocolate and bath oil. The packs were supposed to be a gift to say thank you and we are thinking of you all, not charity packs.

The response has been amazing, both from the companies and the nurses and I'm so pleased this worked. I honestly feel like doing something and keeping busy has helped me a lot too. Creating a job and a focus has been a way to get through this Lockdown and loss of work. It feels good to be doing something for the NHS, but it doesn't feel like anywhere near enough when I deliver the packs and see who they are going to.

Amy

I'm an illustrator and designer. Several illustration jobs have been put on hold for now, but I am lucky in that I still have some art commissions to work on, plus a steady flow of design work.

I worked with Sally (at Sweet Theatre Ltd) in 2014 when she wanted to create some Shakespeare-inspired chocolate bars and had a vision of featuring the leading ladies from the plays. She got in touch and it was right up my street as I love painting girls and beautiful eyes!

Sally got in touch again a few weeks ago saying she wanted to do a Florence-inspired bar to go into care packages and to commemorate Florence Nightingale's 200th birthday, with proceeds going to the NHS. I was glad she got in touch because I wanted to find a way to help too.

I had a look at photos of Florence and other artists' impressions of her. We thought loose ink would look classic and fit with the theme. I worked from a reference photo of Florence and then added my own style to it. I wanted her gaze to be the main focus of the illustration. She was a really inspiring lady!

I was glad to do something that will hopefully make people smile. I feel very passionate about the NHS too, and hope in some small way, the bars will bring some joy. I'm also really proud to be doing something to help boost NHS funding, but I do wish they had what they needed without people having to do things like this and hope this crisis will encourage that to be reviewed. We are indebted to every single person who works for the NHS.

Laura

> " The packs had to be more than practical help – they were a gift to say thank you and we are thinking of you all.

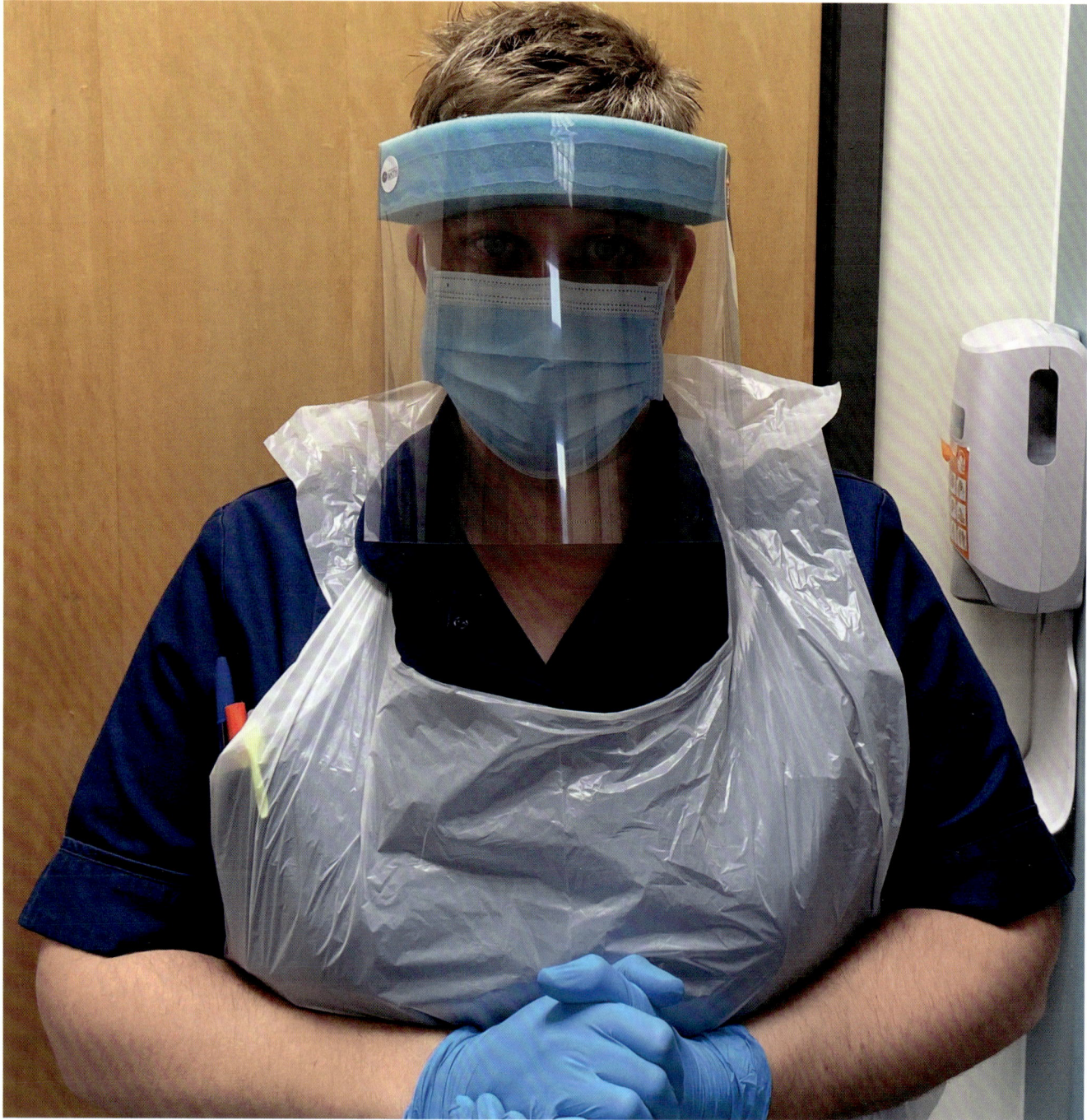

ANDREA MORGAN
Sister (Fracture & Orthopaedic Outpatients) / Bath

Usually, my area sees approximately 3,000 patients a month with Orthopaedic conditions and trauma injuries. I work in a very busy department working 8 a.m.-6 p.m. four days a week. The department is full each day with up to 12 clinics in the morning and another 12 in the afternoon, staffed with a mixture of Health Care Assistants and trained nurses.

Back in March, I was moved to a non-patient-facing role due to my medical condition at the start of the pandemic. Unfortunately, I then received a government letter to shield.

Thankfully, I was able to go back to work at the start of August. I had felt so guilty at not being there for my colleagues and not being able to do my bit to help.

A lot of changes happened within the department during my absence. Clinics were reduced or cancelled completely. Telephone consultations were implemented and some staff were moved to other areas in the hospital, like ICU, to help where they were needed.

Now, all clinics have been reinstated, although patient numbers on clinic lists have been reduced to allow social distancing in between patients. My job has not changed, but the way I work has, to support government guidelines. I have to wear a face mask from the minute I arrive at the hospital until the minute I leave and I need to wear full PPE when in contact with patients so that's also gloves, apron and eye protection.

It's very real, it's happening and it's very frightening. I feel very anxious dealing with patients. Especially as my wife and I are both in the extremely vulnerable category. I worry that I'm putting her at risk doing my job.

But there are some lighter moments. We have protective plastic screens up that surround the reception desk with a 4 inch gap at the bottom. A patient (in her 80s) decided to bend down and tried to fit her face in the gap because she thought she had to speak through it – luckily she had a mask on!

As a group of nurses and HCAs, we've become very close and supportive of each other. Knowing we are doing our bit to protect our patients and each other is what makes me proud to be an NHS nurse. The public support has been heart-warming and overwhelming – the clap evenings always made me tearful in a happy way. I love my job, but going home to my wife and cat at the end of a long, busy day is blissful.

> 66
> It's very real, it's happening and it's very frightening, but we are doing our bit to protect our patients.

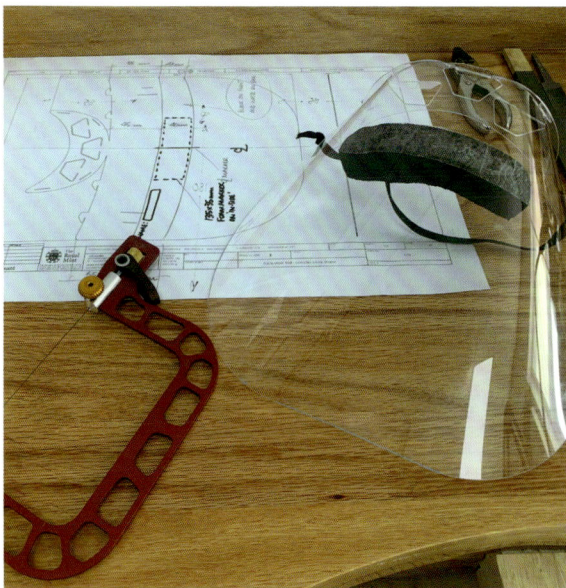

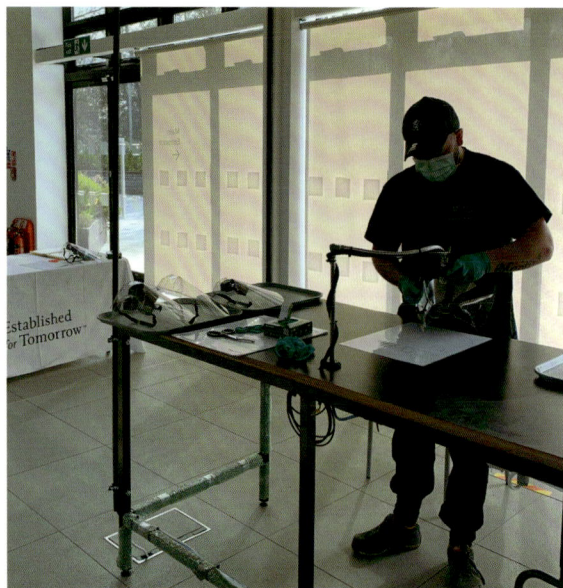

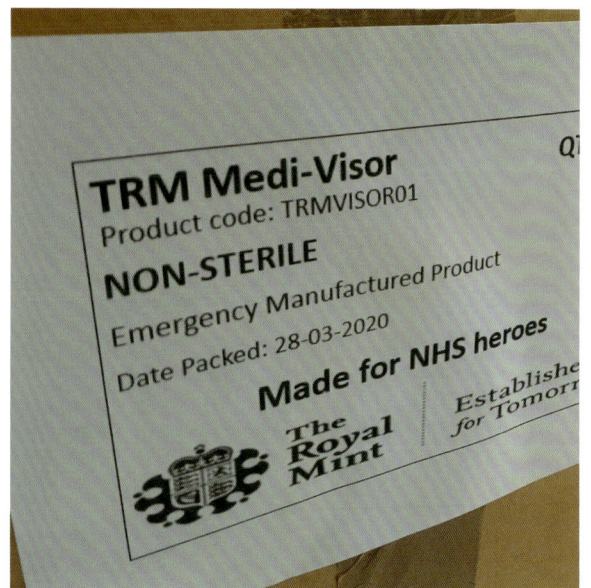

TRM Medi-Visor

Product code: TRMVISOR01

NON-STERILE

Emergency Manufactured Product

Date Packed: 28-03-2020

Made for NHS heroes

The Royal Mint — Established for Tomorrow

THE ROYAL MINT

When people think of The Royal Mint, they usually think about the coins in their pockets but we've been making all sorts of useful products for the nation for over 1,000 years and have a team of skilled designers, engineers and production staff.

We wanted to play our part in the fight against Coronavirus and to support the NHS. Some of our colleagues have family that work for the NHS and it really focuses your mind on the challenges they are facing and the opportunity we have to support them.

We started searching for protective medical equipment we could make on-site that would help NHS workers keep the nation and themselves safe and pledged to make almost 2 million medical visors, as well as supplying other essential PPE from our stores.

Together – and in consultation with staff at the Royal Glamorgan Hospital – our team turned a rudimentary visor design into a working model that was comfortable and durable, in just 48 hours. We then became the first firm in the UK to secure BSI safety approval.

Within a week we were manufacturing thousands of visors per day, working with our key suppliers to source the components needed to make them.

We transformed our visitor attraction into an emergency production line and have been making over 100,000 medical visors a week exclusively for the NHS. It's also meant we were able to keep manufacturing jobs open whilst our normal production was scaled back.

We are extremely proud that so many of our medical visors are in use at so many hospitals across the country.

Anne Jessop / Chief Executive

We are incredibly grateful to The Royal Mint for this work. The equipment will be vitally important for our frontline staff to protect themselves and others as they work to respond to the Covid-19 pandemic. It is also an excellent example of teams working collaboratively to provide safer environments for our staff and patients.

The generosity of organisations such as The Royal Mint, as well as our communities, has been humbling and I would like to thank everyone for their continued support for our staff and the NHS.

Dr Sharon Hopkins / CEO of Cwm Taf Morgannwg UHB

> "
> I applaud The Royal Mint for refocusing their efforts and working around the clock to play their part during this national emergency.
>
> *Rishi Sunak / Chancellor and Master of the Mint*

MANCHESTER UNITED FOUNDATION

Supporting Manchester United's community plan, Foundation coaches have been involved in distributing food donations across the region. This includes food banks and schools, plus a sizeable donation to the NHS Manchester Foundation Trust Charity, a family of nine hospitals across Greater Manchester.

At the beginning of the crisis, the Foundation and Club packaged 30,000 items of food and drink to deliver to Stretford Food Bank, Salford Royal Hospital and a number of other local charitable organisations in Manchester dealing with the impacts of the coronavirus pandemic. Staff cleared the stadium's bars, kiosks and kitchens of all perishable goods stocked for use up until the summer and loaded them into a fleet of Foundation vehicles with volunteer drivers on hand to make the deliveries.

As part of #ACITYUNITED, the Foundation donated £50,000 to the Trussell Trust, a network of over 1,200 food bank centres, including 19 in Greater Manchester as part of a joint fan-led initiative with Manchester City.

The Foundation also delivered over 60,000 prepared meals free of charge for NHS staff across Manchester in a joint initiative between United, Manchester United Foundation, Mealforce and the club's catering supplier, Bidfood and involving over 80 permanent and casual club staff, who volunteered to prepare the food in the kitchens at Old Trafford. Staff and facility costs were covered by United while all other costs were underwritten by Manchester United Foundation.

Foundation vehicles were also dispatched to Salford Royal NHS Foundation Trust and the NHS Manchester Foundation Trust Charity to deliver over 3,500 Manchester United gifts as a thank you to NHS staff including hospital cleaning and backroom staff.

Where possible, Foundation coaches continued to support partner schools that remain open to children of key support workers and those who are vulnerable.

More recently, the Foundation committed £100,000 of funding to be used to purchase bulk supplies, which have been delivered to a number of local food banks and food clubs.

"The Foundation is dedicated to supporting the local community; we continue to adapt and diversify at this most challenging time to enable our workforce to assist those who need it most.

"While many of our regular programmes have been disrupted by the pandemic, Manchester United Foundation is doing everything possible to continue helping the communities that we serve during this period of elevated need.

"I am incredibly proud of how united our workforce is; the number of staff volunteers wanting to support this initiative has been overwhelming and I thank everyone for their commitment to this inspiring scheme."

John Shiels / Chief Executive

> The Foundation is dedicated to supporting the local community and we continue to adapt and diversify at this most challenging time.

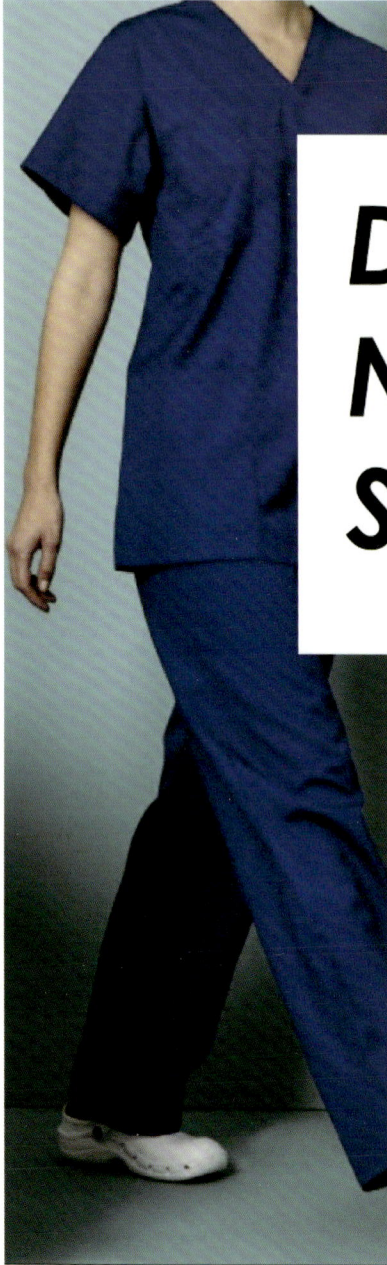

DO YOU NEED SCRUBS?

WE'D LOVE TO HELP

We are a voluntary community group who love to sew and are making scrubs to order for NHS staff across the UK. to find out more information visit

www.scrubhub.org.uk

#scrubhub
#DresstheNHS

COULD YOU SEW SCRUBS?

THERE'S A SHORTAGE

Do you have garment production experience? We are a network of voluntary community groups making scrubs to order for NHS staff across the UK. To find out more visit

www.scrubhub.org.uk

#scrubhub
#DresstheNHS

THE SCRUB HUB

Following a request through a local WhatsApp group from a local doctor in need of scrubs, a team of four neighbours who work in the charity and fashion sector, organised a small-scale production line for scrubs with local volunteers in East London.

It had emerged that there was a shortage of scrubs (special hygienic clothing) for NHS staff amidst the Coronavirus crisis. Many doctors, who don't usually wear scrubs, needed to buy their own for use during this time but a lot of suppliers had run out of the medical uniforms.

Brooke Dennis, Maya Ilany, Annabel Maguire and Rebecca Zehr were joined by a team of over 50 volunteers, all working to help meet a shortage of scrubs for NHS staff living and working in North East London. The initiative had a huge response from the public and the team also assisted hundreds of volunteers from across the country to set up their own local 'Scrub Hubs' to meet the demand in their own community.

In the course of a month, over 100 hubs were set up according to guides produced and shared by the group. Across the UK, thousands of scrubs were delivered by local sewers for local health care workers.

> 66
>
> I'm very tired after a day at the Nightingale but I'm thrilled with my new scrubs. They making working easier and help keep my family safe
>
> **Dr Katie Ward**

The planning, production and delivery all had to meet the requirement of this unprecedented isolation period. Fabric cutting was done in isolation, meetings happened over Zoom, decision making over WhatsApp and email, and our delivery volunteers 'knocked and dropped' sewing kits to local seamstresses on their exercise breaks. We had to be agile to adapt to these new and quite unusual circumstances. It was a challenge to keep the work flowing, but the community spirit and bonds within the group are strong despite many not being able to meet properly in person.

Challenges came up in different areas. At first, it was managing the massive influx of both volunteers and orders from doctors, and then it was trying to source fabric because the readily available supplies of cotton drill were dwindling in the UK. We realised the sheer magnitude of the situation across the country.

The biggest win was delivering our first batch of scrubs and getting fantastic feedback from the doctors. Seeing their relief and the direct help we had given was really special and spurred us on. There were lots of happy tears.

Another milestone was when the second Scrub Hub set themselves up using our guidelines, We then realised that our local initiative could be successfully replicated across the country, meaning more doctors and health care workers would benefit.

We are truly grateful for the opportunity to put our skills to use and support NHS staff on the frontline, who are working 24/7 to keep us all safe. We have been overwhelmed by the sheer number of people who heeded our call from all across the UK, and it's been heart-warming to see many set up their own, local Scrub Hubs.

We hope this scrubs shortage will be addressed and solved as quickly as possible and that NHS staff will be provided will all the tools and equipment they need to do their work but we are doing the best we can to help plug the gap in the short term.

We also hope our community effort might highlight a little about how scrubs are normally sourced through a global supply chain and whether a partnership between the NHS and UK manufacturers could be fostered and developed beyond the crisis. We'd like to champion a 'made in Britain, ethical scrub'.

Photographers offered 'Doorstep Portraits' – often in return for food bank or charity donations – to capture memories whilst we were confined to our homes ...

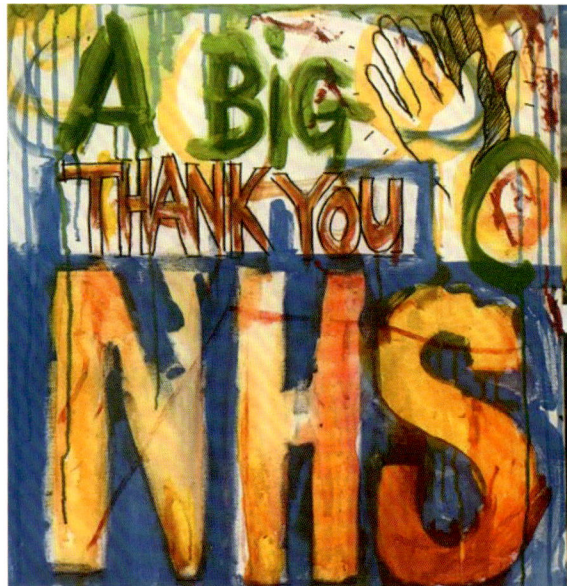

BONHAMS

Bonhams 'Blue Auction', held in aid of the NHS Charities Covid-19 Urgent Appeal, was a not-for-profit digital auction with pledges generously donated by the UK's leading actors, musicians, artists and sports people.

More than 60 pledges were listed including Afternoon Tea with the cast from 'The Crown' and lunch at Claridges with Dame Joan Collins and Christopher Biggins; a 'University Challenge' quiz hosted by Jeremy Paxman; artwork by Anish Kapoor, The Connor Brothers and Ronnie Wood; special passes to any live show with Jools Holland and his orchestra; a walk-on role in 'Call the Midwife'; a night at the opera with Joanna Lumley; tickets to the 2021 British Film Festival and racing suits from six times F1 World Champion Lewis Hamilton and upcoming star Lando Norris as well as a VIP experience a the 2021 British Grand Prix. And much much more.

The appeal raised over £400,000 and Bonhams waived all charges which means 100% of proceeds are going to the appeal which will help support the health and wellbeing of NHS staff and volunteers supporting Covid-19 patients in ways above and beyond which NHS funding can ordinarily provide – including wellbeing packs and gifts for staff and volunteers on wards and departments and supporting the cost of travel, parking and accommodation for NHS staff and volunteers.

"The NHS staff and volunteers are heroes to us all. We at Bonhams are honoured to host this initiative and to donate the skills we have at our auction house to support those who are working so hard for us on the frontline."

Patrick Masson / Managing Director for the UK and Europe

66

When I was approached to support the auction, I really wanted to help out, so I phoned round a few of my co-stars from the television show 'The Crown' and the result was the creation of 'The Alternative Royal Family Tea Party'.

Olivia Colman

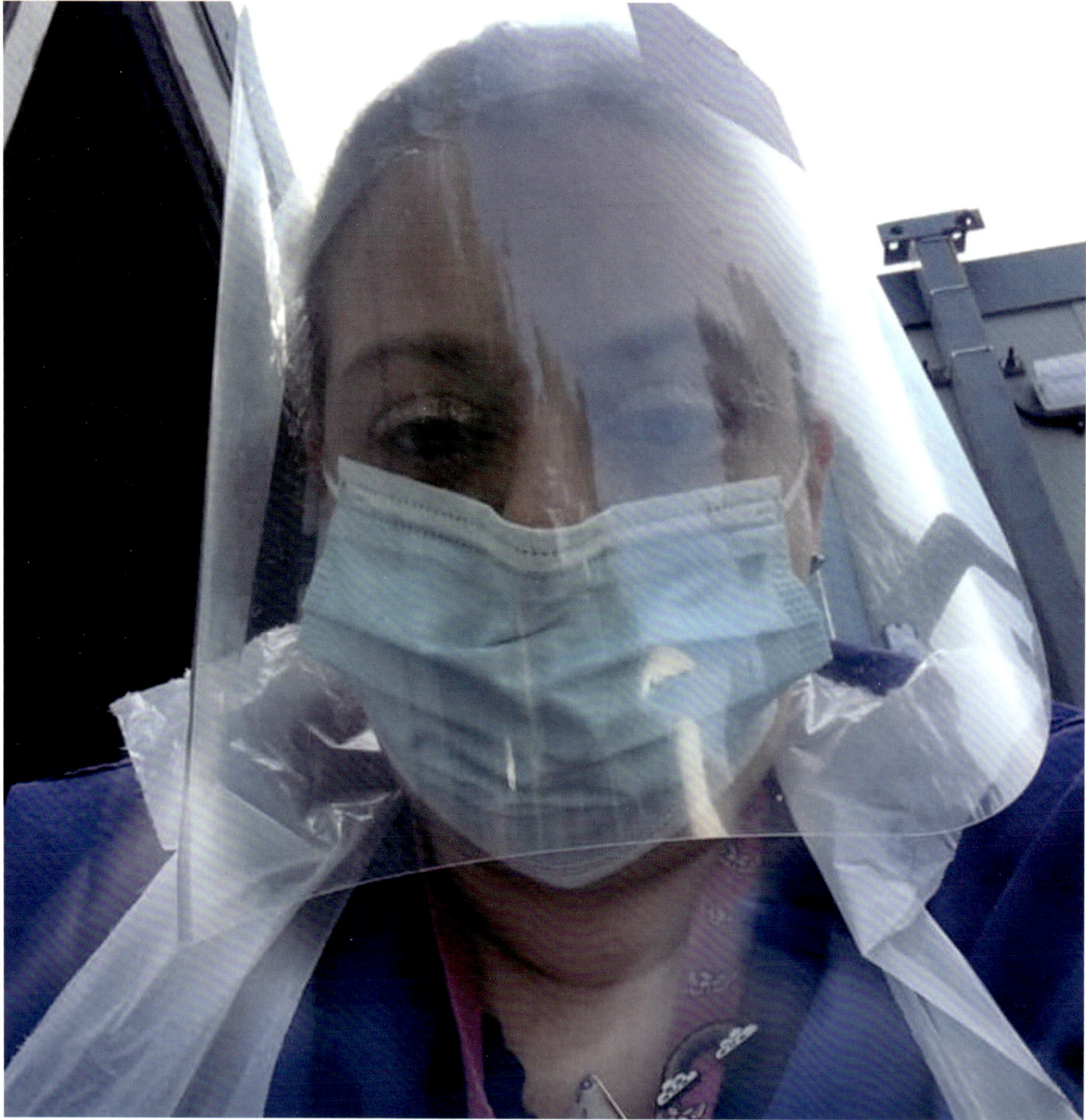

JESSICA NEALE
Health Care Assistant / Harlow

Normally I spend my days doing blood tests, ECGs and checking results for MRSA status and urine results. We'd also manage the notes going to the various areas that will be dealing with the patient for surgery or further investigations so the notes are in the right departments for the surgery to proceed as planned. We try and make the process as easy and as smooth as possible and try to put patients at ease too.

Our job changed completely with Covid. We were no longer doing any part of our job anymore. One of the things we were trained to do was to test the masks that staff would be using in Covid situations to make sure they were safe.

I also did shifts in ITU which was very daunting as it was very different to what we usually do but was a good insight as to what the nurses go through every day. The patients were all ventilated and it made it all very real especially as one patient was the same age as my husband and I could just picture him laying there with no way of family getting to see them or know how they're doing.

The next day I was just covering the reception in the day unit were we had been relocated and I actually cried, feeling almost guilty that I was just there while I knew the work people were doing upstairs and how hard it was with all the PPE on.

We were then asked to help with Covid swabbing patients that were going to be operated on and we're still doing that, with patients coming to a drive through swab area which we call 'The Pod'. Patients are swabbed prior to surgery and must then self-isolate. They're retested 72 hours before surgery and if all is clear the surgery can go ahead.

It's been emotionally challenging as we're were coming to work some days not knowing if we would be asked to help on wards or ITU but you feel a mixture of guilt and relief to be left to carry on with the mask testing and swabbing.

My team has been amazing and it's been nice to meet staff that you would never normally come in contact with. I hadn't long joined the pre-assessment team but we have been there for each other and I am so grateful to them for appreciating me. I've proven myself to be a team player, always volunteering for extra days or early starts to catch the night staff to be tested. And even though I fractured my ankle, I have been coming in with my moon boot on – still doing my job!

We are starting to do a few more surgeries now at the hospital and patients are starting to come in for their pre-op checks while the pre-assessment nurses are doing telephone assessments. Our Covid critical state has reduced completely so things are trying to get back to semi-normal but still continuing to stay safe. Hopefully slowly things will keep getting better but it has definitely been a hell of ride.

> " Our job changed completely with Covid. It's been daunting and emotionally challenging and it's definitely been a hell of a ride.

ZANE POWLES MBE
Assistant Headteacher / Grimsby

I support the head and deputy with the day-to-day running of the school; supporting staff in class, giving pastoral support to children and teaching some intervention classes. I also run a Resource Base supporting children who have SEMH/SEND needs and have been excluded from mainstream education.

The changes to my job – WOW these are massive. I've been nicknamed 'Captain Covid' due to my role in school! The changes at school, physically, have been immense due to staggered start and finishes; separate lunches and staggered playtimes for every bubble; changes to learning areas and how staff are able to support children; one way systems and how to get 300+ children through 8 toilets and washing their hands without anyone crossing bubbles is a mammoth task in itself. The teachers at school have been awesome and the children have been absolutely immense and adapted to all the changes.

My plan to get food delivered started as soon as the government announced that all schools would be closing on March 23rd. The concern as soon as we heard that was – how are we going to make sure the children get their free school meal? How are we going to make sure all is ok at home?

This is when I decided to print off a map, plot addresses on the map and deliver every meal, every day to all of those children. Staff would make all the buns up and pack them into my rucksacks and I had a bin bag fastened to me that was full of crisps. In the second week, jacket potatoes, tins of beans and meat hampers were added to the load.

At the same time, I also delivered home learning packs to children that didn't have devices or online at home and checked on our vulnerable children to make sure they were safe.

This continued for 17 weeks pretty much the same, rain or shine, every single day. It amounted to delivering over 7,500 meals, walking 550 miles and carrying more than 4 tonne in weight.

The response was were amazing and something that I did not expect. They had posters in their windows, would come out and clap and wrote messages on their garden walls and on the roads and cars beeped their horns. The school arranged a surprise parade for my penultimate day, with everyone singing the Proclaimers song '500 miles'. I had no idea this was happening and it was one of the best days of my teaching career.

The feedback was immense and appreciated but at the same time very overwhelming. I started this to support our children and families because it was the right thing to do. I am quite a private person so when I started getting phone calls from media companies, lovely supportive comments on social media and parents being so nice, I started to really struggle. I was just doing something that was the right thing to do and was part of my role as a teacher – to support our children, as much as I can and in any way I can, all the time, no matter what.

I think the best part for me was when my three children would message as they had seen something on the TV or in social media and would say how proud they are of me, that they love me and could see the difference I am making to families. For me, the actual getting out, seeing children and families benefiting from our efforts was all I needed. Seeing their smiles and appreciation, chatting randomly to parents about general stuff and knowing that I was there for them. I also saw my role, compared to theirs, as easy. I was walking some miles and carrying a fair bit of weight but it was nothing compared to being stuck in the house 24 hours a day with children for weeks. They had the tough part of the deal and that I was making that easier for them was all I needed.

I feel totally honoured to have been chosen to receive an MBE. Not in my wildest dreams did I think this would ever happen. I still feel a little uncomfortable about receiving it as there are thousands out there that do so much but I was a Grenadier Guard and have guarded all the royal palaces many many times, done lots of royal ceremonies and four 'Trooping of the Colours', so it will be amazing to go back on the other side of the fence.

> "
> It's my role as a teacher to support our children as much as I can and in any way I can, all the time, no matter what.

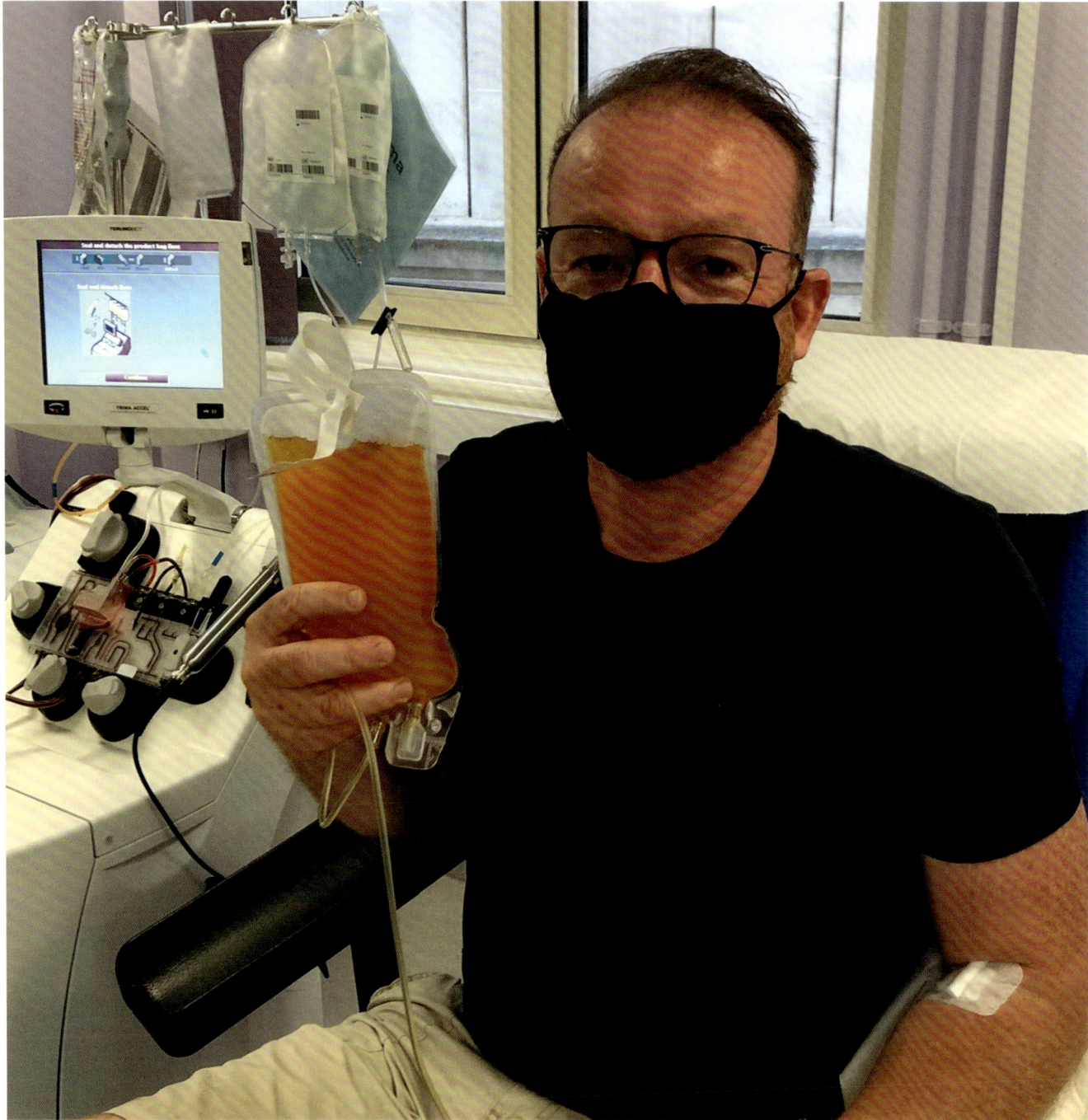

DARREN BUTTRICK
Covid Survivor & Plasma Donor / Staffordshire

Just before Lockdown, I had the darkest day of my life. I had a temperature over 40 and just could not breathe. I was rushed to hospital by ambulance. On arrival, I was admitted to ICU and told that I needed to be put into a coma and ventilated to save my life.

Thankfully the doctors and nurses at New Cross Hospital in Wolverhampton did just that. I was frightened for my life. I was crying and begging them not to let me die.

I'm 48, in good health and with no underlying health conditions. They said that all this was a positive but they were dealing with an unknown virus. They said they would do everything they could to save me but I needed to prepare myself and my family for what could be the worse possible outcome. My oxygen level was at a very worrying level and my body was very poorly.

I had 15 minutes to call my wife, three girls, parents, two brothers and sister and some close friends. My daughters had an idea what was happening but I didn't want them to know how serious it was. Those calls were very emotional and hard. I still have messages people sent telling me to fight for my life, that they loved me and would be praying for me.

Two messages from the time always stay with me. One of my daughters had no idea about the severity of my illness and said: "Dad, please have a nice sleep and come back soon". That message still breaks my heart today when I read it. And the CEO of the company I work for messaged to say "Darren fight for your life, every one of us is also fighting for you".

I cried and once again begged the nurses who took me to theatre to not to let me die. They held my hand and kept saying "Fight this and we will help you fight it. Stay strong".

I was in Intensive Care and ventilated for a week. After 5 days, I was taken off the ventilator but my body didn't react well to this, so they had no choice but to sedate me and reventilate me for a further two days. During this time I was awake and conscious and could see everything going on in intensive care. Seeing other patients in comas and on ventilators all around me was very upsetting. It was really distressing seeing just how bad this virus had taken hold of some people.

I had what I would call 'out of this world' care by two nurses. When I was successfully taken off the ventilator, they let me Facetime my wife from their personal phone so she could see me. That was just amazing – they were angels. I hadn't seen my wife for a week and for her to see me recovering and off ventilation was a memory we both won't forget.

I was taken to a high dependency ward for two days and remained on oxygen before being discharged.

I owe my life to the doctors and nurses at New Cross Hospital. The NHS saved my life, along with my fight and determination and the love and support I received from family and friends, which helped me through this.

At the end of April, I had a call from the NHS asking if I'd be willing to take part in plasma donations to help with the trials. It was a no-brainer for me – I had been saved and now wanted to give back. On 2nd November, I donated plasma for the tenth time and will carry on giving back to help others as I was helped on that very dark day.

We have some tough times ahead but I hope my recovery story gives everyone hope, confidence and faith that there is life after Covid. I do pray for everyone suffering Covid or other illness, and for those that did not make it, or whom are still suffering, I send love. Stay strong, safe and well.

> The NHS saved my life and now I want to give back.

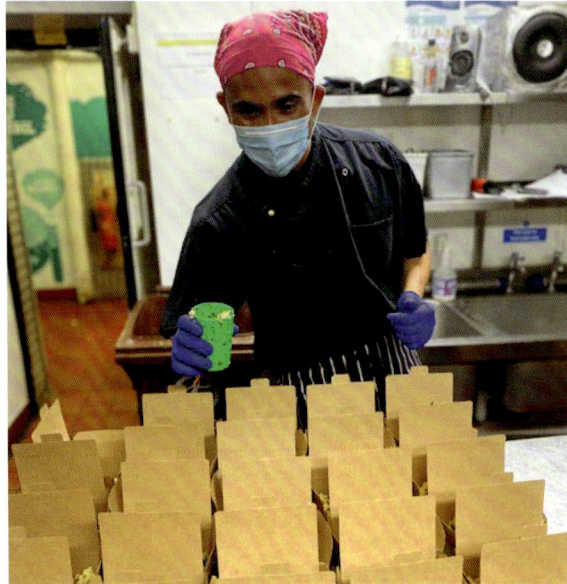

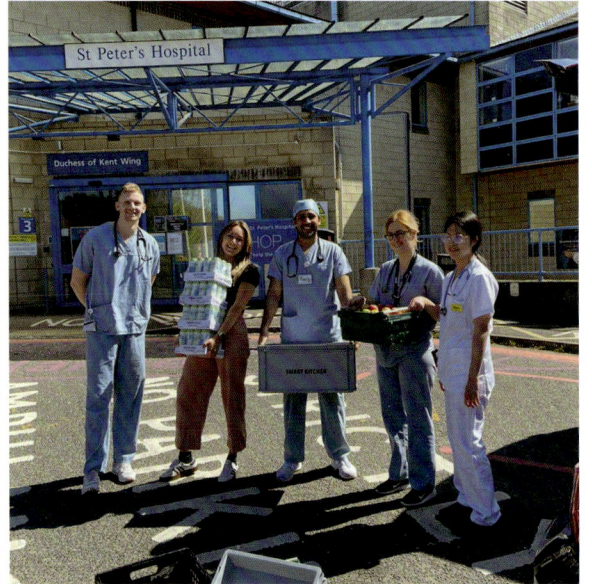

LULU DILLON
Cook-19 Founder / London

The film I had been working on as a PA had been suspended indefinitely, so I was out of work for the foreseeable future. My friend Clem (an NHS doctor) had been moved to work on a Covid ward. She was spending her days off learning about ventilator logistics and had a week of night shifts ahead.

To help a little, I went shopping to stock up her freezer and cooked her a lasagne. It seemed to really mean something to her so I decided to call all the NHS medics I knew and ask if I could cook for them too. From these conversations, I got a sense of the pressure they were under and decided to ask for donations from friends and family so that I could keep cooking for NHS staff beyond my immediate friendship group.

The donations came thick and fast and the message was very clear – people wanted to help the NHS. So, Cook-19 (a feeble pun on Covid-19!) was born. It is a crowd-funded community with food that is a gift from people who feel indebted. Every morning I cooked and then spent the afternoon delivering food parcels to medical staff. The response was overwhelming.

Within a week, Cook-19 grew apace. My family helped shop for ingredients and deliver food. My 84-year-old shielding grandma baked butterfly cakes. A great family friend, Angela Hartnett, wanted to help. She is widely renowned for her Michelin star restaurant, and began cooking at home with her chef husband.

But if we were going to do this properly, we needed a professional kitchen. Angela had a friend who catered for huge events and had the kitchen space and equipment to enable us to scale up safely. They agreed to help; and then three of my oldest friends volunteered to organise distribution and our volunteer workforce, with people driving across London daily to deliver food to hospitals.

We received an email from the wife of an ICU anaesthetist who was worried about her husband and his colleagues who were often living off vending machines for 15-hour shifts. Feeding a whole ward was not a commitment we had foreseen, but we couldn't ignore the request. So we started doing safe, contactless drops of 100 meals every 24 hours so that those in the ICU would be fed through the day and night shifts.

Members of the public have donated over £120,000, Fortnum & Mason donated 800 Easter eggs and people I've never met before have volunteered to help. We had 15 volunteer drivers and around 30 chefs volunteering at any one time – including every chef at Angela's restaurant.

The frantic pace of our expansion left me little time to reflect why I was so moved to support the NHS. My mum, Heather, who was my best friend and remains my hero, died of cancer when I was 21. It was the worst time of my life and NHS nurses and junior doctors devotedly cared for her, eased her suffering and supported me through every hour. It was my mum who taught me to care about others, to listen to their struggles and to work to change things for the better. If she hadn't instilled in me the vital joy there is in bringing people together to do good in the world, none of this would have happened.

In a world that might feel gloomy right now, the fact that we've been able – through the hard work and generosity of so many – to look after those that look after us, feels special.

This started when I cooked my friend Clem her favourite meal, and now over 140 volunteers have delivered almost 75,000 meals to the NHS. Our admiration of the courage, strength and selflessness of the NHS staff we support has never waivered. We believe there is magic in the nourishment of good food, cooked by good people. Food that is given with no strings attached, but with the hope that it gives strength to those that receive it. Food cooked with love by those that give their time freely, who use the skills they have to create something for others that says "We're thinking of you, we're here for you, we thank you".

> " We believe there is magic in the nourishment of good food cooked by good people, given with hope that it gives strength to those that receive it.

Do all the good you can,
by all the means you can,
in all the ways you can,
in all the places you can,
at all the times you can,
to all the people you can,
as long as ever you can.

// JOHN WESLEY

MARK SHOTTON
Postman / Bruton

I've been a postman for 10 years and I love it. It's a bit different now and sometimes difficult to maintain the 6ft distance, but once I'm out and about on a round delivering, I still love it like at the best of times.

There's definitely more post going about. Some of it's essentials but there's all sorts. Although to be honest, it depends what you call essential. For some, ordering garden paint might not be essential but for that person, if it gets them out in the garden, into the fresh air and helps their mental health, then perhaps it is essential to them.

> There's precious little to smile about at the moment so if I can put a smile on someone's face, I feel like I'm doing something worthwhile.

The whole dressing up thing was almost a mistake. Someone saw a video online of a postman who had done his round in fancy dress, and asked if it was me. It wasn't – and I said it definitely couldn't be me anyway as I don't have any fancy dress outfits.

So then the fancy dress outfits got donated! Friends, people on my round and even a local costume hire company got involved.

I didn't really have any excuse then so I did a round dressed as Superman. The reaction was fantastic. In fact it was bloody awesome. People were driving past waving and beeping and excited to see me every day, in all sorts of different outfits. It really bought the community together for what was not really very much effort – I was just doing my job.

I live on my own and suffer with depression. All of this Covid and Lockdown nearly drove me mad, but feeling like I was doing something good for the community really helped.

There's precious little to smile about at the moment so if I can put a smile on someone's face, I feel like I'm doing something worthwhile.

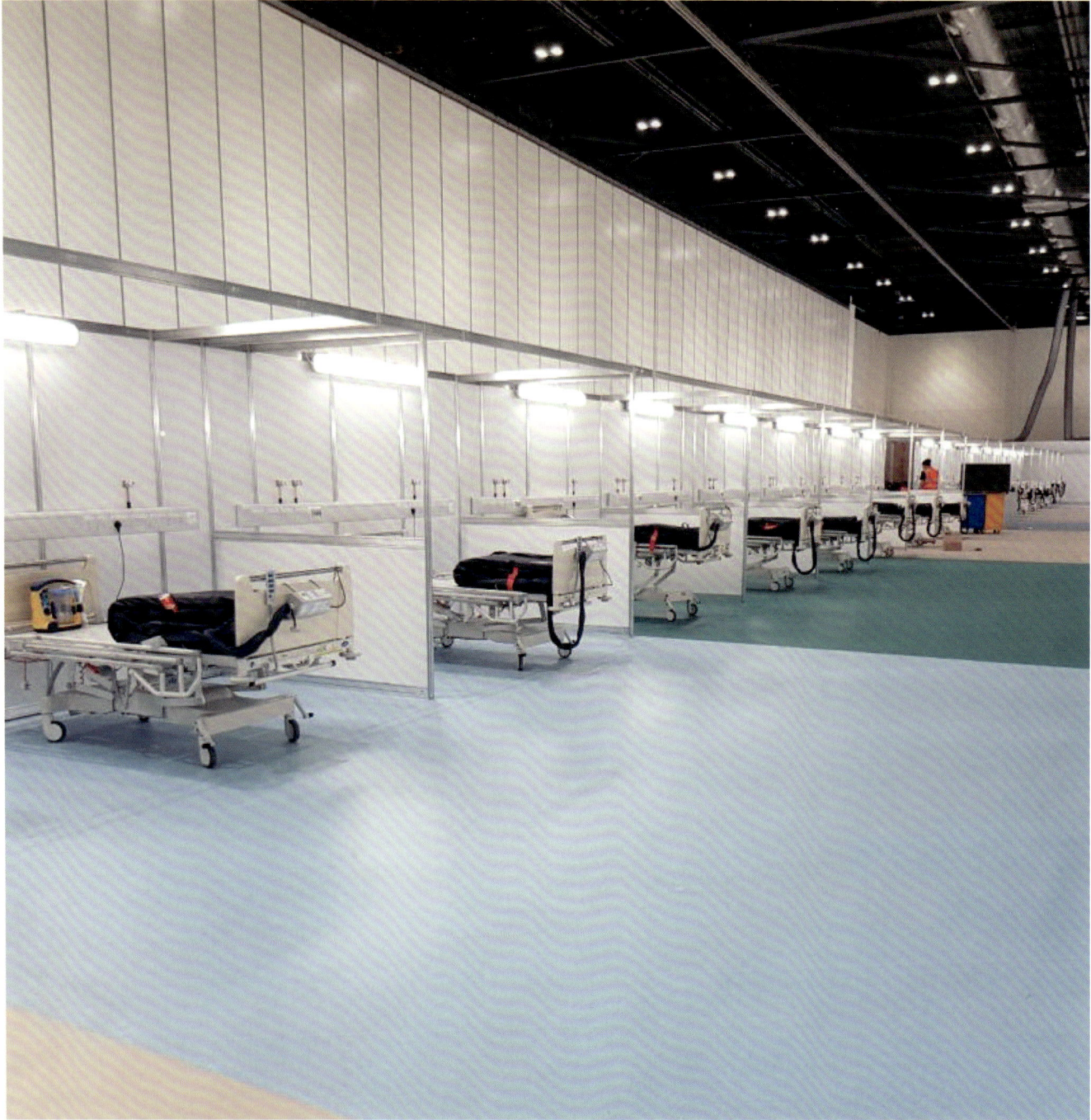

TREVOR BLAKE
Exposure Events & Global Experience Specialists / Redditch

I have a story to tell that may bring a warm feeling to your hearts.

With the onset of the current crisis, my client company GES was tasked with helping to build a temporary field hospital at the London Excel Exhibition Centre. No small task but one that we jumped at, given the chance to help.

The hospital would create an additional four thousand hospital beds and, with other hospitals already reaching capacity, it may be needed sooner rather than later.

It was reported by various newspapers that The Army transformed the Excel event centre into the Nightingale field hospital, and whilst indeed they were instrumental in the organisation and transformation, it was also the sweat and hard work of hundreds of event people who made it possible. Hard working contractors from stand builders and carpet fitters to electricians and plumbers.

Whilst working on the project, I happened to create a LinkedIn post saying how the Excel was really starting to look like a properly equipped hospital and that within another couple of days it should be fully functioning.

And that's where the story gets even more interesting.

I really didn't expect what was about to happen because of that post, but I can hand on heart state that it has left me a lot more optimistic about humanity in general.

Within the space of one day, the post garnered over one million views, vastly surpassing my own LinkedIn network. It quickly went viral with people passing it to their connections and them to theirs and so on and so on. It literally exploded!

And then it happened. Firstly started the influx of connection requests and, upon accepting these, came an influx of messages followed by message after message from businesses, self-employed people and people on furlough all wanting to help out!

It was overwhelming in all honesty; over 2,500 messages, some simply wishing myself and my team well, some asking how they could help on the project and offering their services – electricians, gas engineers, IT professionals, private nurses and even a surgeon. It was mind blowing.

One company offered to donate four hundred motor homes to the NHS for the staff working at the hospital, another to supply, for free, any furniture they may need to set up temporary offices and breakout rooms. One company offered to donate anti-microbial matting and another, two container loads of sanitizer and protective masks. And this is just a fraction of what was offered – the list is huge.

All in all it was an absolute eye-opener and a true testament to how humanity puts aside the petty issues and greed in the face of a crisis and pulls together as a team. It was truly inspiring and has left me feeling very warm inside.

I hope that where possible everyone is managing to self-isolate and that by doing this we can beat this virus. And remember that even in our social separation we can all work together to make this situation easier. Keep in touch with loved ones by phone or video call regularly and more than anything look after each other where possible. At the end of the day this will drive home to us all, through this period of separation, just how lucky we are to have each other.

> It was a true testament to how humanity puts aside petty issues and greed in the face of a crisis.

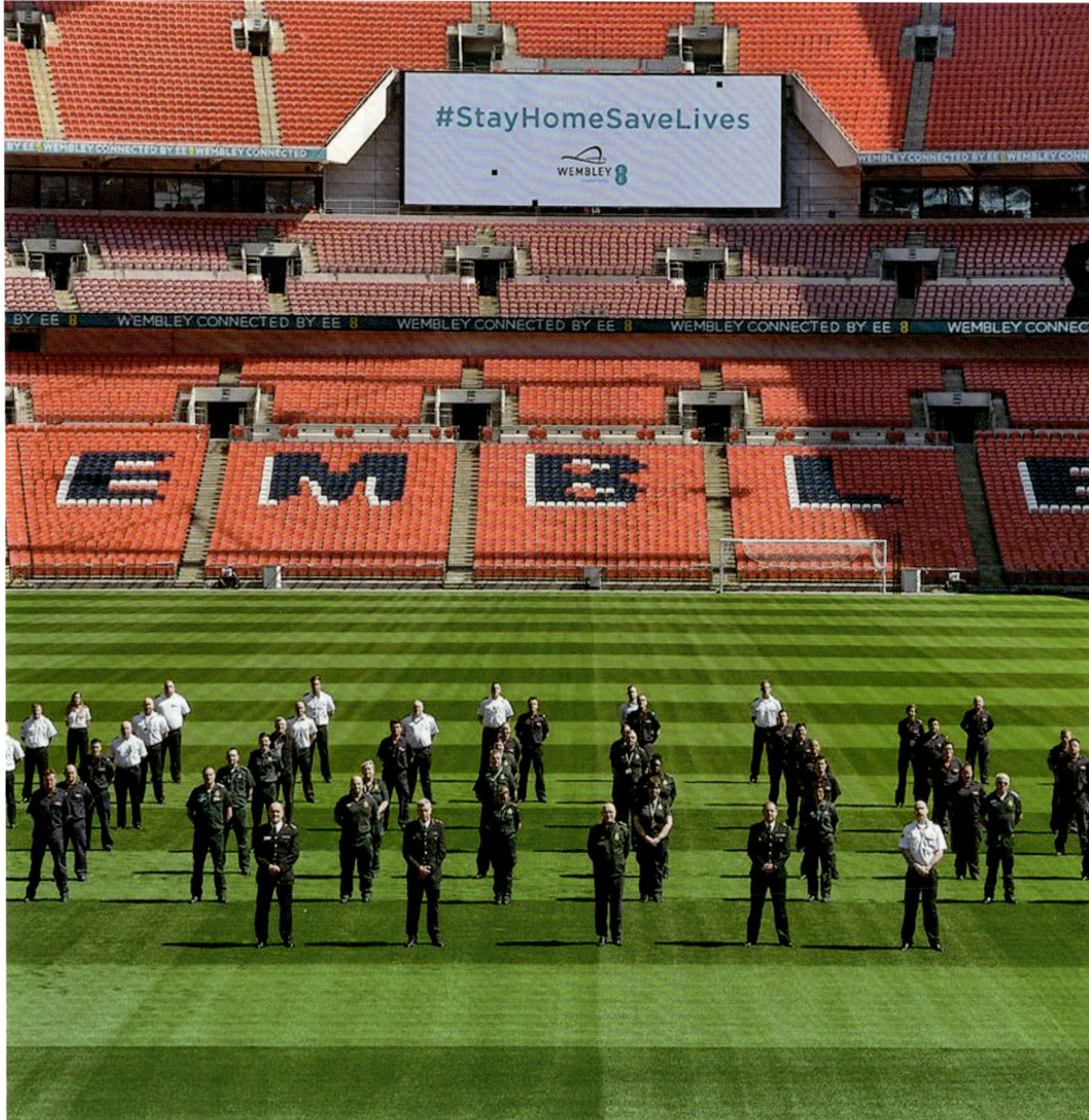

DAVID O'NEILL MBE FINSTR MICPEM
Deputy Assistant Commissioner / London Fire Brigade

The outbreak of the global Coronavirus pandemic led to the greatest blue light collaboration ever seen between London's three emergency services. The London Ambulance Service, Metropolitan Police Service and local authorities asked the London Fire Brigade for assistance in response to the unprecedented demand placed upon them.

I was asked to explore ways in which we could support blue light partners and a list of options was drafted up for discussion at the Commissioner's Continuity Group and then presented at the multi-agency GOLD/Strategic Coordination Group.

I was then asked to lead our response, Operation Braidwood, which was delivered by operational staff volunteers across three distinct areas – Ambulance Driver Assist, the Pandemic Multi-Agency Response Team and Mortuary Body Handling.

With Ambulance Driver Assist, we had volunteer Firefighters co-crewing the additional ambulances procured in response to the pandemic. Over 300 operational Firefighters were detached to the London Ambulance Service for six months to act in the role of driver/assistant. Wembley Stadium was the venue selected to conduct familiarisation training for these volunteers. In groups of 40, each 'batch' underwent familiarisation in ambulance driving, casualty handling and the issue of PPE.

Our Firefighters were then allocated to an ambulance hub and, to date, over 95,000 incidents have been attended by London Fire Brigade volunteers. At peak, an extra 168 ambulances were available to Londoners as a result of this arrangement.

The Pandemic Multi-Agency Response Team saw multi-agency teams responding to Covid related deaths in the community to investigate the circumstances of the death, certify the death and prepare the deceased for undertakers.

And the Mortuary Body Handling saw us provide assistance at temporary mortuaries. We had a lot of enquiries from recently retired London Fire Brigade staff expressing an interest in helping with the cause in some way. This role seemed an ideal opportunity to use those ex-officers to fulfil the request for support.

Additional roles were also developed for non-operational volunteers to support their operational colleagues with call handlers helping to answer calls at control as well as supporting the welfare of operational staff in their volunteer roles with a programme of 'buddy checks'.

Operation Braidwood is just one of the operations being undertaken by the London Fire Brigade to support the pandemic. Other initiatives include facemask production, PPE distribution and the delivery of food parcels and medicine.

The urgency of these projects has required the secondment of staff from various departments within London Fire Brigade HQ and unprecedented collaboration between the Brigade and our blue light partners, alongside the NHS, City Hall and local authorities. The success of Operation Braidwood could not have been secured without the support of staff and the various representative bodies to prepare and secure risk assessments, PPE, training, operational guidance, rota management, facilities issues and welfare.

We are proud to have worked together like this to do our bit.

> 66
> The pandemic led to the greatest blue light collaboration ever seen and we are proud to have worked together to do our bit.

JAMIE CHRISTON
Chief Operating Officer / Chester Zoo

As COO of the UK's biggest charity zoo, there isn't really such a thing as a normal day anyway, but my job changed massively with the outbreak of Covid-19. The day job went from planning exciting projects to make our zoo even better for the animals and our visitors and to carry out our long term mission of preventing extinction, to putting everything on hold, switching into crisis mode and trying to save the future of our zoo.

All of the vast amounts of planning and all of the logistical challenges associated with caring for 35,000 incredible animals and managing a huge 128 acre site continued, but we had to do it with a much smaller team, with social distancing measures in place. And then we had to close altogether.

It was eerily quiet around the zoo without any visitors at all. It was also a little sad that, as the beauty of our zoo came to life as spring turned into summer, hardly anyone else could share these changes and so many lovely moments with us. The animals definitely missed seeing our visitors' smiling faces.

For our keepers, it's been business as usual providing the animals with the world class levels of care they receive every day. But for our management team it's been very different – furloughing staff, working out the logistics of how we can open in a Covid-secure way to how we can save the zoo. We're so lucky that we have a fantastic team of people behind us, and I can't thank them enough for their relentless energy during such an uneasy time.

Chester Zoo contributes over £83 million to the regional economy, supports over 1,700 jobs, protects wildlife in more than 30 countries and engages hundreds of thousands of young people – who'll be responsible for the future of our planet – every year, so what we do is important far beyond the zoo itself.

We lobbied the government to allow us to safely reopen, after three months of closure with no income really pushed us to the brink. That included the launch of our multi-channel campaign to save our zoo – it's been a real rollercoaster period in the zoo's history but we had an absolute determination that Chester Zoo would survive this pandemic, for our staff, animals and plants; for conservation, education and science; and for continuing the zoo's vital mission to prevent extinction. It's felt overwhelming at times, there have been a lot of early mornings and sleepless nights, but we have given everything to save our zoo.

The public well and truly came to our rescue, getting behind our campaign and it's amazing to see so many people continue to fundraise for us. I can't express how thankful everyone at the zoo is. Every kind donation, every word of support, it really is making a huge difference to us.

Persuading the government to allow us to reopen is something we won't ever forget. Words can't describe how much we were taken aback with the sudden U-turn, and we were absolutely elated to be able to reopen our gates to the public. It was our lifeline and not an exaggeration to say it really did help us to save our zoo. It's been just phenomenal to see how much love, passion and energy we've been shown from the public.

Reopening was a detailed, military operation, balancing ensuring that we continue to provide an optimal visitor experience, with cost cutting and income generation, as well as trying to maintain our species-saving conservation work. Each day comes with new challenges and tweaks to operating processes.

It was great to see our first returning visitors and hear how delighted they were that we were open again. It was also vital for the zoo's financial survival and a huge relief. There's a real buzz of excitement about the place again now but there's also still a long way to go before we're fully back on track and we're having to pause lots of major projects. The financial damage suffered has left a deep scar and the road to a full recovery remains uncertain but now we've started to safely welcome visitors back, we've some renewed hope that this great charity zoo has a future.

> 66
> We had an absolute determination that Chester Zoo would survive this pandemic and the public well and truly came to our rescue.

BRAIN TUMOUR SUPPORT

Brain Tumour Support is uniquely dedicated to supporting anyone affected by any type of brain tumour, at any point from diagnosis and for as long as support is needed. We're here not just for patients themselves, but also families, carers and loved ones. The charity's origins lie in one family's own devastating experience which resulted in a pioneering support service that has developed over the course of seventeen years.

We've been impacted massively by Covid. We had to radically adapt our ways of working right across the charity to ensure we could continue offering support. This meant a much smaller team and, as our community is already medically vulnerable, operating without any of the face-to-face support which has always been at the heart of our service.

Receiving a brain tumour diagnosis is like a bomb going off. It disconnects you from everything, and life changes. But being in contact with others in a similar situation helps to connect to life again. For many people, being part of a regular support group is a motivation, a lifeline. So we needed an alternative and, whilst virtual hugs and virtual cake aren't quite the same, we've still been able to bring people together via Zoom.

In fact, this enforced change has proved positive for those who've never been able to attend real-world meetings for reasons such as mobility and travel issues – these virtual groups have actually given them the chance to connect and feel less isolated.

Of course support comes in many forms and hosting groups is just part of our service. Our team's specialist knowledge, training and sheer passion for what they do means that on a daily basis they are also giving one-to-one support, advice and guidance or sometimes simply being a listening ear that understands. And when an extra level of help is needed to get through what so many people describe as 'the darkest of times', we offer a specialist counselling service for individuals and families.

For the many thousands of people who cannot wait for a cure, the chance to find the right support is truly life changing – some have said life saving.

Of course Covid has not only affected the way we can deliver support, it has wiped away much of the usual income stream needed to fund that too. So many of our fundraising plans and events had to be cancelled, postponed or rethought, and naturally there are many people worried about jobs and income, who can't be as generous in donating to charities at the moment. So at a time when our support is really needed more than ever, as a charity we have also had our own fight to survive.

Our fantastic fundraisers, old and new, continued to be there for us, as just two examples from Lockdown show: Katie Tucker, her husband and son took on a fundraising head shave together and achieved an amazing £3,800. Having been supported as a family when their 9 year old daughter Tori had a brain tumour and sadly died in 2006, their loyalty to the charity is as strong as ever.

And then there was grandad Paul Mason, an amazing man, facing self-isolation just 9 months after being diagnosed with grade 4 brain cancer but determined to keep himself motivated and to help others. He set out to walk a marathon circuiting his garden with just his dog beside him, and raise funds for Brain Tumour Support. Starting on March 29th and completing it in 19 days he was indeed the original Captain Tom! Aiming to raise £150, his final total reached £3,250. Paul more than completed his challenge but sadly lost his brain tumour battle at the end of July.

Our supporters have kept us here throughout Covid to help others, and they continue to inspire us every day in our vision that no-one should feel alone when facing the effects of a brain tumour diagnosis.

> 66
>
> Dealing with the repercussions of brain tumours is extremely stressful, let alone with a Lockdown too. The virtual meetings have helped me feel less lonely and isolated. It's lovely just having a chat with other people who understand.
>
> *Emily*

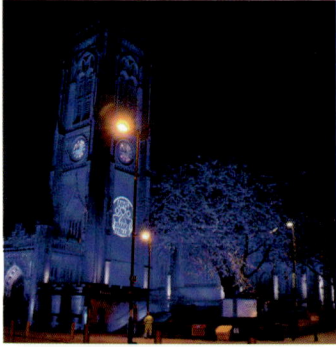

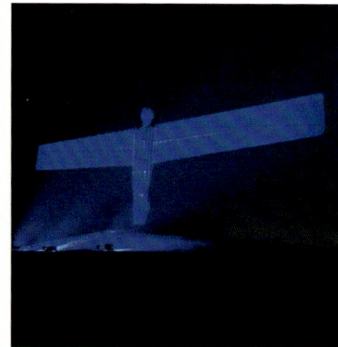

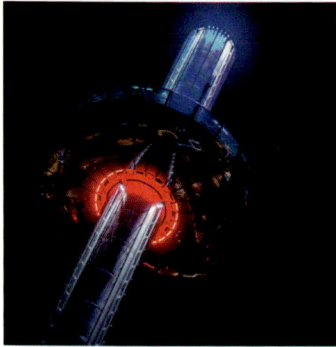

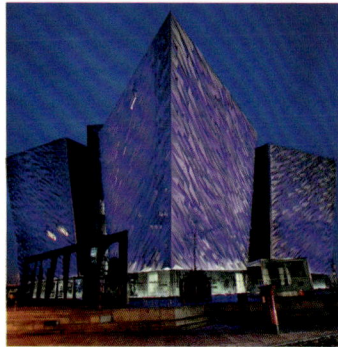

A collective from the events industry co-ordinated the 'Make It Blue' campaign, lighting up iconic buildings and landmarks in support of the NHS ...

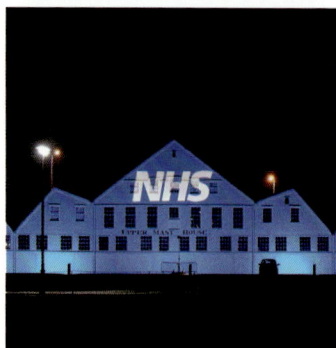

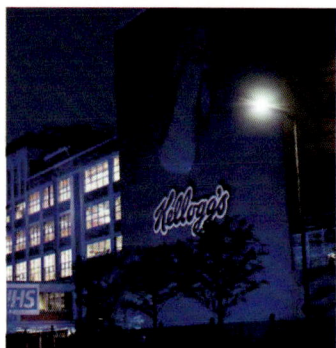

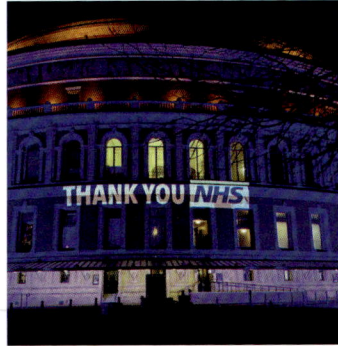

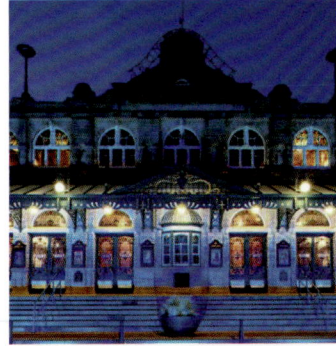

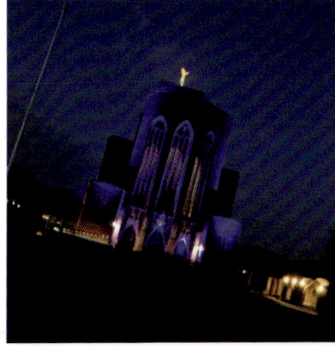

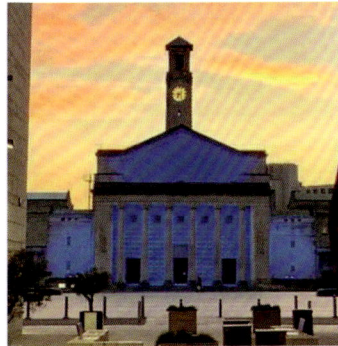

THE BIKE SHED MOTORCYCLE CLUB

When the Bike Shed Motorcycle Club was forced to close its doors in London, we decided to mobilise our community into a volunteer group to provide free courier-style services to support the fight against Covid-19. Indian Motorcycles also offered to cover the cost of services we couldn't get for free, and even threw in a couple of bikes with full luggage for anyone who could make good use of them.

Motorcycles are used by first responders, couriers and food delivery drivers because they are fast and efficient, so we are using our bikes to collect PPE parts for assembly, deliver assembled PPE gear to front-line healthcare workers, along with food and medicine. Soon we will be distributing NHS lung-capacity testing kits, to see which unwell people might be better off in hospital than at home.

Team Rubicon UK are working with the government and British Red Cross to coordinate tasks, and we are working with them to help those most in need get connected with our unique services.

There are lots of groups out there using Facebook and WhatsApp to coordinate volunteers, but for motorcycle riders the missing piece of the puzzle was having a mobile app that collected rider's details with full safeguarding and legal checks, and tracking jobs for the pickup and delivery clients.

We worked with a consultancy company, for free, called Wavestone, who researched lots of apps, and after going through half a dozen, they connected us with Gophr who repurposed their commercial courier app for our use, again for free. Huge thanks to both companies for their help, support and hard work over the weeks of research and testing.

We have hundreds of active volunteers already signed up to the app, covering much of the UK and with more joining every day. Our riders are mostly professionals on Lockdown, with a wealth of useful life experience and who happen to ride a motorcycle for pleasure or as a commuter. They are doing this volunteer work to help the country and to take some of the strain off front-line health workers.

> *When it all goes wrong, it's only right that those of us who are able to help step-up to do our part to support the community.*

STAY ALERT > CONTROL THE VIRUS > SAVE LIVES

PROFESSOR CHRIS WHITTY
Chief Medical Officer for England

To be really clear, it is absolutely critical that every individual, every household and every firm takes these precautions seriously.

You cannot, in an epidemic, just take your own risk. Unfortunately you're taking a risk on behalf of everybody else. It's important that we see this as something we have to do collectively. This is not someone else's problem. This is all of our problem.

We, through the extraordinary efforts of the whole population, got Covid rates right down. They are now rising again, especially in those aged 17 to 29. If we stop social distancing, Covid comes back. We all need to protect others.

There has been a remarkable, ongoing response from the medical profession to Covid. The second wave will be challenging and their continuing work to reduce Covid and non-Covid harm is massively appreciated.

I have an absolute confidence in the capacity of science to overcome infectious diseases – it has done that repeatedly and it will do that for this virus.

> This is not someone else's problem. This is all of our problem.

THE SAMMUT FAMILY
Fred, Essjay, Raegan & Ripley / Doncaster

I work in the rail industry and so am classed as a key worker and can continue my role despite Covid. However, I have been instructed not to attend sites because the majority of what I do has been deemed 'able to be done from home' for now, via telephone or video call. We have had to do a makeshift office in the living room which me and Essjay share.

We have two young children, who are both at a very demanding stage and provide us with different challenges. When we found out that we'd both be working from home, we had to put some structure into our day. Not only for me and Essjay, but for them as well, so they wouldn't turn feral! One of us works from 8 a.m. till 1 p.m. and the other from 1 p.m. till 5 p.m. The person who was not working would be looking after the kids.

Ripley just loved exploring the playroom, painting and drawing and, of all things, folding hand towels!!!!! This kept her busy for ages and was good to see. Raegan had times planned for when she was doing different subjects. Thanks to the school she goes to, there is everything we need to give to her but the problem is how I/we choose to deliver this. It turns out Essjay is a much better teacher than me. I seem to repeat myself, which gets Raegan frustrated, then me as well. It seems we are both learning and getting used to it.

The most challenging thing is being under each other all the time. We try and get through this is by keeping our exercise up and all having our own 'alone time'. Things still boil over sometimes but the main part is that we understand that this is happening.

Raegan has had great support from the dancing school she goes to and they are constantly posting videos in a private area where she can go into watch, learn and copy. She also likes to be outside so the good weather has helped massively. If it was bad I don't know what we would have done.

I would say that the best bit for me is the fact that I can spend a lot more time with the kids, watching them develop in their own ways. In particular Ripley – she is at a great age where her vocabulary is growing day by day, and she is learning about how to deal with different things.

The funniest moment is when Ripley said "Raegan" for the first time. We'd been trying to get her to say it for weeks, then one random moment on a random day she said it. The house went crazy. I will never forget the way we all reacted.

Another good thing is that we have been doing more walks, bike rides and garden activities together as a family – time which would have normally been filled by rushing through the days going to swimming, dancing, toddler gymnastics and other things, making everything a blur. This has really slowed us down which has been great.

My brother and his wife are paramedics in London and have both contracted and recovered from Covid-19. I use this as a reminder that we will win this battle. The strength of the all the NHS staff is now clear for us all to see.

> It's very weird because I am used to my teacher Miss Middlebrook but it's good being home schooled because we have two snack times at home and only one at school. The best part so far is playing with my sister a lot and being hugged a lot by my mummy and daddy but the worst part was not having my friends around on my 7th birthday. I will definitely be excited to go back to school as I will be able to see my friends and teachers.
>
> *Raegan (age 7)*

MARCELLA WHITTINGDALE
Newsreader / BBC South East Today

My normal working day involves going to the studio and working on the bulletin I've been assigned to present that day. Contrary to popular opinion, we don't just rock up and read the news! We have to craft the bulletin that we read on TV so as well as fact checking, writing and research, I'll also work on the scripting to make sure it sounds right for the way I present. And of course it all needs to fit to specific timings. When the time to go on air comes close, I'll put my TV makeup on and go into the studio to rehearse.

Since Covid, news reading has changed in as much as we used to present the programme double-headed. Now it's a solo affair just like presenting the early or late news (I do a combination of all of those). I also go out on the road reporting and if I'm out filming we take our temperatures every day and make sure all our interviews are done at a distance of 2 metres. Obviously we wear masks where we need to.

We don't edit together any more. The cameraman and I would usually sit in a van together and go through the rushes – now I sit in my car and he passes the microphone through an open window to record a voice track!

> It's been a privilege to be able to work throughout Covid, with viewers thanking us for keeping them informed and entertained.

The newsroom is a lot emptier than it used to be too. Not everybody has to come into work so a lot of my colleagues who I used to see are now working from home. Several of the desks have been removed so it's physically impossible to sit too close together. There are disinfectant wipes and hand sanitisers on every desk. There were also fewer programmes and bulletins to present and all our meetings are by Zoom even if we're in the office because not everyone is.

It feels sad not to see my colleagues as much as I used to. And a large swathe of what we report on is Covid related. But apart from that and all the signage around everywhere reminding us to be vigilant, we are working in pretty much the same way.

One of the biggest challenges we found, as I'm sure it's been for many working mums, is childcare. As a family we relied very heavily on grandparent power, which now we can't use. My children really miss that and so do I.

I wasn't furloughed but I was on screen less as some of the bulletins were removed for a time. I was also juggling home-schooling two primary school children, so having fewer shifts meant I could concentrate on them. As a freelancer I felt it financially – PAYE freelancers (you need to be one to work for the BBC) were not eligible for any government schemes.

I feel it's been a privilege to be able to work throughout Covid and the earlier Lockdown. So much of my identity is tied up in my work and it's also a great feeling when you get emails or messages on instagram from viewers thanking us for being there and keeping them informed and entertained.

BARBOUR

Barbour is expecting to make at least 50,000 PPE disposable gowns by the end of May in our factory in South Shields, producing between 1,000-1,500 disposable gowns a day. In addition, we're making 2,000 scrubs and have sourced 20,000 face masks through our supply chain for the Trusts to distribute, making a total of 72,000 PPE items to support the fight against Covid-19. There is no charge from Barbour to the Trusts for any pieces of PPE.

Following a call to the Royal Victoria Infirmary (RVI) on the 6th April to see how Barbour could help, the first quantity of PPE disposable gowns was delivered to them on the 10th April. The factory is now working six days a week with twice daily deliveries of disposable gowns to the RVI and other North East NHS Trusts for them to distribute and use.

"Everyone has a role to play in fighting Covid-19 and I wanted my daughter Helen and I to play our part by turning our South Shields factory over to produce PPE product for the NHS. I would like to thank Professor Sir John Burn and the Newcastle Hospitals and Northumbria Healthcare Trusts for their guidance and assistance in helping us facilitate this.

"I am very grateful to my staff for their overwhelming support. Their welfare is our most important priority and we are limited in the number of people we can have in the factory at any one time. We undertook a strict risk assessment to ensure that we are adhering to social distancing and that all staff are fully protected whilst undertaking this important role.

"The factory, where we normally make our classic wax jackets is no stranger to adaptation. During both World Wars, we turned the factory over to make military garments to assist the war effort. We are pleased to once again be able to make a difference and this time, to support the NHS".

Dame Margaret Barbour / Chairman

> Everyone has a role to play in fighting Covid-19. We're now working 6 days a week making disposable PPE gowns.

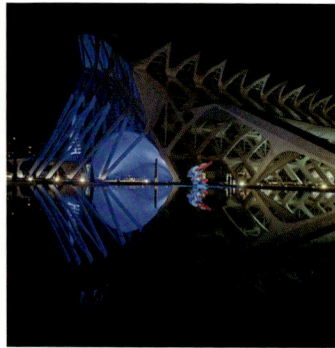

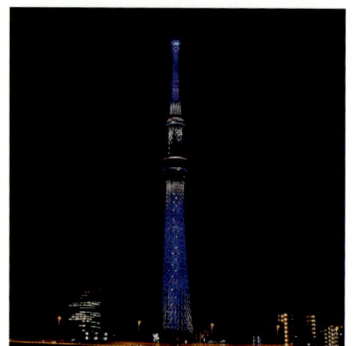

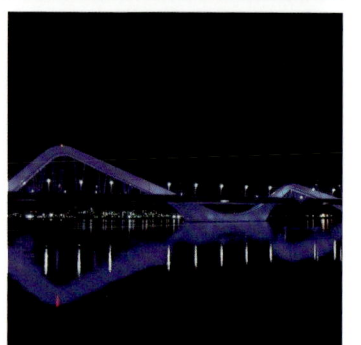

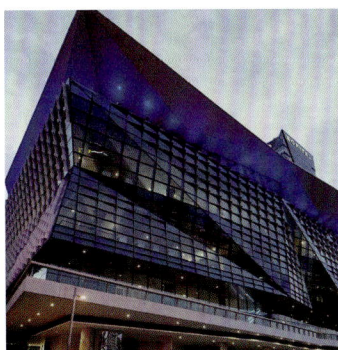

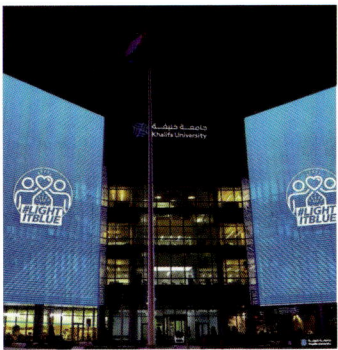

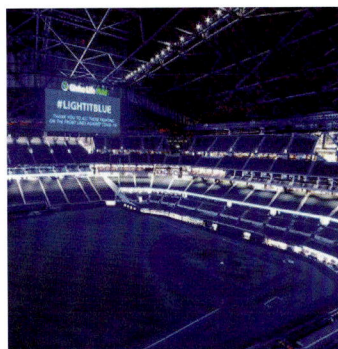

... and they did the same all over the world too – from America to Australia and everywhere in between!

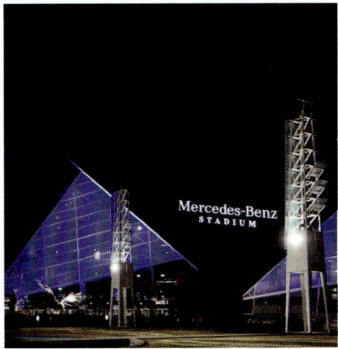

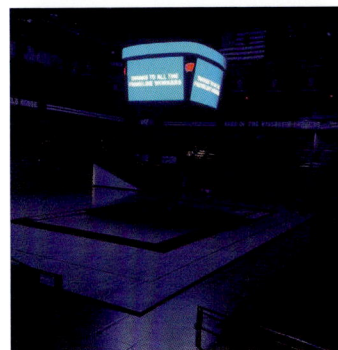

THE INDEPENDENT BUILDERS' MERCHANT GROUP

The Independent Builders' Merchant Group is the largest independent builders merchant group in the South East. Bringing together the experience and capabilities of Parker Building Supplies, Chandlers, Fairalls and Stamco Timber, we have 39 branches operating from the Midlands to the South East, primarily serving trade customers with heavyside building materials, civils, roofing and timber, as well as an array of ancillary product lines.

As independent builders' merchants (and proud of it), we felt it was our duty to somehow get our branches open in some capacity so that they could support our customers and help them to provide vital services to their own customers as well as institutions like the NHS.

We reopened branches that had been closed so these essential services customers had support as near to their sites as possible. We also knew that they needed a quick response so we prioritised their orders and even delivered stuff in cars. We made sure we kept trading so they could keep working.

Amongst many other examples, our Maidstone branch pulled out all the stops to stay open in order to support a customer working on a temporary extension to the morgue at the hospital in Ashford, whilst our Haywards Heath branch supported one of our largest customers with the build of a temporary ward at the hospital there.

We were hugely proud of the efforts that our people made to get back to work in the face of so much uncertainty in the wider world. We were delighted but not surprised at how they rallied round to be there for their customers when so many weren't. That is the essence of independent merchanting and it remains the driving force of our business.

Allun Pittingdale / Managing Director

> 66
>
> We were delighted but not surprised at how our team rallied round to be there for their customers — that's the essence of independent merchanting.

ASH ELRIC
Amazon Fulfilment Centre / Doncaster

I'm a master scuba diver trainer. I've got more than 11,000 dives under my belt and I was working as a scuba diving instructor in South East Asia when the virus outbreak prompted my return to the UK. I'm also a yoga instructor and have worked as an English teacher. I speak Thai and Japanese fluently so I've worked across the Far East.

The Covid pandemic turned the whole world on it's head and everything my career was based on just got closed off. It seemed like Amazon was one of the only places taking things in their stride so I applied for a job with them to help tide me over.

Lots of companies were having to furlough staff but Amazon was actually taking them on! Amazon added 3,000 new permanent roles across its UK network of fulfilment centres, sort centres and delivery stations and will add a further 7,000 new permanent roles by the end of 2020 across more than 50 sites. That's in addition to the 20,000 seasonal positions available for the festive period.

I feel extremely fortunate to have been able to get back on my feet since joining Amazon.

Amazon has reacted quickly to changing circumstances, introducing thermal imaging cameras and one-way systems throughout the building. These precautions haven't been put in place because of a Government mandate but because Amazon took the initiative. The people are great and there's a lot of support and training. The cleanliness and modernity of the warehouse are unlike any place I've worked before.

I'm working with colleagues from all over Europe, South Africa and America. I've made new friends from all over the world and we've all come together. I'm really proud of that.

> " Lots of companies were having to furlough staff but Amazon was actually taking them on!

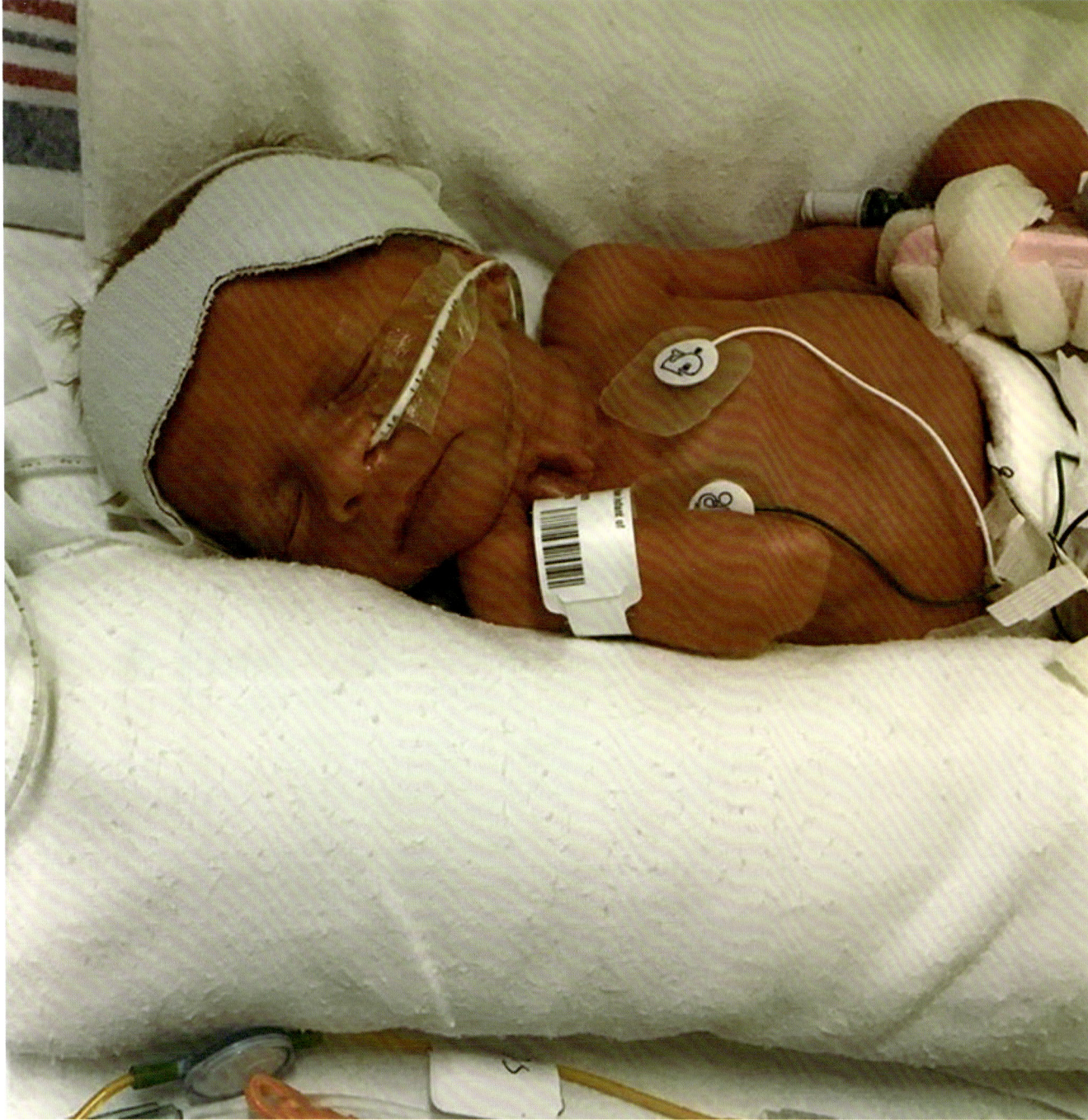

LUCY, MIKE & BABY JACK DICKIE
'Lockdown Baby' / Hackney

We were expecting our first baby and were just starting to get prepared with some of the big items like the pram and cot. I still had 7 weeks of work to go as a Deputy Headteacher, so hadn't even started to think about packing a hospital bag.

My waters broke just after midnight at 31 weeks and 1 day. We were rushed in and my fluids were very low. I also had a temperature and cough and we were put into isolation. I was very ill and was kept in for observation to make sure we didn't go into premature labour. The baby settled down and my symptoms stopped, but we were told there was no fluid left. He'd also turned from head down to breech. It was highly likely that I would need a C-section at 36 weeks and we had to be hugely careful for infection before then.

We were going to be allowed home but I hadn't felt him move. They found his heart beat was fluctuating. Due to all the complications of no fluid, Covid, breech etc., we were then prepped for an emergency C-section with the top consultant. The staff were amazing and talked us through every step. We just took each step at a time until we were on the operating table. Labour was 11 minutes and Jack was born at 4.09 p.m. His Dad was wonderful at keeping me focused and smiling throughout. The staff were incredible and they showed him to us over the screen before he was put in the incubator and again when he was in it.

Jack is now in isolation in an amazing neo-natal unit with the best care, and although it's unbearably hard to not see him, I know he is safe and well and that's all that matters. He needed a little help to breathe but had his tube taken out that night and is now breathing well and feeding through an IV with milk too.

It was terrifying though. Each day and hour took a new turn, with new information. Gradually, our birth plan disappeared but we didn't care. As long as he was OK and put first, nothing else mattered. I put full trust in the team and my body to make the right choices and get him out safely. We are the first Covid-positive mother with a premature baby at Homerton which is why everything has been so complicated about how and when we can see him. It's totally new.

A huge amount happened and changed in such a short time. We were not prepared for a 31 week delivery so staying calm and having small focuses and little wins each day helps. I'm going through every step with my husband by my side, making decisions which are best for our baby and making them calmly so we can be ready, prepared and in control for him.

It's incredible to have a son. He is gorgeous with his Dad's hair and nose, and his Mum's legs! He's also very curious and grabbing about when the team are monitoring him. I can't wait to touch him – whether that's a hug, a feed or a small stroke. I'll take anything! We can't wait to bring him home, hopefully by Christmas (and to a new house as we are also moving!). We can't wait to be near him, nothing else matters.

The midwife team in Homerton delivery suite were amazing. They supported me with everything from washing, staying calm, taking bloods and having to make big decisions. They were there before, during and after everyone else – they were the constant. The doctors and consultants were wonderful, full of knowledge and honesty whilst listening to small questions and keeping us informed. They had full PPE on but it never felt awful or unkind. It was hard but they made it work and showed me such care.

Now, the neo-natal team are working around the clock to keep Jack safe and well. The app they've set up for daily updates and the phone calls with them have really helped us feel reassured.

Not having touched Jack yet and only having seen him for the shortest time has been really hard. But knowing where he is helps, and we're doing things at home to feel close to him like expressing food and getting clothing ready. We are trying to find the positives. The love, support and help from friends and family has been amazing but it's been very hard not to be able to have my mum here to help as I'm quite immobile. My husband is keeping our whole world together right now – I already knew he was great but this is a whole new level of marriage and team effort! And actually, it's love. Love for our son and for each other, that's what is getting us through this!!

> It's unbearably hard not to see him but he's safe and well and that's all that matters.

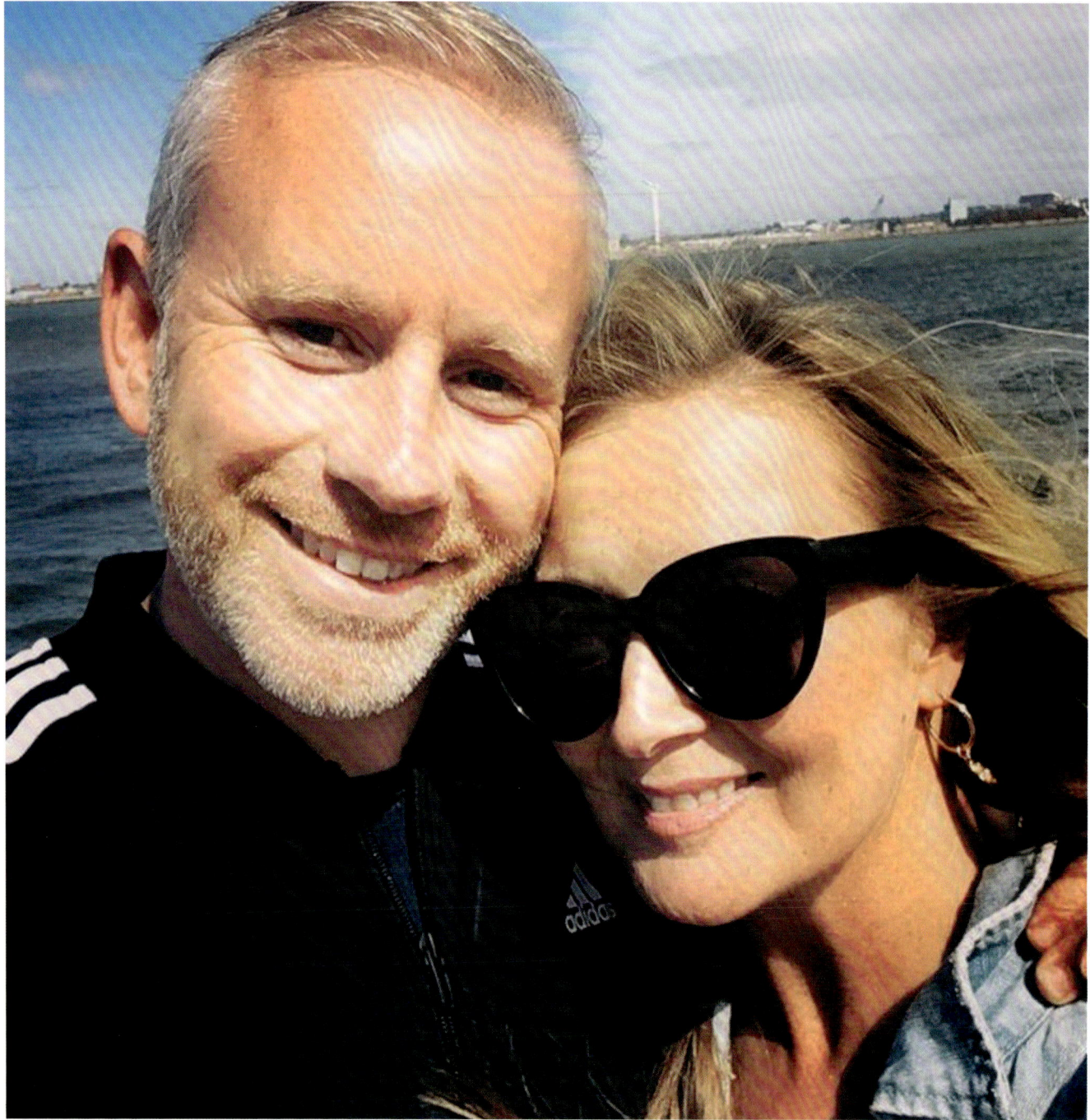

MATT KELLY
Author of 'Our Heroes' / Wigan

Amongst all of the dark moments that the pandemic has brought, there have been some glimmers of hope, where human kindness reminds us that when we come together as a society, that we are unstoppable. Working for Wigan Council, I have seen first hand that when we are united with a common goal, there is nothing we can not achieve together.

Since this crisis began, we have all been faced with seemingly impossible situations, where the most needy and vulnerable in society have had nowhere to turn, particularly when we were in the midst of the national Lockdown.

But that's when the magic happened. Neighbours finally got to know each others after years of awkward smiles once a week when putting out the bins. Random acts of kindness, showed us that we were not alone and that no one had been forgotten.

I was truly humbled by the kindness shown to me in response to the poem I wrote in tribute to our incredible NHS, who fought the virus so bravely to protect us all from this dreadful disease.

Originally, I wrote the poem for my partner Jill, who is part of a District Nursing team responsible for delivering vital medical care in the community. I often write poems in birthday cards for family and one night, having been inspired by Jill's work and the clap for carers, I came up with a line for a poem about Covid. And then another. It just flowed out of me. I sent the poem to Jill and one of my best friends, Paul. They both posted the poem on social media and the rest is history!

It's hard to tell how far and wide the poem reached, but it has been seen over a million times and I have received some beautiful messages from around the world. The poem was used in posters on hospital wards, it was sent on thank you cards by hospital managers to NHS staff, it was made into a song, interpreted in dance and was re-created by school children and nurses each reading a line in a video.

Incredibly, the poem was also used as part of a beautiful piece of artwork created by Scott Tetlow, outlining the history of Manchester. The artwork is being used to raise money for the Royal Manchester Children's Hospital and I am so proud to have played a small part in that project.

The highlight for me was when Christopher Eccleston recited the poem live on BBC's The One Show. I was literally jumping up and down in my living room when he had finished speaking!!

I have formed some fantastic friendships on this journey. The filmmaker Tom Woodward, whose video of the NHS poem went viral, has now made several other powerful videos based on poems that I have written. For example, we created a video for Yorkie Dad's, who are a support group for fathers in the York area. When I was approached by Matty Lewis from Yorkie Dad's, we created an incredible project together and formed a lifelong friendship along the way.

The most important thing I have learnt from the kindness shown to me after I wrote 'Our Heroes', was the overwhelming love we all have for our wonderful NHS. When this is over, we need to remember how we felt about our nurses and our carers during the darkest moments we have faced as a society since the end of the Second World War.

"We love you, our heroes, lest we forget".

> 66
>
> I wrote the poem in tribute to our incredible NHS, who fought the virus so bravely to protect us all from this dreadful disease.

NUMATIC

We're normally known for our vacuum cleaners – most famously our Henry vacuum. We make over one million vacuums every year but we're also a leading brand in the design and manufacture of other commercial cleaning products too.

We obviously, like everyone, had to adapt our site and how we work on a day to day basis but as a team we were also determined to do our bit and to do something to help and protect our communities.

The Numatic teams have been working around the clock to provide support to the Government and the NHS. We urgently retasked our Research & Development Teams, Production Specialists and Manufacturing Teams to work across projects where we could help in the Covid-19 crisis, including the development and provision of face masks, face shields and free loan of cleaning equipment for NHS cleaners.

Our Design and Manufacturing teams worked hard to quickly develop a face shield that is effective, comfortable, reusable and can be manufactured in high volumes immediately. They were developed with, and are currently in use by, Worcestershire NHS Trust, West Midlands Ambulance Service, Birmingham Children's Hospital and The Gibraltar Health Authority.

We then had hundreds of volunteers from colleagues across the workforce to help with assembly. We started off making around 50 units a day but they're now in full production and we're working towards producing 10,000 per day.

I cannot thank the team here at Numatic enough for their efforts in getting an additional product into production for our NHS in these unprecedented times,.

Simon Lawson / Managing Director

> 66
> We were determined to do our bit and do something to help and protect our communities.

Try to be the rainbow in someone else's cloud.

// MAYA ANGELOU

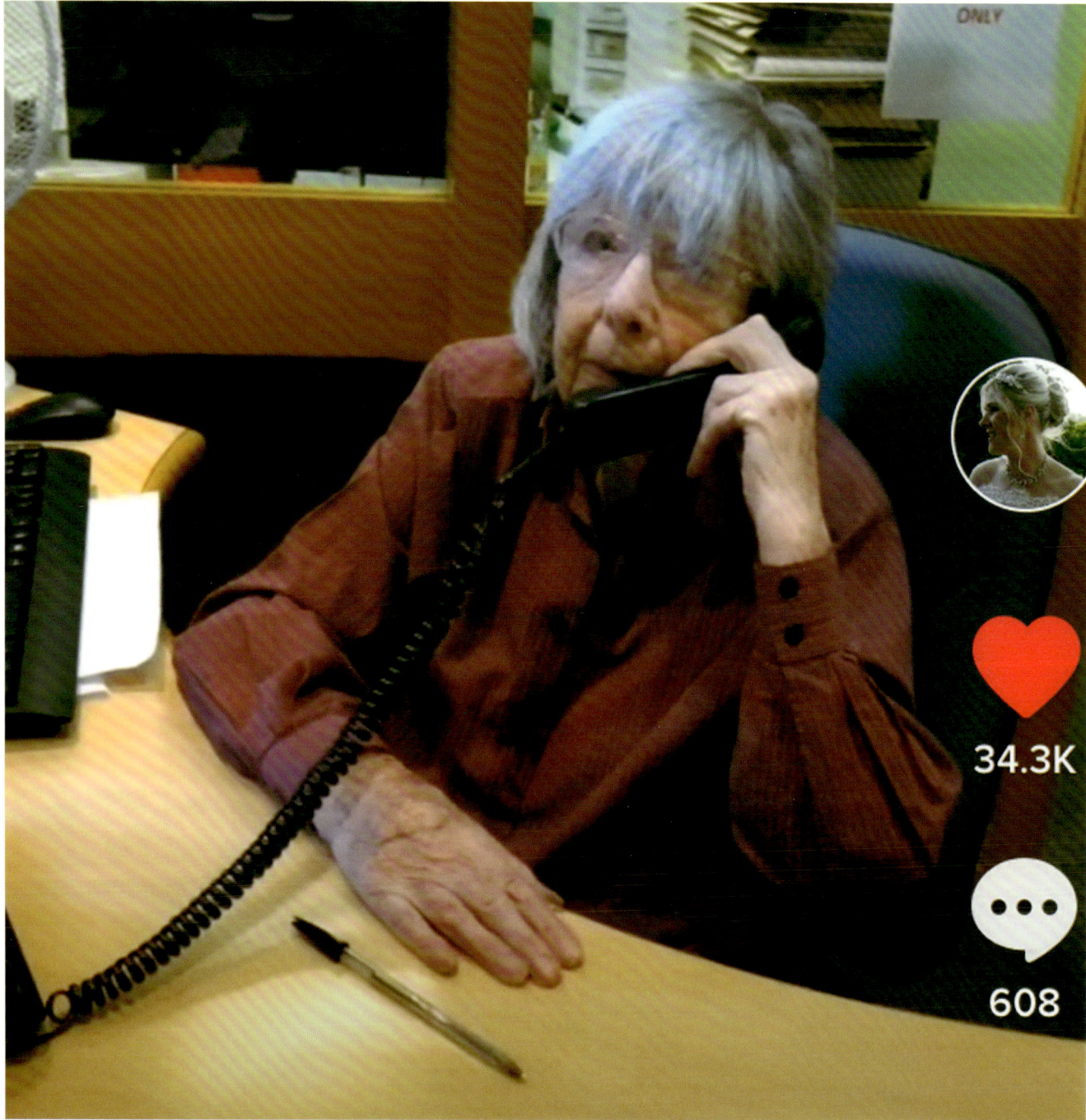

TEAL BECK HOUSE

Residents at Anchor's Teal Beck House in Otley are filming videos (with the help of the care team) of dancing and acting along to extracts of classic songs such as Queen's 'I've got to break free' in a series we are calling "TikTok Fridays".

The videos were initially a simple way for the residents to have a bit of fun and show their families they are well but have become hugely popular, with one video to Dolly Parton's iconic '9 to 5' getting more than a quarter of a million views! The videos have also seen many positive comments from viewers left charmed by the performances.

While TikTok Fridays have become an example of how residents in care homes are still enjoying life and having fun, the videos are not the only thing the residents have been getting involved in. There has been a wide selection of enjoyable social events, including exceptional tea parties, cocktail afternoons and a regular nail salon.

The care team have also used their social media skills to arrange regular virtual meetings (via Zoom, Skype and FaceTime) for residents with their families.

"I'm just so delighted that people are enjoying our TikTok Fridays! It was a brilliant idea by my deputy Emma and colleague Rachel. It's been incredible how keen everyone is to take part and has been so much fun to make.

"It started as a way of lifting the mood during Lockdown and now it's become the highlight of the week! Everyone is keen to watch the latest video and my team keep outdoing themselves with each one!

"It's not been an easy time for anyone, and we've been doing what we can to make sure our residents are happy and entertained. It's so nice to think these videos are bringing joy to people outside Teal Beck House and all around the country as well."

Louise Bulcock / Manager

> 66
>
> I've always loved a bit of Dolly and Queen so getting to dance along to them is brilliant. It's been a really nice way to have some fun but also show my family that I am ok, having fun and being well looked after.

June Longley (age 96)

SARAH BOWERN MBE
Deputy Head of Costume / English National Opera

There is really no such thing as a normal day in theatre! My main role is costume supervisor of our new productions at the ENO. So it's my job to take the 2D costume designs on paper and realise them for stage. My day often consists of fabric sampling, shopping, arranging costume fittings, liaising with costume makers and working on budgets. If it's early on in the process, it may also involve researching and developing costume ideas with the designer.

We were just about to open our production of *Rusalka* when we were all sent home from the Coliseum and put on the government furlough scheme. We've been back to work to put on ENO *Drive & Live* – a drive-in production of *La Bohème* at Alexandra Palace – and my job has changed massively. My job usually involves being constant close contact with performers and we have had to totally rethink our approach to costuming with the Covid restrictions.

Being asked to leave theatre and not knowing when we would be back was very daunting. Theatres and the Arts in general are in a very precarious situation because our industry requires large amounts of people inside buildings. You can't help but worry that you might not have a job to come back to and sadly this has been the case for many of my peers in the Arts.

> *Many didn't know when their next paid costume job would be and yet they volunteered their time and talents regardless.*

We saw on social media that people were turning their skills to making PPE and I asked our full-time team and regular freelancers if they would like to help me make some scrubs.

To begin with there were about 10 of us and at our busiest we had over 60 people sewing to make scrubs, masks, hats and visors. The team was made up predominantly of costume staff, but we also had props and stage management sewing too. Some of our stage and lighting crew became our delivery drivers taking PPE directly into hospitals.

We started a 'Go Fund Me' page and I asked for £750 so we could make 100 sets of scrubs. We ended up raising over £27,000 and making 1,700 sets of scrubs and thousands of visors and hats. We collaborated with a group called 'NHSherosupport' who gave us all the intel on which hospitals were in more need of PPE so our scrubs went directly to those most in need.

I'm incredibly proud of what we achieved. The team grew bigger every week, many of them not knowing when their next paid costume job would be and yet they volunteered their time and talents regardless. It brought us all closer together and united different departments in the organisation.

Also seeing the photos the medical staff shared of our scrubs on Facebook and Instagram was so uplifting and spurred us on to make more. We received great feedback (especially about our funky pockets!). I'm so grateful for the patience of my family. For four months our kitchen became scrubs headquarters! My daughter even helped sew hats to match our scrubs.

I was shocked, overwhelmed and delighted to be on the Honours List. It's a lovely reward of recognition, not just for me but the whole scrubs team who just really wanted to put our skills to use, to help our wonderful NHS and do something significant in such difficult times.

PUT YOUR BINS OUT IN YOUR BALLGOWNS

Angie Emrys-Jones, Alison Davey & Victoria Rogers

Angie was meant to be going to a charity awards night but it had been cancelled because of Covid. To stay positive, she decided to put the ruby red, full-length dress she'd been planning to wear on anyway and shared a photo on Facebook.

In Australia, Victoria saw it and thought how lovely she looked. She suggested that, when Lockdown started, we should start a movement to wear everything in our wardrobes. Alison thought this was a fantastic idea too, so the three of us set up a video chat to brainstorm.

Eventually, we decided we wanted to encourage people to dress up when they were doing mundane household chores. People were going to need some cheer and this was something silly they could do in their own homes that was happy and positive. Plus, it gave them a reason to get out of their pyjamas in the morning!

We set up a Facebook group and called it 'Put Your Bins Out in Your Ballgown'. We planned to post photos of ourselves every day, 'dressed up to the nines' whilst doing boring things like hoovering, cleaning or taking out the bins.

At first we just invited friends to join but numbers quickly grew as people shard it. By the end of the first week, we had 10,000 members all posting their glamorous pictures. And it wasn't just Australia and the UK – we had photos popping up from all around the world and lots of positive comments about how it was helping to put smiles on peoples faces.

One woman was hanging out the washing while another washed her car. Some women whipped out their wedding dress for the first time since they got married. And men were getting glammed up too, wearing wigs and their wives' dresses.

We started to pick daily themes such as colours, movie stars and characters, and as the weeks went on people got more creative with their outfits. There were drag queens, inflatable unicorns and hula girls, all parading the streets with their bins in tow – and several celebrities got involved too.

We have people of all ages taking part, from little kids to 90-year-olds. The group is a diverse mix and everyone is so accepting of each other which is incredibly heart-warming.

It's given people something to look forward to in this rather bleak time. We want people to live in the now. If you're saving a special candle or glam heels for a rainy day, this is that rainy day so get it out! Let's live and enjoy our best china or sparkling wine.

It's a shame it's taken a pandemic to do this but we hope, when it's over, we can continue the kindness and fun. We need to live life to its absolute fullest but for now, we'll keep dressing up and spreading joy from the safety of our homes.

> "
> People were going to need some cheer – this is that rainy day!

FIRST BUS

First Bus is one of the UK's largest bus operators. During Lockdown, from April to June, our entire team worked hard to keep services running, providing over 18 million customer journeys and 3.2 million bus trips whilst our call centre colleagues handled over 32,000 calls from home.

We were delighted that three of our colleagues were recognised in the Queen's Birthday Honours for their services to the community. All three were awarded a British Empire Medal (BEM) for providing selfless services to others.

When First Wessex implemented no less than 13 pandemic-related schedule changes across Dorset – an unprecedented figure within such a short timescale which would normally take weeks of preplanning, followed by a two-week rollout period. Aaron Sparks, a First Bus scheduler, pulled out all the stops to ensure these last-minute changes were done in a way that kept safe and reliable transport services running for key workers. He worked with the team at Dorset County Hospital to ensure schedules were supportive of their shift patterns so that NHS staff were able to get to and from work during these very difficult and challenging times without any extra inconvenience. He made sure that everyone (drivers, hospitals and customers) had the latest timetables. He even visited bus stops himself to make sure customer information was up-to-date.

In York, Chris Koksal who works on the York Park & Ride, responded immediately to the call for NHS volunteers when on furlough, and was signed up as soon as the scheme was launched. It proved to be the beginning of hundreds of hours' availability and volunteering throughout the pandemic. After a week logging on and off via the 'GoodSAM' volunteer responder app he decided to leave it 'on' permanently, rather than limit his time to a few slots during the day.

The Government advice was to only go out once day, but he was shopping so often and his face became so familiar that some security guards at a local supermarket became suspicious until he explained he was a GoodSam. After little more than a month from the start of the scheme he had clocked up 750 hours of volunteering time and he completed at least one volunteer duty every day over the two months he spent furloughed, totalling more than 80 trips to fetch shopping or collect prescriptions for elderly and disabled people in York.

As Covid-19 hit, all canteens which had previously served hot meals to staff across First Eastern Counties' depots, had to close

and Simon Taylor, a driver from Great Yarmouth, decided he wanted to help support his fellow colleagues by providing meals, free of charge. He enrolled himself on a Food & Hygiene Diploma Course at his own cost. With the support of the company, he bought large industrial cooking pots and utensils in order to set himself up making meals, which could then be heated up on company premises for all the staff at the Great Yarmouth and Lowestoft depots. On his 'rest' days, he set himself the task tof preparing 80 meals, and this ongoing venture proved so popular with staff that Simon set up a 'JustGiving' page for donations to the local air ambulance service, enabling grateful eaters to give back to a service which had helped a number of staff in the past.

"I am really delighted that they've been honoured in this way for their outstanding dedication to others; delivering Covid-critical services to their communities and colleagues. This fantastic recognition also shines a well-deserved spotlight on the role played by all our bus workers throughout the ongoing pandemic. We are so proud of their collective commitment and hard work and extend our thanks to all our staff."

Giles Fearnley / Managing Director

> "This fantastic recognition also shines a well-deserved spotlight on the role played by all our bus workers throughout the ongoing pandemic. Our entire team worked hard to keep services running and we are so proud of their collective commitment and hard work.

John Stoddart / Together Campaign

ARCHBISHOP JUSTIN WELBY
Archbishop of Canterbury

We are good in this country at holding our nerve and steadying one another. But a pandemic is something else; you can't touch the virus, see it or even know where it is. As in epidemics throughout history the effects of this fear disturb us very deeply and dread comes upon us. The answer to conquering that fear is the love we receive. The UK has a culture of caring so let's show that love through kindness.

All of us now face a common threat, Covid-19. The question is how do we find hope in these difficult circumstances? Hope comes from both what we can do and who we are.

We need to listen to the science so we know how to reduce the risk and above all we must look after one another, knowing that in an uncertain world with a new virus we are best protected with honesty, compassion and care.

We can go out of our way to be attentive to neighbours and to those who are vulnerable. We can shop for one another. We can

help at a food bank. Everywhere, people are reaching out to one another in a way almost unknown in decades. More than that, they're doing so while social distancing. I am overwhelmed and overjoyed at the humanity and kindness.

There is one more thing that everyone can do. Something you would expect from an Archbishop. I make no apology for saying "pray". Even if you can scarcely imagine how, pray! Pray for yourself, for those you love, for friends and neighbours.

The coronavirus pandemic has hurt families, communities and nations across the world in so many ways. So many have suffered from the virus, been in hospital or mourn someone who is gone. So many people right across the country are anxious about food, employment, are isolated from loved ones and feel that the future looks dark. People right across the Globe feel the same uncertainty, fear, despair and isolation. But you are not alone.

Whether we are confident and brave, or doubt-filled and fearful, God is the source of love and hope. May the wisdom of God lead the doctors, nurses and researchers, that they may know God's protection; and that the love of Christ will surround us and take away our anxiety and give us His peace. May He hear us and heal us. We are not only the Church of England; we are the church FOR England.

After so much suffering, so much heroism from keyworkers and the NHS, so much effort, once this epidemic is conquered here and around the world, we cannot be content to go back to what was before as if all is normal. There needs to be a resurrection of our common life, something that links to the old but is different and more beautiful.

> *The answer to conquering that fear is the love we receive. The UK has a culture of caring so let's show that love through kindness.*

From the Archbishops of Canterbury and York's call for a National Day of Prayer & Action, 16th March 2020, and the Archbishop of Canterbury's Easter Sermon, 12th April 2020.

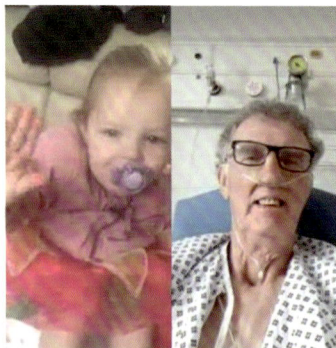

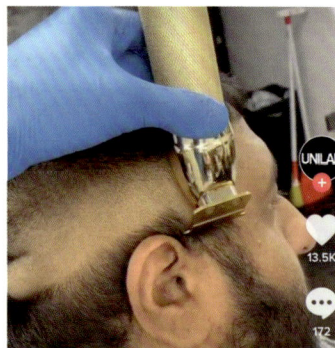

We went digital – from online quizzes and exercise classes to virtual meetings and TikTok challenges. We kept in touch with FaceTime, Zoom and Teams, often with varying degrees of success ...

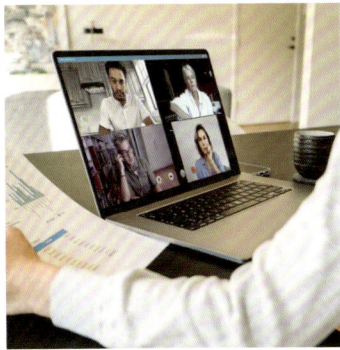

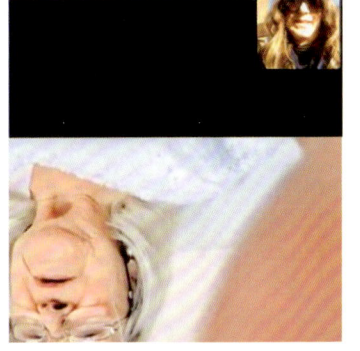

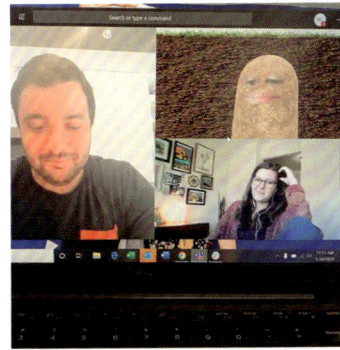

TIM LOUGHTON
Member of Parliament / East Worthing & Shoreham

I've been an MP since 1997 and have held various positions during my time in Parliament – Shadow Minister for Environment, Shadow Minister for Health & Children and Parliamentary Under-Secretary for Children & Families. I currently sit on the Home Affairs Select Committee and chair a number of All Party Parliamentary Groups, so before Covid I'd be up at Westminster a lot as well as out and about within my constituency.

When Covid hit, so much of the day job just fell by the wayside and it was simply about doing what was needed in the immediate moment.

My whole office was completely overwhelmed with questions and requests for help. We became the recipient of every query going from people needing food boxes to someone wanting to know if it was OK to drive to the Midlands to collect a new car.

Penny Mordaunt, the Paymaster General, co-ordinated a Monday morning call for MPs so we could clarify the practicalities of the latest guidelines and we had regular zoom calls with the police, the hospitals and councils to plan and manage logistics. Very quickly, my team had to develop significant additions to our website to provide Covid advice and support.

People were asking what they could do to help. We directed them to the various community hubs to offer their support there, like knocking on doors to check people were OK, doing pharmacy runs, delivering shopping and that sort of thing.

Then I saw a news feature with a nurse in tears at the end of a long, difficult shift. She'd gone shopping on her way home but her local supermarket had already had its shelves emptied and she couldn't even get hold of the basics. It made me think that we were doing all these things to help people stuck at home with their shopping and other needs but, although they could, in theory, access priority shopping hours, there were some simple but practical things that could be done to help NHS staff.

Along with a team of mostly local councillors including the Chairman of Adur Council who was also there every night, we set up the Shopital. Basically, this was a pop-up shop outside Worthing hospital, stocked with essentials that NHS staff could buy as they left work and then just go straight home.

We worked out a list of 50 key lines with the manager from the local Sainsburys and, every day, they put stock aside for me. Milk, eggs, bread and tea bags – that sort of thing. And loo rolls! I'd load my car up and deliver it all to our 'shop' so we could offer the hospital workers an easy way to at least get the basics they needed.

To make it work, we had to be there when they finished their shift at 8 p.m. and as the days went on, we had offers from local businesses to help with evening meals. A local Indian restaurant gave us 50 meals every Thursday and the chef from a local canteen that was temporarily closed, gave us dozens of home cooked ready meals. A local bakery let us have all their leftover bread at the end of the day to give away free.

I think it helped. We had nurses in tears telling us how much of a difference it made. It was quite a small, simple gesture on our part but it was really touching how much it was appreciated.

Overall, it has been – and still is – the most extraordinary national effort. People have come together to support each other, we've got to know and helped our neighbours, and I really hope we can continue this as a peacetime network, not just for the duration of the pandemic.

> " We set up a pop-up shop outside the hospital so NHS staff could get the basics they needed as they left work.

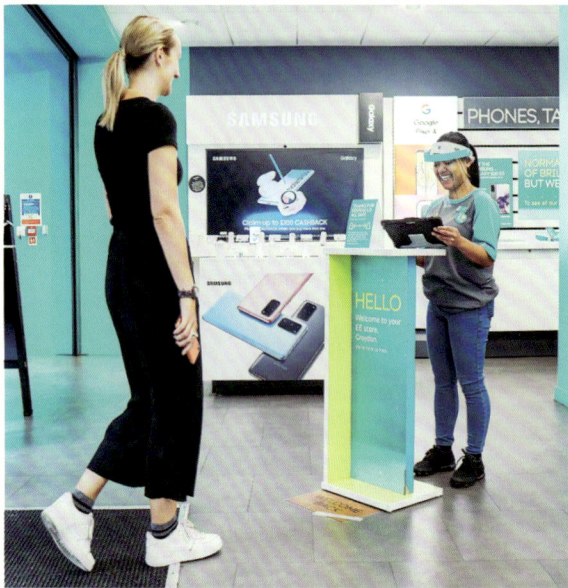

BT, EE AND PLUSNET

This year has been like nothing anyone of us has ever experienced. Our purpose across BT's Consumer brands – BT, EE and Plusnet – is to 'Connect for Good' and that has driven how we have supported our customers, our country and each other through these exceptional times.

Digital technology has never been more important. The beginning of Lockdown saw a surge in demand for the networks and connectivity we provide. We saw a 45% increase in traffic for communication apps such as WhatsApp, Houseparty, Skype and Teams on our EE network alone. From our engineers maintaining masts to our people serving our customers in our contact centres and stores, we've done everything we can to keep the UK entertained, productive and safe through the coronavirus pandemic – as well as keeping everyone connected to the people and things that matter most.

We've set ourselves a bold ambition: to help 10 million people in the UK make the most of life in the digital world by 2025. To that end, BT launched our Top Tech Tips campaign in April with ITV to help teach the nation vital digital skills needed to stay connected at home via video shorts fronted by famous faces including David Walliams, Angellica Bell and Clare Balding. We ran our Top Tech Tips every weekday during This Morning and the evening news.

We have connected and supported millions of parents needing to be teachers and juggle day jobs. BT's Learn at Home webpage saw a 1,100% spike in April. We also partnered with the Department of Education to help 10,000 underprivileged children with six months' free internet access to help them study.

A BT Work Ready two-week placement for those looking to kickstart their careers hasn't been practical for most of this year, so we're running regular webinars instead. And we live-streamed a special Work Ready event, with advice on finding a job, taking charge of your career, and staying motivated from Maya Jama, Chelcee Grimes and Jack Parsons, CEO of The Youth Group. Meanwhile, our Work Ready courses have given 40,000 business owners and employees digital skills training during Lockdown.

We free-rated websites supporting victims of crime and domestic abuse, as well as NHS and Government websites. We offered unlimited calls, texts and data for vulnerable customers, as well as roaming credits for customers stranded abroad.

We've offered free, unlimited mobile data to NHS workers. More than 270,000 NHS staff have taken up our offer. We hope this has given NHS staff one less thing to worry about.

Our BT Sport customers gifted a total of £1m to the NHS Charities Together Covid-19 Urgent Appeal, using their customer credits for paused BT Sport subscription payments. Elsewhere, we responded to more than 100 bespoke requests for help across various central government departments, including bringing high-speed connectivity to the Nightingale field hospitals around the country.

BT donated baby monitors to hospitals to help medical staff communicate with patients at a distance to minimise the spread of infection. And BT's Adastral Park – our research and innovation hub near Ipswich – coordinated a major effort to 3D-print thousands of protective visors for frontline health and social care workers in the east of England.

Volunteers from our BT contact centres in Gosforth and Doncaster made weekly calls to local care homes to help combat loneliness among socially isolated care home residents in an initiative we called Care Home Companion. We worked with Crisis to provide 400 phones with pre-paid credit to the homeless and delivered more than 1,000 tablets to enable relatives to see and speak to their loved ones being treated in intensive care units. That made more than 15,000 calls possible, including a touching proposal.

We also supported an unprecedented volume of calls coming into our 999 call centres, experiencing volumes typically seen on New Year's Eve (traditionally the busiest day of the year).

I'm so proud of how all of my colleagues continue to be there for the communities they live and work in, supporting and caring for those who needed it the most, as well as for each other.

Marc Allera / CEO, BT's Consumer brands

> "
> We've done all we can to keep everyone connected to the people and things that matter most.

MINNIE KLEPACZ BEM
Ophthalmology Matron & BAME Lead / Bournemouth

When I first arrived in the UK in 2001, I was already working at the NHS as an overseas nurse. I knew my job had many benefits. Not only was I working in one of the world's leading healthcare systems, but I was also be providing high-quality care that is freely accessible to everyone in the UK. Early in my career, someone told me that my ethnic background might mean it would take me longer to get to a senior position – I took this as a great challenge to progress and a few years after I started, I had worked my way to becoming matron for ophthalmology at the Royal Bournemouth Hospital, now University Hospitals Dorset NHS Trust. Today, I also lead the hospital's BAME network and am proud that in my own little way, I can provide support to my colleagues.

It is often said that crisis and disasters bring out the best in people. This truism is being confirmed every day in the middle of the pandemic, with countless reports of compassion and selflessness all over the world.

Today, being a Filipino nurse in the middle of a pandemic means having two faces: one is worrisome and the other proud. The side that is proud comes from my heritage – growing up in the Philippines we are used to facing all kinds of calamities, but we always rise above the waters, and support each other in any way. However, the side that is worried springs from the fact that staff from ethnic minority backgrounds, especially Filipinos, are highly disproportionately affected.

But the best way to not feel hopeless is to get up and do something. With that in mind, I set my worries aside in order to support to my colleagues. I actively contributed to – and encouraged our BAME members to undertake – our staff Risk Assessment Tool to help ensure staff are protected by the correct PPE. Beyond the physical protection, we have provided information, guidance, and support for mental health wellbeing for the many staff feeling overwhelmed and anxious.

Outside of my daily matron duties, I have provided support to local Filipino communities groups and myself and other Filipino nurses founded the group Filipino Nurses Association UK to help each other and fellow Filipinos experiencing difficulties both at work and home. I cooked food and delivered groceries and medication, and home-cooked meals with the help of my husband who drove me around. Equally important is the emotional support I provided to my community.

The people I supported have no family here so we became their family. For us, having a Filipino family means you are not alone and you will never be left in need. We have a tradition of bayanihan (being a community, a spirit of unity among Filipinos), and that was exactly what we did during this pandemic. We might not have our blood family with us daily, but we provide each other with support when needed.

I was recognised by Her Majesty the Queen and awarded the British Empire Medal for my services to Nursing during Covid-19. I am truly humbled and honoured but share this with all my amazing team, all NHS staff, all Filipino nurses across the UK and around the world and our local communities who tirelessly work above and beyond. I also want to share the honour to our Filipino colleagues who lost their lives during the pandemic – I dedicate the award to their family and friends.

I am thankful for my personal support system. My mom is my prayer warrior and guides me on what to do and my husband provides me with overflowing love and tremendous support.

I will continue what I have been doing, helping my colleagues and the Filipino community. Despite my own worries, I have tried to see how I can support people, what act of kindness and humanity I can provide. If people need help, then I'll help them. I will go out and make good things happen.

> 66
> Fill the world with hope, and you will fill yourself with hope. Take the challenge of paying it forward. It takes each one of us to make a difference.

BISCUIT THE BEAR
The Pike Family / Castle Cary

Our daughter's bear was in our front garden for weeks during Lockdown doing all sorts of activities and poses – he was always keeping neighbours guessing what he'd be up to next!

We came up with the idea because people were putting bears in their windows and Ferne had this giant 5ft bear so we thought we'd put him on the front lawn over Easter weekend, just to wave at the children as they went down the lane and make them smile.

At first we thought we'd do it just for the Easter break but then people were coming past for their hour of exercise and lots of people stopped to take photos, so we just carried on. It was quite easy to come up with ideas for when it was sunny but when it was windy or raining it was really tricky!

We just wanted to bring a smile to anyone who passed our place.

> I didn't want Biscuit to get ruined or stolen but now I'm glad we put him out because it made people smile.
>
> Ferne (age 10)

REX & SELINA TAYLOR
Self-isolating / Derbyshire

Selina has Alzheimer's and gets worked up sometimes so I sit with her and we hold hands and sing to each other. She really depends on routine and doing the same things at the same time every day. She usually goes to a day care centre twice a week but she can't do that now so I'm her full-time carer. Singing gives us something regular to do together.

Selina and I have been married for more than 60 years and are very much in love. We met when she was 19 and I gave her my seat on a crowded bus. We've now got 5 children, 11 children and 5 great-grandchildren

We'd been self-isolating for 2 weeks and wanted to let our family know that, although it wasn't easy, we weren't too bad and that we were healthy and well, and in good spirits. They usually helped a lot with Selina's care but we'd had to stop seeing them. We sang to them through the window a few times and then we decided to record a video for them.

We've got an Alexa and we asked it to find us something to sing by Vera Lynn. 'We'll Meet Again' came up and we thought it's just perfect.

My son, Rob, helped me put it on Facebook to cheer the family up and it just went barmy! It's had more than 3 million hits and so many lovely comments from all around the world – that's the power of the internet. I'm astonished by the response. It was just a bit of fun really but if it's put a smile on someone else's face then that's brilliant.

We're all going through some very, very tough times and it is absolutely scary. But we will come out of this and we will be in a better place. As long as people do what we are doing and try not to spread it, it stops people dying when they don't need to. Do as you're told and let's stick to it, but most importantly, keep your chin up.

> " It was just a bit of fun, but if it's put a smile on someone else's face then that's brilliant.

IN LOVING MEMORY OF SELINA TAYLOR 1937-2020

We shared social media posts like this ...

My hobbies include long scrolls down my phone, talking to my pet, binge watching Netflix, singing in the shower, staying in my PJ's too long, being tired all day? then not sleeping at night, drinking everything but water, ordering stuff online, reading about new diets while eating cake, and making lists of things I will never do...

And the people stayed home. And read books, and
listened, and rested, and exercized, and made
art, and played games, and learned new ways of
being, and were still. And listened more deeply.
Some meditated, some prayed, some danced.
Some met their shadows.
And the people began to think differently. And
the people healed. And, in the absense of people
living in ignorant, dangerous, mindless, and
heartless ways, the earth began to heal.
And when the danger passed, and the people
joined together again, they grieved their losses,
and made new choices, and dreamed new images,
and created new ways to live and heal the earth
fully, as they had been healed.

KITTY O'MEARA

STEPHEN PHILPOTT BEM
Strategic Lead Rough Sleeping / Birmingham City Council

This summer marked 30 years of me working with people who are homeless, but I only started working for Birmingham City Council in February. Birmingham has a long and generally successful history and commitment to working with people who sleep rough and to preventing homelessness. Consistently throughout the 2000s, the number of rough sleepers was only in single figures on any single night. Then, numbers started to increase and in 2018 we found around 90 people sleeping rough in Birmingham, but we managed to reduce that to about 50.

The council works with organisations across the city to provide outreach services, hostels, housing advice and healthcare. There are many others providing things like independent outreach and soup runs. A normal day would be visiting homeless services, meetings with commissioners and other local authorities, writing bids and planning the coordination and delivery of services.

On March 26th, Luke Hall, then Minister for Rough Sleeping and Housing, called on local authorities to get 'everyone-in' by that weekend to protect the most vulnerable rough sleepers. For me, that meant a strategic role had then to become much more operational and my leadership much more hands-on. Many services had to change the way in which they operated and so were less available to the most vulnerable. We had a night-shelter with a shared dormitory that could not remain open. The main day centre couldn't operate safely with the number of people it was seeing in the building. Additional accommodation was required to deal with the closure of the night-shelter. We had to ensure there was space in our emergency hostel and that we had space for all rough sleepers who sought accommodation. We needed to be ready for any surge in demand and had to act fast.

> "
> The crisis brought out the best in many people and we were able to achieve things which, under normal circumstances, would have been impossible.

We teamed up with the Holiday Inn in the city centre to provide rooms for people. It was great to be offering good quality hotel accommodation, en-suite rooms with TVs, and 3 meals a day. I spent the first couple of weeks mainly sat at the coffee bar in the lobby of the Holiday Inn coordinating staff, homeless people and liaising with the Holiday Inn staff. Their job changed from looking after their usual clientele of business people and tourists, and they responded wonderfully.

From the beginning we were also thinking about what do we do when this period is over? Planning for a positive move-on, arranging tenancies and supported accommodation, and even reconnecting people with friends and family. No one left without extra support and the offer of accommodation to move on to.

We were still going out to engage with anyone rough sleeping though. The streets were very quiet. I spent one late night walking the streets and could not find a single rough sleeper.

There were challenges for all. Lockdown is stressful, fear and anxiety grew, hotel rooms can be an isolating experience for those used to socialising on the streets, but there was also a feeling of excitement across a sector that is often battling for outcomes and success. For a time, things were moving fast and in a positive way. We had no deaths from C-19 in the homeless population and very few infections. And some of the most long-term rough sleepers accepted help and came off the street for the first time in a very long time, which was great. We were able to achieve things that, under normal circumstances, would have been impossible. The crisis brought out the best in many people and created a flexible, pragmatic and outcome-orientated approach. It felt like what we were doing was not just important in the moment, but also making lasting changes. Rough sleeping in Birmingham is currently lower than pre-Covid-19. It's still challenging and there's still work to do, but the advice service is now set for the long term. There is accommodation and support for all who need it and we are ready for the winter.

It was a surprise getting on the Honours List, but I accepted in the hope that it would be a reflection on all the people, including the homeless, working together through this strange time. I hope in some ways it helps going forward, so that homelessness is prevented rather than relieved in a crisis like Covid-19.

TANYA FEWKES & ALESSANDRO SQUARCINA
Staff Nurse & Charge Nurse / Sheffield

We both work at Chesterfield Royal Hospital and, on a normal day, I would look after both elective and trauma orthopaedic patients, caring for them pre- and post-operatively. Alex works on a Surgical Assessment Unit, assessing and caring for patients needing emergency surgical procedures.

Covid changed things on both of our wards – elective surgeries were cancelled until later dates; visiting was suspended, leaving patients and their relatives worried and anxious; PPE became mandatory, and the admission process and way the hospital runs changed completely. Teams were split and merged, staff were designated to new areas and wards were moved around in order to cater for Covid.

Throughout all of this, there was a feeling of worry and anxiety about the unknown and the fear of bringing Covid home to our families. We also understood that the public were depending so highly upon the NHS and seeing us as a beacon of hope.

On the flip side however, it wasn't all negative. As many of my colleagues say "Nursing made us friends, Covid made us a family". Teams became stronger, we all shared a common sense of purpose that left us with an overwhelming feeling of appreciation for each other, despite the greater responsibilities. On top of this, we were recognised for the caring and compassionate profession that we are.

Nursing is often described as a job however, as many patients have told me, "it's your vocation". To be able to help people at their most vulnerable time is an honour, and nursing through this pandemic will be a part of my career that I will never forget.

During this pandemic our wedding was also cancelled – not once but twice – leaving us utterly devastated. The magical feeling that should surround your wedding seems to have dissolved into a sense of numbness. The dream of your big day is all taken away as a result of social distancing and guidance to keep people safe. We have now rebooked our wedding for 8th August 2021 and are hoping that it will be third time lucky. We will get our happily ever after …

And as the saying goes "every cloud has its silver lining" and we are now expecting our second child, due in March 2021. To make it even more joyous, it's a girl so we now have been blessed with a child of each gender!

> 66
>
> Our wedding has been cancelled twice but we will get our happily ever after and it's been an honour to help people at their most vulnerable.

PAUL HUGHES
Funeral Director / Leeds

I am the Operations Director and CEO at the independent funeral company, Hughes Funeral Services in Leeds. My normal day at work would usually be 8 a.m.-6 p.m. and involves running staff meetings, making sure arrangements are checked and in place for the day, as well as some administrative work. But my true vocation is as a Funeral Director, which means that I will also be arranging funerals with bereaved families and conducting these arrangements in due course.

As a small family company, we employ twenty full-time staff and are very fortunate that our team appreciate the importance of looking after the bereaved and their loved ones at an incredibly difficult time in their lives and take pride in carrying out their duties with dignity and respect.

Since February 2020 my workload has increased dramatically, as myself and my fellow directors have taken on additional roles in managing both health and safety and training for all our staff. We also have to keep up to date with the legislation, set by government and the three local authorities we deal with on a daily basis.

For the whole team, our workload and our hours have also increased dramatically due to the unfortunate demise of so many with Coronavirus. It also took more time to explain the rules and regulations that would affect the funeral of their loved one to each and every bereaved family.

As a result of Coronavirus, we were unable to meet face-to-face with many families because of the restrictions and self-isolation. Like many other professions, consultations took place via telephone calls and email which was very impersonal and, unfortunately, not as consoling as sitting down with someone in the comfort of their own home.

As a company our aim was to try and keep everything as normal, as traditional and as respectful as possible to enable families the right to say goodbye in a manner befitting the life of their loved one. The one positive coming out of this is the fact that the families that we have been called to serve have appreciated everything we did and are still doing in trying to make their loss a little less stressful.

We were quite lucky, as last year we created a Service Chapel with live streaming facilities at our Funeral Home. This would normally enable up to 120 mourners to attend a service. However during these uncertain and very difficult times we have only been able to provide a safe environment for up to thirty people to attend and to pay their respects and say goodbye to their loved one, so the live streaming has been good to have.

Although we provided training, counselling and full PPE for all our staff, they were aware of the inherent risks involved in the duties they had to carry out, and I have to reiterate how proud I am of each and every one for how they have performed, looked after each other and helped those they were called to serve.

I asked my staff how they were feeling in these crazy times, and what made them feel a little better and more positive. They answered quite categorically that working in a small team with trust and friendship helped them immensely and going home to their families gave them the security and normality they needed.

> Our aim was to try and keep everything as traditional and respectful as possible to enable families to say goodbye in a manner befitting the life of their loved one.

TEST
AREA 2
10

Penlon

PACKAGING
Penlon
HANDLE WITH CARE
Medical Equipment

VENTILATOR
CHALLENGE
UK

PENLON

On January 29th 2020, the UK recorded its first cases of Covid-19, an aggressive strain of the coronavirus that had not been previously identified in humans.

As the virus took hold, so too did the demand for equipment to treat the sick, and by mid-March the Government had established that up to 30,000 ventilators may be required for the UK's Covid-19 patients.

It would soon become apparent that this was a serious issue because the UK does not make a suitable critical care ventilator, and established international providers were struggling to cope with their own domestic and international demand.

On March 17th the UK Government issued a 'call to arms' and the Prime Minister called on British manufacturing to help step up ventilator supplies to save lives during the coronavirus pandemic.

An appropriate technology specification was drafted and the Rapid Manufacture Ventilator System (RMVS) was conceived. Using our ventilation expertise, Penlon quickly responded by proposing the ESO 2 Emergency Ventilator, based on the existing AV-S anaesthesia ventilator platform.

The purpose of the ESO 2 is to save lives by ventilating the sickest patients until they are strong enough to be transferred to one of the limited number of ICU ventilators available for recovery. The first ESO 2 prototype was demonstrated less than a week later and the 'Ventilator Challenge UK' consortium was formed to manufacture the ESO 2 in large numbers, with a number of the UK's leading technology and engineering firms partnering with specialist manufacturers to build existing, modified or newly designed ventilators. The challenge was primarily one of ramping up from 500 AV-S ventilators a year to over 500 every two days!

In a matter of days, we successfully transformed our company from a daytime batch production business to a 24/7 operation providing technical back-up to the consortium manufacturing sites and final testing and despatch of the ESO 2 to the NHS.

By April 13th, after receiving MHRA approval, the first ESO 2 production units were despatched and just a few days later, installed at the newly established 4,000 bed NHS Nightingale Hospital in London.

Today, our UK factory in Oxfordshire is dedicated completely to the ESO 2 project. Penlon's regular business of Anaesthesia Systems, Patient monitoring, Laryngoscopes and Suction and Oxygen Therapy will only recommence when the ESO 2 delivery objectives have been met. Thereafter, we plan to offer the ESO 2 overseas, wherever the need for Covid-19 treatment exists.

In the longer term, we believe that a UK-manufactured ICU ventilator would help in any future pandemic and the company are investigating how the development of this product can be funded. Penlon is looking to the future, and to establishing itself as a world-class manufacturer of Anaesthesia and Respiratory devices for the global market.

We have certainly been on a journey which will be a very big part of our history and we are delighted to have been given the opportunity to dedicate our lives, 24/7, to the task of making the ESO2 for the NHS. We would also like to pay tribute to the dedication of NHS staff, the Penlon workforce, Ventilator Challenge UK members, and all key workers around the world.

Craig Thompson / Head of Products and Marketing

> 66
> The challenge was ramping up from 500 ventilators a year to 500 every two days! We have dedicated ourselves 24/7 to making the ESO2 for the NHS.

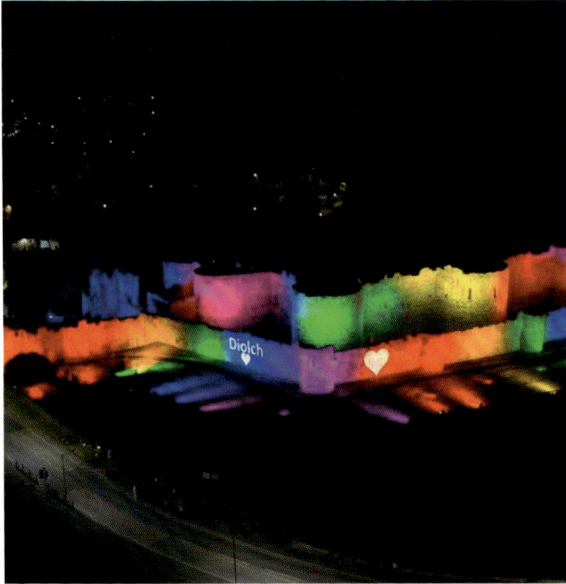

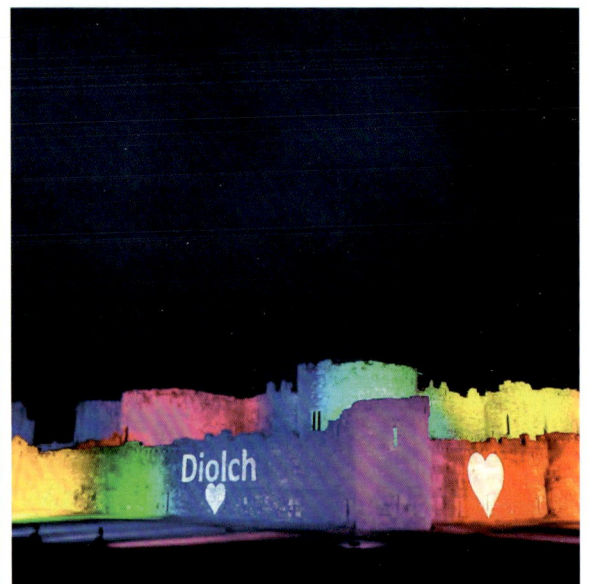

PETE WHITEHEAD & WILL KELLY
Illuminated Events / Snowdonia

Illuminated Events are an outdoor lighting specialist based in North Wales. In mid-March, all of our upcoming work was completely cancelled. Our company ground to a swift stop and now has a very uncertain future.

Both of our partners are key workers – Will's partner (Nerys) works for the NHS and Pete's partner (Beth) works for BT, both providing essential services for our community. We found ourselves watching them going to work each day and feeling pretty helpless that there was nothing we could do to help. We also started seeing people volunteering to build hospitals, deliver food to vulnerable people and a whole host of other amazingly good, kind deeds.

In Wales, our emergency Coronavirus Hospitals are called Esbyty Enfys – or in English, Rainbow Hospitals. Rainbows are a great positive sign of hope, a symbol of unity and a symbol that represents everyone, from the NHS to all of our keyworkers. We were seeing rainbows appear all over the country.

We have the largest resource of outdoor lighting equipment in North Wales, and as our own way of being able to volunteer and do something positive for our community, we took it upon ourselves to start lighting up the local landmarks in our home area with rainbow lighting each Thursday (all for free). This was to symbolise our Rainbow Hospitals and to say a heartfelt thank you to all of the real heroes who are working so hard right now to get us all through these troubled times.

Other people are doing much bigger, better and far more important things right now but this was a little something we were able do with the resources we have around us. To help in our own very small way. It's been lovely to see the positive morale boost that our rainbow lighting brings to people.

We make a point of not publicising which landmark we are going to be lighting up next and we very much encourage people not to come out and see what we are doing, but instead to "please stay at home and enjoy the beautiful pictures posted on social media".

We have lit up lots of iconic sites including Bangor University, Pontio Theatre, Conwy Castle, Llanrwst Bridge and Tu Hwnt I'r Bont Tea Rooms (the little ivy covered house next to the bridge), Caernarfon Castle, Portmeirion Village and Beaumaris Castle.

We have been overwhelmed by the huge positive response from the local community and we are incredibly appreciative of all of the hard work that so many volunteers have put in behind the scenes to help each project happen.

On behalf of Illuminated Events, we would like to offer our sincere thanks to all of those volunteers for the wonderful things that they helped make happen – and above all, we would like to offer our sincere, heartfelt thanks to our wonderful NHS and key workers who are working selflessly to help us through these troubled times.

> Other people are doing much bigger, better and far more important things right now but this was a little something we were able to do and it's lovely to see the boost that our rainbow lighting brings people.

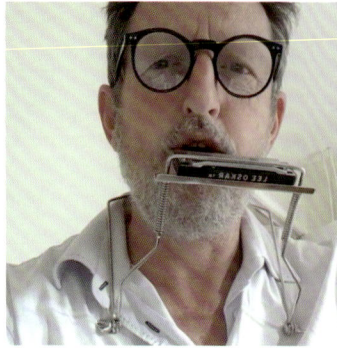

A country pub's open mic night went virtual — and ended up with over 7,000 performers from more than 30 countries all around the world. Music is the glue ...!

ALFIE JOEY
Breakfast Radio Presenter / BBC Radio Newcastle

Usually, I'd be on air with a co-presenter – a 'double header'. We'd have a team around us with producers, news readers and travel presenters – our 'posse' – and we'd have music, news, fun and games. All the usual breakfast radio stuff.

With Covid, everything changed. As part of national plan, there was no more double headers, no more team, no guests – I was on my own. My producer was there through a screen but it was quite hairy, as I now had the pressure of pressing all the buttons! I really missed the crack and the camaraderie of having everyone around.

Shows were extended from 3 to 4 hours to help make things run more smoothly – and that's a long time on your own! It was set up so that if any of the local presenters became ill, coverage could be picked up and carried on by another one of the local stations.

I usually cycle into work but with the much earlier starts, I decided I felt happier driving in. However, the dreaded 'Lockdown paunch' soon crept it in so it was back on the bike every day, which was actually really good for me.

Another good thing to come out of it was no more after-show meetings! Instead, we just got on with making more radio.

I think with things like this, you suddenly realise why local radio is so important and why, as a local radio station, you exist. A bit like with floods or snow or school closures, you can feel people turning to you and tuning in for help and updates. A lot of commercial radio has stopped being local – it's networked from London or wherever – so it's local radio that really offers people company with character.

I do some stand up comedy, so I tried to be a bit of Jeremy Paxman and Chris Evans at the same time. I could be interviewing Sir Keir Starmer one minute and then following that with a phone-in game of Blankety Blank. We were there to entertain and inform so we had a big job on our hands but it felt like we were really making a difference.

My mam doesn't have a TV and for many like her, radio might be the only way they have of keeping in touch. The late night show also came into its own as people weren't going out so we were there to keep them company. I felt privileged to be there for my audience – it's not my show, it's theirs.

> With Covid, everything changed. And with things like this you realise why local radio is so important.

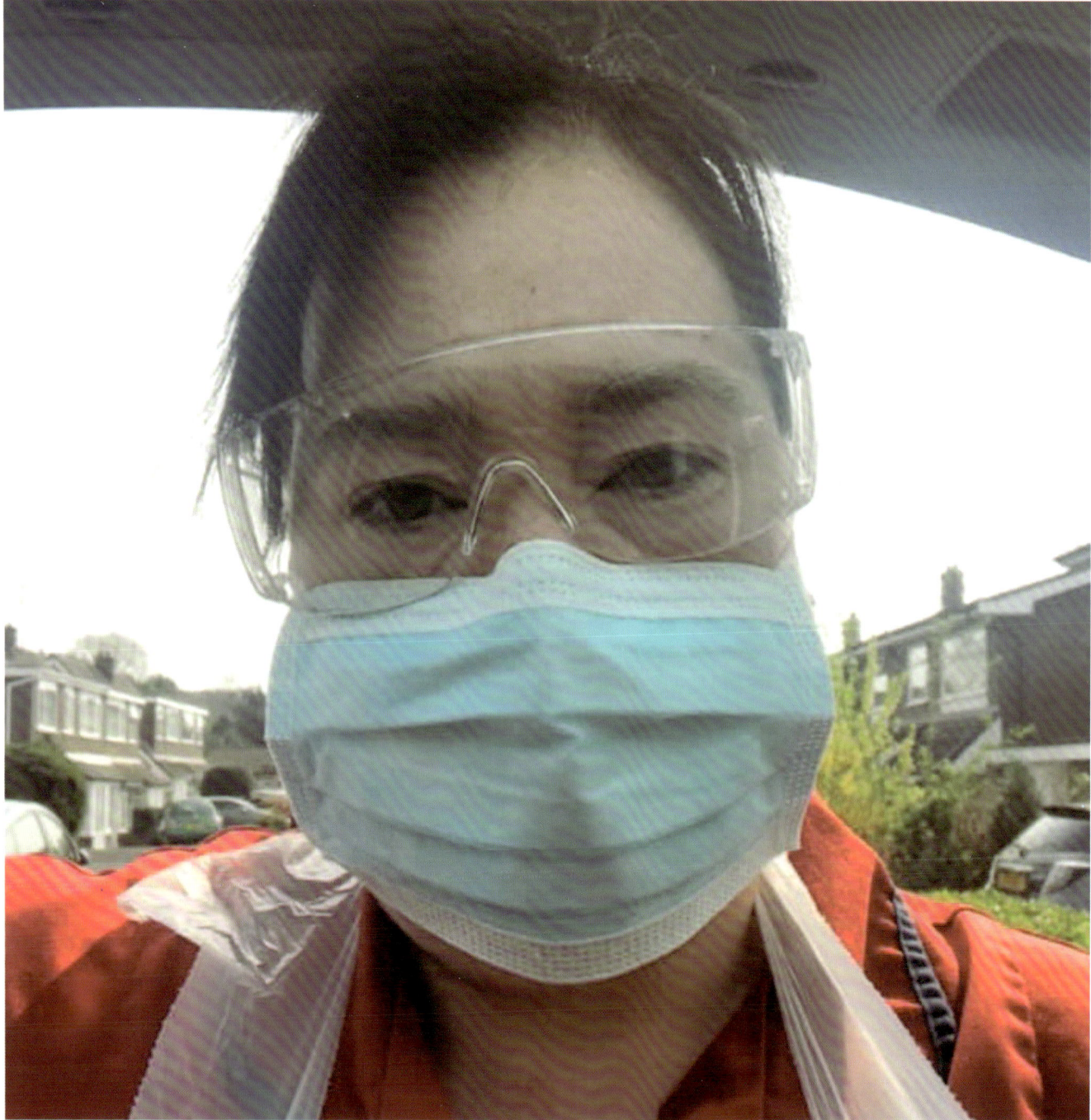

ANGELA NICOLL
Paediatric Nurse / Stockport

I work for Stockport NHS Foundation Trust and am a specialist community practitioner / senior paediatric nurse / paediatric palliative care lead. I co-ordinate and deliver care to children who are end of life or who have complex health needs. I am responsible for a variety of teams whose role is to keep our most vulnerable and fragile children well and at home where they belong.

I have always enjoyed caring for others and like to make a difference in the lives of the people I meet. My passion for caring for this vulnerable group of children has always been there, ever since I was sent to a residential unit for disabled children on work experience from school 30 years ago.

No two working days are ever the same for me. I loosely plan to work Monday-Friday from 7 a.m.-3 p.m., but due to the nature of my role work often follows me home. I provide 24/7 phone support and visits for all of the families under my care so that we can keep these children as well as they can be and at home.

> " I am so grateful to have the equipment I need to keep me and my family safe, but how scary is it now for the person who you are caring for? They can no longer see the smile on your face or the love and care you are trying to give them.

Covid has meant that I have had to take on extra roles at the hospital as well as my day-to-day job. I'm working harder to manage these children safely at home, delivering services that we didn't before. This is involving more hours and has intensified the work that I do when I'm in. In addition, I'm emotionally propping up the 60 staff within my teams and making sure they are well supported. As you can imagine, everyone is scared and having their own wobbles despite having to try and carry on as normal.

I won't lie – going to work at the moment scares me. I have my own children, one of whom is classed as vulnerable, and I am petrified of taking anything home with me. However I have to put this aside because I have too many vulnerable families and children to support.

Times are very stressful at the moment and I guess what gets me through is the team spirit, colleagues looking out for one another. Being able to spot when someone's having a bad day and lifting their spirits a little. Also, the look of relief on the families' faces when we manage to keep their children at home and away from the hospital, the thought of which terrifies them all.

We do now have access to the correct PPE and I am using this to keep myself and my family safe. Wearing it is hot and sweaty and some of us have to wear it for 8 hours at a time. I am so grateful to have the equipment I need to keep me and my family safe whilst carrying on with my job, but today it's really hit home – it saddens me that we need to do this as it creates a barrier to the love and compassion we are trying to give to the children and their families. Delivering palliative care is emotional and difficult at the best of times, but how scary is it now for the person who you are caring for? They can no longer see the smile on your face or the love and care you are trying to give them. However, I am rewarded knowing that we are managing to keep these children safe at home.

So my message is simple – please just do as you are told and stay home, then hopefully we can get back to business as usual, as quickly as possible.

NICOLA & MALCOLM CUMBER
Covid Survivor / Dorset

Malcolm is a Veterinary Practice Manager and a retired Metropolitan Police Officer. We've been married for 32 years and have 4 children and 3 grandchildren. We've also got our dog Crumble, who works as a PAT dog. We visit Dorset County Hospital and Weldmar Hospice every week and the children, patients and staff absolutely love him – everyone loves a Crumble cuddle every week!

Malcolm was in hospital for 2 weeks. After falling ill, he was admitted to a ward where he tested positive for Covid-19. He deteriorated very quickly, so he was then transferred to ICU for 6 days where he was put on a ventilator. Malcolm doesn't remember too much about it until they slowly started giving him less sedation, but he does remember feeling grateful to be alive. After leaving ICU he stayed on a ward for a week to start his recovery.

I couldn't see Malcolm for the whole time he was in hospital. My children wanted to come home to be with me but I asked them to stay away as I didn't want them being at risk. It was inevitable that I got Covid-19, as I looked after Malcolm before he went into hospital. I had Coronavirus symptoms, coughing, I felt like someone was sitting on my chest, I lost taste and smell and felt completely exhausted. It was a very difficult time for me, dealing with my own illness and being out of my mind with worry and not knowing what was going to happen to Malcolm.

I was so excited and emotional about Malcolm coming home. I knew that we were soincredibly lucky to have him come through this nasty disease. The first thing he wanted was a cup of coffee, but he was so disappointed as it tasted awful due to having a lack of taste.

The last few days have not been very good. He has been home a week and his breathlessness was getting worse and he got a pain in his leg. I called the GP who came to our home within 10 minutes. He gave Malcolm an injection and took a blood test and realised very quickly that he has a DVT (deep vein thrombosis), blood clots on his lungs and an infection – but with antibiotics and blood thinner tablets, he is now showing signs of improving.

With the care of the GP, ambulance, doctors, nurses and all the equipment in ICU, Malcolm is coming through this awful virus and we cannot thank these people enough for what they have done to save this wonderful man's life.

> When Malcolm came home after not seeing him for 2 weeks, it was the best reunion anyone could ever ask for. We came so close to loosing him and we are eternally grateful to the NHS staff at Dorset County Hospital. I am the happiest wife ever.

AUGMENT BIONICS

Augment Bionics is a medical devices start-up founded at the University of Edinburgh, focused on building high functioning and affordable 3D-printed prosthetics for transradial amputees and individuals with below-elbow limb differences.

We know that 3D printing can change lives and that's why, in the midst of the Covid-19 pandemic, we began to 3D-print and donate essential protective medical equipment in response to national shortages. Now, we are using injection moulding to achieve the same goal but at a hugely increased capacity – a jump from 1,000 to 10,000 shields per week. This will enable us to officially supply NHS and governmental bodies around the UK which are experiencing shortages.

Before Covid-19, it was business as usual. We were developing 3D-printed bionic prosthetics with the goal of democratising access to quality medical devices. When we pivoted to producing face shields, none of us knew what we were getting ourselves into or how much we would learn. We only knew that Covid-19 was serious, that healthcare workers desperately needed critical PPE and we wanted to help.

In just three months we went from a single 3D printer (12 shields/day) to injection moulding and die cutting (2,000 shields/day). As part of our donation initiative, we provided over 60,000 medical face shields to 62 different NHS locations across the UK. In addition, we distributed a further 60,000 face shields abroad, where the effects of the Coronavirus had also taken hold and where they were struggling to secure their own PPE.

Although at times overwhelming, this work has allowed us to have an enormous number of rewarding experiences. The daunting gap between the seemingly infinite demand for equipment and the inadequate supply, encouraged us to continually increase our production capacity. This required countless design iterations, process optimisation, supply chain logistics and, most importantly, communication with healthcare workers as well as other quick-response PPE manufacturers.

We encountered many obstacles and setbacks along the way, some of which threatened to stop the project dead in its tracks. However, with the unwavering perseverance of the Augment Bionics team and our committed volunteers, we managed to overcome those challenges to successfully see the project through to conclusion.

As our production grew, so did our public profile. We have been featured on several global media outlets including CNN and Sky News. This media exposure bolstered the crowd-funding efforts and it also meant that a large number of healthcare workers found out about our work and reached out for help.

With £110,000 raised, over 120,000 face shields produced and countless people protected, we can proudly say that this project has been quite exceptional.

None of this would have been possible without the generous donations and support of our communities. Before recognising the outstanding group of people and organisations involved in this project, we would like to express our thanks to Latymer Upper School. They helped us raise crucial funds for our project and provided access to their facilities and equipment. Our initiative could not have been as impactful if it wasn't for their support. With their help, we've been able to do our part in protecting our true heroes and it's been heart-warming to be able to make a difference.

> We just knew that healthcare workers desperately needed critical PPE and we wanted to help.

MARTIN LEWIS CORONA VIRUS FUND

We face an unprecedented challenge to our health, economy, businesses, personal finance and way of life. And many of those who normally help society – our charities – are going to face similar pressures right now too. To try and help, I released £1 million from my personal charity fund to provide grants to help offer immediate poverty relief.

Small and local charity projects such as foodbanks and charities engaged in community aid and financial advice as well as churches, schools and NHS trusts could apply for grants from £5,000 to £20,000 to help with specific coronavirus-related projects.

I also appealed to any high net worth individuals and organisations to donate a minimum of £10,000 and up to a maximum of £100 billion (well I could hope!). As I was so busy with the live Money Saving Expert coronavirus advice programmes, I set up an administration process to make this happen and to make sure help was spread across the UK as best and as quickly as possible.

The response was incredible. In the first week we had nearly 7,000 applications requesting around £74 million and the work for the team I hastily arranged was staggering.

In the end, we had just under £3.5 million to distribute – BOOM! That's £1.9 million from my charity fund (I increased it from the original donation) and I'm delighted to say that we had around £1.5 million more from other high net worth individuals and firms.

Sadly though, that left us only being able to fund about 5% of the applications received. Simply picking who to give the money to was a Herculean and intimidating task.

However, we did help over 400 small charities and community action groups that included the obvious and most-needed food banks, domestic abuse charities and cancer groups plus projects for direct intervention and help by the likes of local community centres, small football teams, charity groups organised by churches, synagogues, mosques, temples and other religious groups, and women's groups across all four UK nations.

I'm so grateful to the brilliant cast of volunteers that worked with me on this and who gave weeks of time to heavily filter applications. Huge plaudits too to the Charities Aid Foundation, which is where I keep my charity fund. It was never set up to do the due diligence needed at this sort of scale and to make this number of small payments at speed. Yet when I asked it, there was no quibbling. They saw the need, took up the challenge and have been brilliant. And my gratitude especially to the charities, who are the real heroes in this tale – the people out there giving food and support, and caring for all those in need at the moment.

> 66
> We distributed grants to small and local charity projects to help offer immediate poverty relief, but the charities were the real heroes in this tale – the people out there giving food and support, and caring for all those in need at the moment.

You can accomplish by kindness what you cannot by force.

// PUBILIUS SYRUS

JAMIE BROGDEN
Listening Samaritans Volunteer / Preston

Founded in the 1950s, Samaritans provides support to anyone in emotional distress, struggling to cope, or at risk of suicide, usually through our telephone or email helpline. We have over 200 branches and 20,000 volunteers around the UK taking up to over 5 million calls a year and we pride ourselves that someone is always available 24 hours a day 7 days a week to help.

There's no such thing as a normal day. Each shift is different. People have many problems they wish to talk about, so you definitely don't know what your shift will entail. From relationship problems, eating disorders or money issues, to work stress, loneliness and bereavement. There are no targets for calls or emails, we're just there to listen and support.

Covid-19 has brought its own challenges. Our Director recently said: "We're going over and above what we would normally do because these are unprecedented times and the impact of Covid overspills in all sorts of ways. People are struggling with isolation and having to adapt to a whole new way of life. Since Lockdown, around a quarter of calls are from people concerned about Covid in one way or another, whether it be loneliness, isolation or mental health. Covid is such an unknown quantity – as a country we've never ever come across this."

Similarly, the financial uncertainty and fears about making ends meet as furlough ends is another pressure for people.

In August, the Preston branch's volunteers were on the phone for almost 400 hours, answering over 1,500 calls and responding to over 150 emails – an increase of around 30% on the same month last year. Around a third of our branch were shielding or caring for family so there was some extra pressure to fill all the shifts. We can't really work from home because this is a confidential service plus it's quite important to be able to get immediate support from colleagues if we have a difficult call and need to offload so we've also had to adapt the space in which we work to ensure social distancing. Support from all areas of the branches has been brilliant. We are all in this together.

The challenge for the organisation is finding different ways of getting our message over and delivering some of our services. Outreach, training, recruitment and fundraising have suffered from lack of public interaction. And the 'caller' has been unable to come in for face-to-face support during the pandemic. Sometimes the simple human interaction, which for years we have taken for granted, has not been able to be there, which I think has been difficult for callers who have just needed this simple reassurance of human contact.

Why do I volunteer? Good question. The simple answer is I like helping people. The more serious answer is that I struggle with mental ill-health. So has my grandfather and father. They never spoke about it or asked for emotional support off others and my father's long-time battle saw several attempts on his own life. I was not willing to do the same so I started volunteering. I don't want anybody to feel they need to struggle alone.

I am always proud to tell people that I am a Samaritan. I am proud of how we, as Samaritans, have just got on with the challenge. On some occasions the callers have been in a terrible state of mind in their own eyes, but after a telephone conversation or an email we often get a thank you for helping, although all we have really done is listen and reflect their own emotions. A simple thank you means the world to me. We have taken them from a possibly dark place to a safer place for a short period of time.

For me, this time is the challenge of our time. We will look back and say did we do the best for me, for you and for all the people we helped. I think Samaritans have stood up to the challenge and, as well as other charities, have worked hard to help the vulnerable keep some normality. And remember, even if you are wearing a mask you still have a voice, and we are still here to listen.

> " Even if you are wearing a mask, you still have a voice, and we are still here to listen.

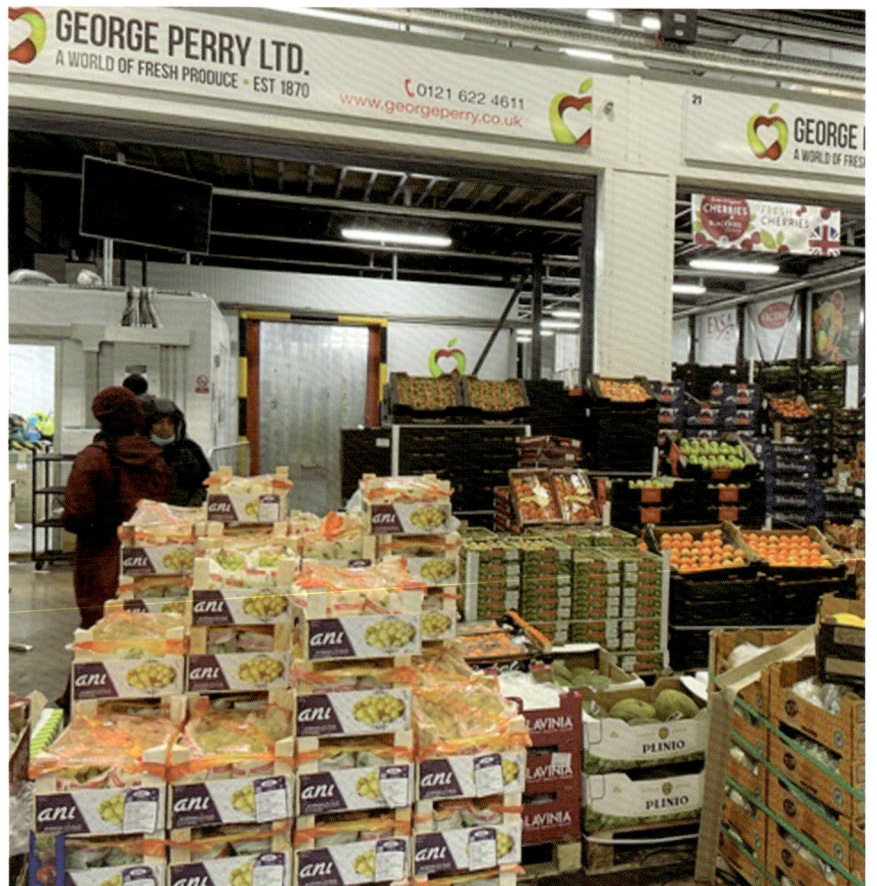

GEORGE PERRY LTD

Established in 1870, George Perry Ltd is the UK's oldest wholesaler of fresh fruit and vegetables. We operate an 18 acre wholesale market, which is home to a wide range of other traders too. As well as the market, we deliver to lots of local supermarkets and our own shops around the Midlands. A normal day usually starts at 2.30 a.m. and sees about 15 lorries making deliveries to around 25 shops each. We also deal with a lot of corporate customers, high end caterers and football stadiums. It's always busy!

I wouldn't say the amount of work we had to do changed that much with Covid – we always work really hard so that's not been much different. But the dynamics of how we work changed. The big contracts, the corporate stuff, the football stadiums. We lost all that. We lost trade catering business worth around £2 million.

I also had to make the difficult decision to close the market to the public to try and reduce the risks to my team and the other traders. I told them all on the Thursday that was what we'd be doing and I got a lot of argument from people. But as things moved on, by the Tuesday everyone agreed it was the right thing to do and we closed at the start of April.

But on the flip side, people were shopping local so our shops, now kitted out with barriers and hand sanitisers and the like, were really busy and we were having to make more and bigger deliveries to local supermarkets. And we found new customers too. Local pubs and garden centres were coming direct to us because disruptions in the supply chain meant they couldn't get some of the smaller orders they needed from their usual places.

We also introduced home delivery around the UK. We've been meaning to do it for quite a while but this sort of escalated the need for it, so we had to sort out the logistics and pull together a new website really quite quickly.

To help those shielding and the vulnerable over-70s, we offered free delivery. We started work as usual at 2.30 a.m., finishing the wholesale stuff by about mid-morning and then making the deliveries. We've always been very active in the community and we do what we can to look after our locals. It was about all mucking in together and looking out for each other.

Our business has had to adapt quite a lot but one of the weirdest things to get used to has been how there's no pattern to things at the moment. We're quite a cyclical and seasonal business so we usually know pretty much what sells at what time of year and in what quantities. But that seems to have turned on its head.

In any given year, we'd usually sell about 80 lorry loads of watermelons but this year we're probably only going to have sold about 10 – I don't know why Covid has made people go off watermelons! And conversely, we'd usually sell about 1,000 pumpkins a year, but this year it will be nearer to 10,000 and I can only think it's because people are spending more time together as a family doing things like that.

We've got through it all with the usual 'wholesale' camaraderie and banter. We've kept each other going and I am massively proud of my team and of the wider wholesale industry. We were absolutely delighted to receive a letter from Parliament to thank us for our efforts but really, we've just kept doing what we do every single day.

Mark Tate / Owner

> We do what we can to look after our locals. It was all about mucking in together and looking out for each other.

RITA REYNOLDS
Covid Survivor / Bramhall

Rita fell ill at the end of March and, after she then tested positive for Coronavirus, we were told to prepare for the worst as her condition worsened.

She was kept comfortable by staff at Abbeyfield care home as 'end of life' drugs were ordered. The staff there were absolutely fantastic but we were certain that was it for her. When you hear everything you hear about the virus and then a 99-year-old gets it, we didn't think for one second there was any way she would pull through.

Then we had the incredible news that she had recovered, we couldn't believe it. At the time, she was believed to be Britain's oldest person to recover from Coronavirus.

As a fairly frail 99-year-old, we can't believe how lucky she is – and that we are – that she's come through it. We have no idea how she did it. It's certainly not down to a healthy diet or rigorous exercise because she's never done either her entire life! She eats very few vegetables or salad but loves cake, biscuits and puddings. However, she's never really smoked or drunk alcohol. At the home, they always ask her what she wants to eat for tea and they joke that they don't know why they bother to ask – every day she only ever wants marmalade sandwiches.

Maybe it was just the luck of the draw, but we've joked that she owes her recovery to her love for marmalade sandwiches. Deurrs, a local manufacturer, even sent her 3 dozen jars of their jam and marmalade to share with residents at the home.

She's just an incredible woman. She was a driver in the Women's Auxiliary Air Force in WW2 and survived a bomb attack on her house during The Liverpool Blitz, whilst hiding under her kitchen table reading a book.

As a family, we feel so blessed. Rita was 100 in July and was delighted to receive her telegram from the Queen.

> "
> She's just an incredible woman. We've said she owes her recovery to her love of marmalade sandwiches!

BECKI GORMAN
M&S Simply Food Store Manager / Cheetham Hill

I've worked in retail since I was 14 and, after studying childcare and working in a private nursery, decided to go back to it. I started as a lingerie manager at M&S in Manchester and worked at that branch for 8 years in various roles, before taking the big step up to become store manager at Hale's foodhall.

Four months later, I found out I had a brain tumour. I had a successful operation in June 2018 and went back to work in August because I love my job and hated not being busy.

I'm currently working in the Cheetham Hill store and my days are always busy. In the morning, I'll help get the store ready and then, once the doors are open, it's all about the customer service. I love the pace and the turnaround of stock because it's a great feeling to see items selling quickly – it shows we're doing a good job.

Working in a food store during the Coronavirus pandemic has been overwhelming. We had such varied information coming through and I had to find a way to quickly deliver those key messages to staff.

It felt a little like Christmas, because of the high volumes of stock that came into the store, but I love working under pressure and so I was in my element. Everything flew off the shelves in the first two weeks – toilet rolls, antibacterial cleaning sprays, tins of beans, soup, flour and sugar. And every day, we filled the shelves until there was no stock left over in the warehouse.

We also had to adapt quickly. For example, staff now wipe down the shopping baskets and trolleys with sanitiser before they are used by customers.

In retail, people are the heart of everything – be it customers or colleagues, there's always great camaraderie in the store. People appreciate one another and people are at their best when they enjoy coming to work.

I also think that it's become a good job for achieving a work-life balance now: there are so many shifts to choose from and opportunities to progress. And it feels like a secure career option too. People will always need groceries.

I wanted to give something back to the NHS because they saved my life so, alongside my job, I signed up as an NHS Volunteer Responder during the Coronavirus pandemic. I do prescription drop-offs and check-in calls with vulnerable people who are self-isolating. I go home after work to look after my two children and make tea, and then put myself on duty via the app on my phone. I also volunteer on my days off.

I'm really proud to have been recognised as a 'Retail Hero' by the British Retail Consortium.

> " Working in a food store during the pandemic has been overwhelming, but people will always need groceries.

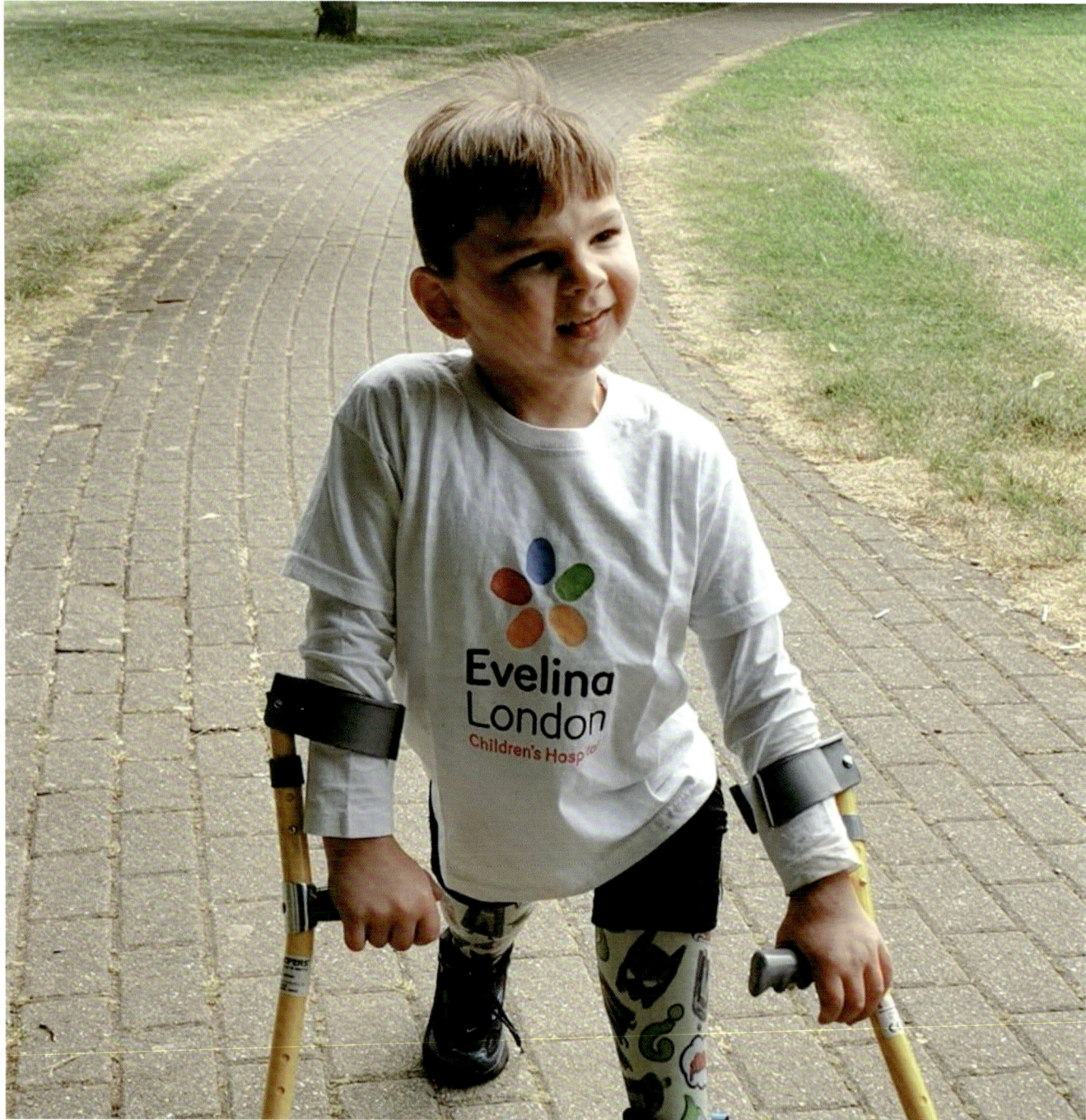

TONY (BEAR) HUDGELL
Charity Fundraiser / West Malling

At 41 days old, Baby Tony was admitted to hospital with multiple fractures of all his limbs, dislocations of several joints, blunt trauma to his face and multiple other injuries. He had been left for anything up to 10 days before he was taken to the doctors in an unresponsive state.

By this time, his poor body had given up to the injuries and he developed Sepsis, toxic shock and multi-organ failure. He was on the brink of death and if it wasn't for the amazing NHS working so quickly and tirelessly for him over the next 3 months, he would not have survived.

Tony – our Bear – came into our lives at 4 months old when he was well enough to leave hospital. We went on to adopt him in 2016 and we couldn't be prouder to call him our son. His strength and determination is incredible.

Sadly in 2017, due to the injuries and infection, he had to have both his legs amputated. He will need multiple operations going forward for the rest of his life and is also deaf in one ear, but he is a happy little boy who loves life.

Over the past few years, he has become very close to Mr Kokkinakis, who leads his orthopaedic team at Evelina London Children's Hospital. They have worked together to help Tony adjust to life as a double amputee.

In June, inspired by Captain Tom, Tony decided he wanted to walk 10 km using his new prosthetic legs to raise money for the hospital that saved his life and has supported him ever since. We thought he might raise £500, but were astounded when he raised over £1 million.

It is incredible to think that just a few weeks before this, Tony could barely take a few steps. He is such a strong and determined boy and we are so proud.

The money Tony has raised will go towards a series of projects that will help the hospital provide specialist care and support for the 103,000 children and young people who come through its doors each year. Funds will be put towards new facilities, cutting-edge technology and research whilst also extending the support the hospital can offer to a wider area.

He was given the 'Good Morning Britain Young Fundraiser' award at the Pride of Britain Awards for what he did, presented by his heroes Ant & Dec.

We'd like to thank everyone who has been so generous in supporting Tony's fundraising and we couldn't be happier that the money is going to a place that is so special to our family.

I'm just so incredibly proud of him and everything he's done has just been amazing.

Paula Hudgell / Tony's Mum

66

A few weeks before, he could barely take a few steps but he walked 10k in 30 days to raise money for the hospital that saved his life.

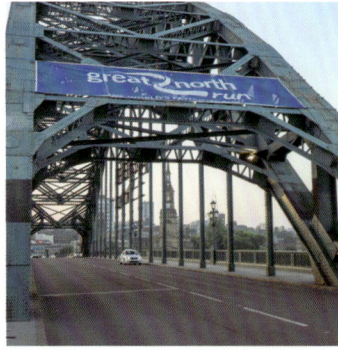

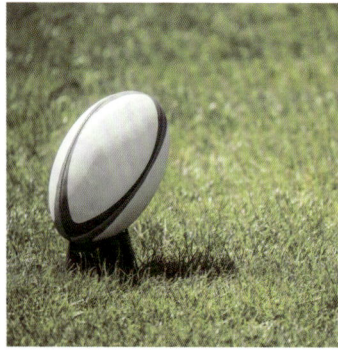

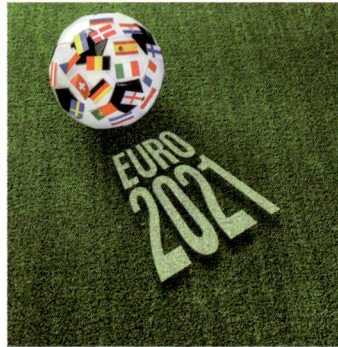

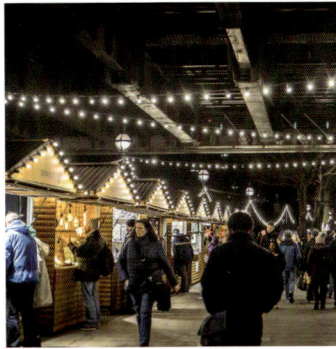

From festivals and sports, to weddings and exams, events and gatherings were cancelled, adapted or went digital; soap episodes were rationed and we even had a virtual Grand National ...

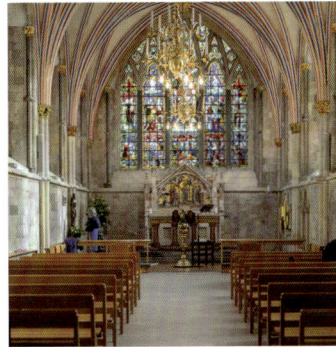

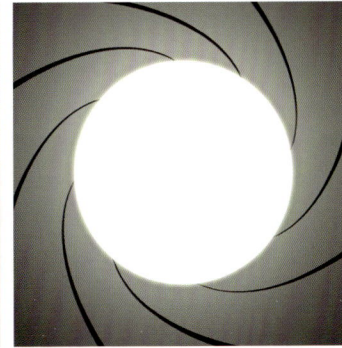

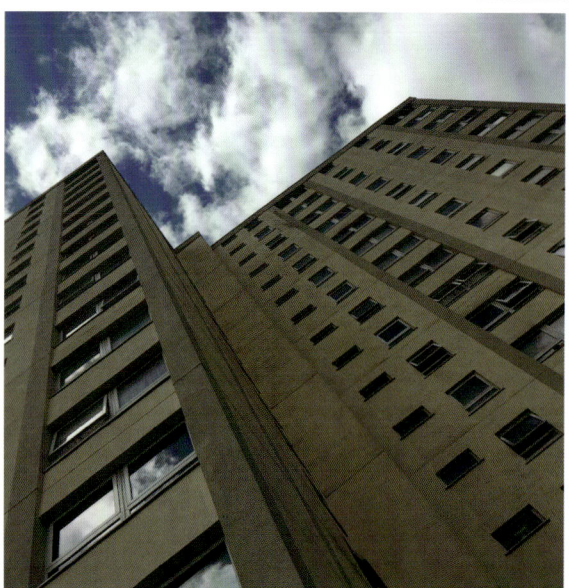
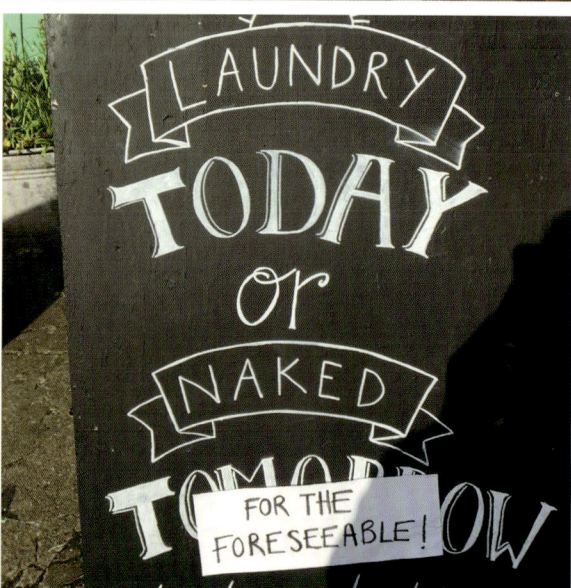

THE LAUNDRETTE ANGELS
'At The Well' Laundrette / Stokes Croft

We (sisters Ellen, Cassie and Lily Grist) founded 'At The Well' cafe-laundrette in 2012, having been inspired by the sense of community we had witnessed in Zambia. We are passionate about building a community over the shared necessity of doing laundry. Like neighbours around an African tap stand or Indian river, people gather here to wash their clothes, get much-needed sustenance, swap stories and build real community.

People heading for the 'At The Well' can often be spotted pulling suitcases or carrying IKEA bags full of laundry. Plenty of people also just come for our brunches, coffees and homemade cakes or just to use our printer. It's a real community affair, with the general laundry activity creating a homely and familiar kind of ease.

In March we were forced to close. Technically, laundrettes were deemed essential services and could remain open, but there was insufficient footfall during the Lockdown to justify a member of staff being on-site. The washers and driers looked set to sit empty and we had to furlough the majority of the team, although a couple of us stayed on to be able to do the odd bit of washing to help regulars who contacted us.

Early on in Lockdown, we saw an article on the local news about a family who were shielding in a tower block in Easton and were unable to safely do their washing in their communal laundry. They had weeks of laundry piling up. Seeing this, we tweeted the news presenter, asking her to put us in touch so we could go and help them. We collected the backlog of laundry and the story was covered on the local news, which described us as the 'laundrette angels'. It was frankly a bit embarrassing but we were determined that this wouldn't be a one-off act of kindness. This was surely not the only family in the same predicament?

A couple of individuals who'd seen the news report kindly got in touch to donate some money to cover our costs and enable us to continue helping the family in the tower during the Lockdown. To help others like them, we started a 'laundry in Lockdown' crowdfunder and were amazed to receive £1,000 in donations in less than a week. This enabled us to go to the Council and offer to help others who had lost safe access to clean laundry.

Anyone phoning the Council's Lockdown helpline and reporting similar issues would be referred to us, but the phone didn't exactly ring off the hook as we imagined it might. Instead, the Council phoned to say that rough-sleepers, who'd been offered emergency accommodation in hotels in the city as part of the nationwide 'Everyone In' campaign, were desperately in need of clean laundry. Many of these individuals were having to just hand-wash their clothes in their shower trays.

We arranged to partner with the Council and two homeless charities, collecting up to nine binbags of laundry a day. It was amazing to be able to return laundry that had been worn for weeks, all clean dry and folded. Returning a car full of clean laundry at the end of the day was a real highlight and kept us going on days where it was a real slog. We reduced the price of each load of washing to that of the washer and drier tokens only, with the Council splitting the cost with the crowdfunded donations, to make each load of laundry free at the point of need.

We've been working with Bristol City Council and local organisations to identify people in the greatest need, and have collected and laundered for them since mid-March.

An Instagram message from one of our clients sums up the impact this is having: "Thank you for helping us – it's making life a lot more bearable having clean clothing so we feel a bit more human and also know that our clothes aren't covid nightmares! I am eternally grateful".

It was brilliant to have a role to play and to know we were making a positive and valued contribution. We were also hugely grateful for every other load of washing we were phoned to collect, not least all those new customers who supported us by sending their duvets for laundry during this period of closure.

> 66
> We saw a story about a shielding family unable to safely do their washing in the communal laundry so we did it for them.

SIR QUENTIN BLAKE

It seems like a time when a few straightforward jokes might not come amiss; so that as I know that people have been putting rainbows into their windows to express solidarity, I took the liberty of borrowing them. You will see that I have supposed that they are real and portable, and I hope they are optimistic too. I can imagine myself submitting them to Punch magazine 60 years ago in the hope that I might get onto the colour pages. Perhaps I don't need to add that they have much more meaning for me now than they would have had then.

ANTHONY COCKER BEM
Maintenance Plumber / Oldham

Everything done at the hospital behind the scenes is, in some way, just as important as what the nursing staff do on a daily basis. The backroom staff (like the Estates department where I work) are the people that keep the hospital running, from making sure the lights are working, that the water is running and doing any repairs needed to maintain the hospital.

At the start of the pandemic I don't think there were many in the entire NHS that weren't scared of not knowing what was out there and what we had to face. We just knew we had family and parents at home and we were scared to take anything home to them.

The Estates department, from plumbers and joiners, to electricians and even painters, were the ones who kept the modern-day hospitals running. Keeping the facilities going, like the nurse call buttons, heating, lighting, removing blockages, repairing taps and fixing heating and general maintenance means that the doctors and nurses are able to care for the patients efficiently and are safe in their environment.

I have worked on many wards from intensive care to the children's wards. I was on the front line at the start of Covid-19 and had to install/repair hand washing facilities – a job which has become crucial in today's environment.

It's been a really difficult time, and as the months have gone on we have all worked tirelessly every day, as well as giving up time where we should have been visiting parents or doing other things. Everyone has made sacrifices just to be able to go to work each day.

On a personal note, going through Covid-19 at the start is one of the scariest things I have ever been through. There were some colleagues who couldn't do their normal day job due to vulnerability, so there were very few of us that went to Covid-19 wards to carry out jobs. You had to make a decision to do the job no matter how scared you or your families were, because nurses needed to be in a comfortable and safe environment, as did the patients they were caring for.

It was a great honour to receive recognition for the work I've done during these difficult times but everyone at the hospital deserves just as much recognition as I do – as well as everyone else that works tirelessly looking after parents, grandparents, children, brothers and sisters even strangers. My parents, my girlfriend Nicola and son Rowan are extremely proud of me and I only wish that my grandparents were still alive to see me receive the BEM.

It is an absolute honour to work for such a great organisation like the NHS, and I will continue to work tirelessly during this pandemic as do all the staff.

> " You had to make a decision to do the job no matter how scared you were because the nurses and patients needed a comfortable and safe environment.

ANTHONY CARDOSO
Eddie Stobart Lorry Driver / Wellingborough

I am a Class 1 lorry driver and usually my loads are containers for items such as TVs, water and electrical goods, delivered to stores up and down the country. My routes are anywhere – I can go from Scotland to Cornwall or into Wales – and an average shift is around 12 hours. I sleep in my lorry.

I've always loved driving and have worked myself up in size to Class 1. Even as a child, my mum recalls me always saying I wanted to drive a bin lorry! I've got dyslexia so any job with too much writing or spelling was never on the cards. I've always been, right from little, a hands-on type.

I'm still driving and delivering things all around the country. The only things that have really changed due to the Coronavirus is longer shifts and a lack of amenities available to drivers. Baby wipes are essential right now! Normally we have a drivers' room wherever we go, to get a cuppa, but obviously we aren't allowed now and have to stay in our lorries. Stobart are good in that they will provide hot meals for their drivers at their own centres.

I'm still working – obviously to earn a living but also because driving is my hobby too, so I'm doing something I love. I'm not scared as such, but I am more tired as the shifts are longer. I'm proud to be doing my bit though. Also, people are being really supportive and having respect for lorry drivers now, that wasn't there before. I think it's made people realise our worth. And the staff behind the scenes have been really important too, because without the people in the transport office, directing the drivers, nothing would go anywhere.

I always watched Stobart growing up and I'm really proud to now be working for them and keeping things moving despite Covid.

> 66
> I'm proud to be doing my bit and people are being really supportive.

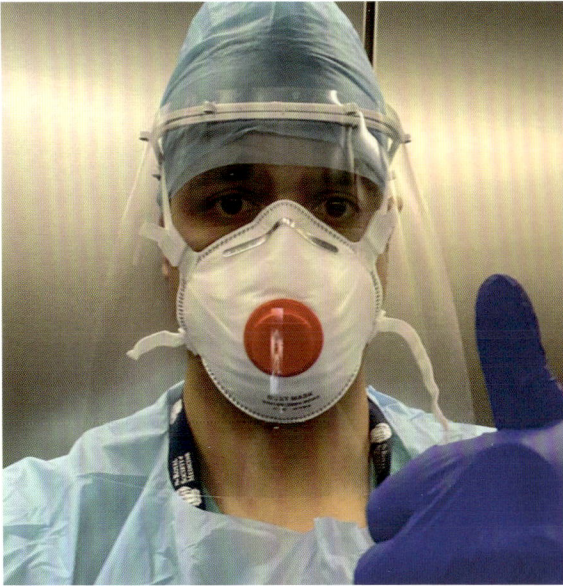
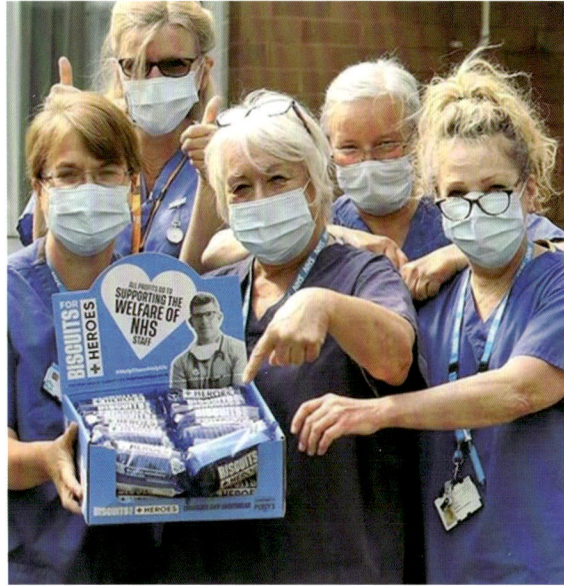

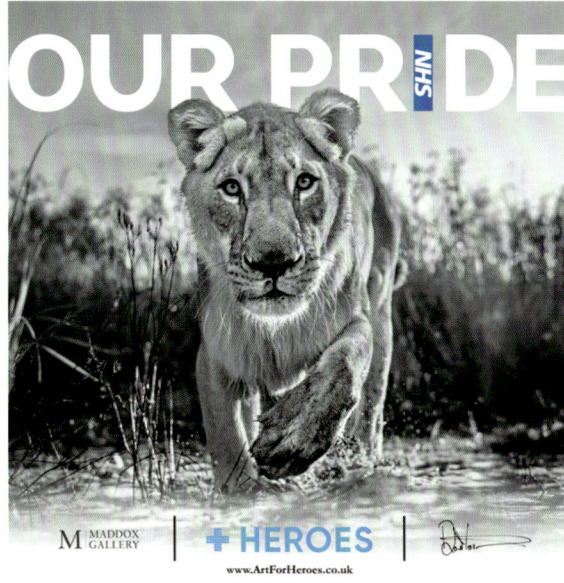

OUR PRIDE

M MADDOX GALLERY | +HEROES

www.ArtForHeroes.co.uk

HEALTHCARE WORKERS' FOUNDATION

Healthcare Workers' Foundation is a charity founded by NHS workers, for NHS workers. We are doctors, musicians, technologists, students, and artists who have come together for one reason: we love our NHS. We love the people that work day in, day out to take care of us. Today, they need our help more than ever and we want to do our best to help them, help us.

We exist to support the welfare and wellbeing of those fighting to keep us healthy and safe during the Covid-19 crisis, and beyond. Our services cover the physical, mental and day-to-day needs of all NHS HEROES, from doctors and nurses to cleaners and porters, either paying for things directly or through a support grant based on need.

We're committed to protecting frontline NHS workers and fund sustainable, reusable PPE so they have the vital personal protective equipment they need. We also work with a number of partners and celebrity chefs to make and deliver food to NHS workers at home and at work, to feed our frontline and their families and bring a little joy.

We've created a hub of mental wellbeing support services across all NHS staff groups and we provide educational resources for the public and clinicians about Coronavirus and Covid-19.

We work with a range of businesses to provide discounted products including gifts, food and travel and we've teamed up with the largest childcare provider in the UK, childcare.co.uk, to deliver safe childcare options so NHS frontline workers can go to work with peace of mind. We're also working with a number of partners to offer free or discounted cab fares directly to NHS workers during the Covid-19 pandemic.

In partnership with Maddox Gallery we launched Art for HEROES, a collaboration of fantastic artists, including photographer David Yarrow and musician Boy George, who donated pieces to raise money for NHS staff.

And, in a bid to encourage people to stay at home, we partnered with agency IRIS and photographers across the UK to launch #StayHomeHEROES, asking people to post their every day domestic acts which, in Lockdown, feel more like legendary triumphs while also protecting the real heroes by staying home.

We're touched and honoured to be supported by such a huge range of business, charities and public figures, who all want to help our NHS Frontline as best they can.

We run entirely on donations. From spare change to large sums, it all goes to supporting frontline NHS workers and we've been blown away by the support and enthusiasm to date. When we launched, we had dreams of raising £1 million to support NHS staff. Week one was a busy one. It fast became clear to us that not only were NHS workers in desperate need of support to make their day-to-day lives easier, but there were also people all around the UK who wanted to help. We raised more than £100K in donations, delivered thousands of hot meals cooked by chefs, as well as hand creams and PPE which had been donated.

By the end of October, we'd raised over £2 million and delivered almost 600,000 items of PPE, masks coverings, food, gifts and services. We've funded thousands of CE-marked 3D-printed visors, scrubs and reusable filtering face coverings; distributed hand sanitiser to GPs and hospices; purchased essential medical equipment for hospitals; granted childcare support and given out over £1 million of food, gifts, counselling and more.

The emerging second wave of Covid-19 is just the tip of the iceberg so we're calling on everyone to show their support by donating to our emergency appeal, so that we can continue supporting healthcare workers at a time that's needed most.

> " To all the NHS doctors, nurses, cleaners, carers, admin, GPs, paramedics — this one is for you.

A single act of kindness
throws out roots in all directions,
and the roots spring up
and make new trees.

// AMELIA EARHART

MARK GARSIDE
Blood & Transplant Driver / Huddersfield

I work between 35-45 hours per week, over a 14-week shift pattern and it can vary from 6 a.m. starts to midnight finishes. A typical shift involves delivering blood, plasma or platelets to various hospitals. We could also be collecting high risk samples from path labs in various hospitals in the North West.

When the need arises, we are called out on a 'Blue Light' which involves taking emergency blood, plasma or platelets to any hospital around the UK where needed. It is a job that gives me extreme satisfaction and is very rewarding.

The job has not really changed with Covid-19. We still carry out the same duties, although it is a lot harder now with social distancing in place and more time consuming gaining access to the hospitals.

I feel scared but at the same time proud to be saving lives and providing a service for the public. It gives me great job satisfaction knowing I am part of a service that helps people and saves lives. It is a very rewarding job that I enjoy immensely.

I work with a great group of people that are always there for each other and pull together. The banter we have keeps us going in these crazy times and I have had amazing support.

I always felt proud to work for the NHS before Covid-19. It is an honour doing the job that I do for our wonderful NHS and makes me proud to be British.

> " I feel scared but at the same time, proud to be saving lives and providing a service to the public.

THE ALVIS FAMILY FARM
Charlotte, Stu & Gracie / Somerset

On our farm we produce beef and lamb, which gets sold into supermarket chains via the Red Tractor scheme and goes mainly to supply Tesco and Aldi with the highest grade meat. We also run a small campsite called 'Gert Lushing'.

My husband is a 3rd generation farmer who farms with his Dad. It's a totally family run business. I'm a farmer's wife and full-time mummy plus I help to run the family campsite.

A normal day would start about at 6 a.m when my husband starts the day by checking all of the animals to ensure they are happy, well fed and in good condition. He usually doesn't come in until 9 a.m. when we have breakfast together with our daughter, then he goes back out.

Each day is different, depending on the time of year. In autumn and winter we often have to move sheep to different grazing as they get mischievous when the grass is getting low.

Spring is usually spent making sure we are ready for lambing and that all the ewes are checked on several times a day to make sure they have not got stuck on their backs or have endured dog attacks. Usually the cattle are out in the fields grazing by late spring and then in the summer we have to plan and organise all the silaging alongside our other farming daily tasks.

None of this really changed with Covid – the farm still had to keep going. It did mean we couldn't meet family and friends and escape the sometimes lonely days in everyday farm life. I didn't get to see my family but we were very lucky to have been able to isolate with my in-laws. It bought us closer and we have continued with more meals and quality time together. Our daughter kept us all entertained daily too.

I'm not sure we felt any more appreciation for what farmers do, but I think it would definitely have been noticed if we were not all working as hard as we always do behind the scenes. It is nice knowing that we can make someone smile with a nice steak at the end of their day.

We also had to close the campsite we've worked really hard to establish. Our farm is in a lovely area of the Mendips, near the beautiful cities of Bath and Wells, so we're always full with campers, caravaners and people staying in our pods. We're also not far from Glastonbury and we were fully booked for that. All those guests had to be cancelled. They were disappointed and we lost a lot of much needed income.

We've reopened again now but obviously have lots of new social distancing measures and deep cleaning processes in place which has been a learning curve. It's just so nice to see people enjoying our facilities again though.

> " The farm still had to keep going but we couldn't meet family and friends to escape the sometimes lonely days in everyday farm life.

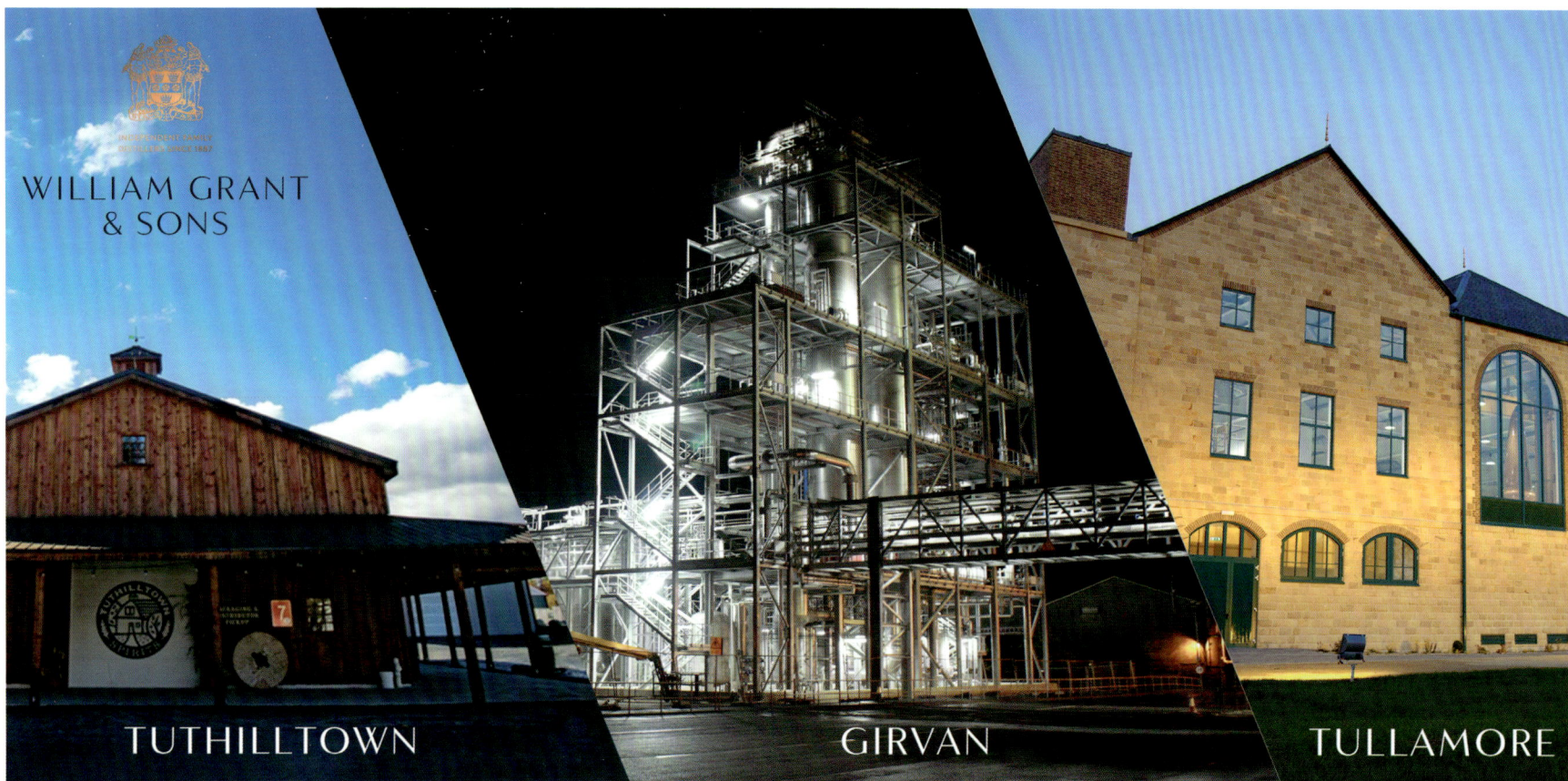

WILLIAM GRANT & SONS

TUTHILLTOWN   GIRVAN   TULLAMORE

66

Thank you to everyone involved in this unbelievably kind donation of hand sanitiser – it is very much appreciated during these uncertain times. This donation will go a long way in the battle against coronavirus for social care in North Lanarkshire, as it will allow us to protect vulnerable adults and staff who are carrying out key work during the pandemic.

Lanarkshire Care Partners

WILLIAM GRANT & SONS

William Grant & Sons is an independent, family-owned distiller headquartered in the United Kingdom and founded by William Grant in 1887. Today, we're run by the fifth generation of the William Grant family and distil some of the world's leading brands of Scotch Whisky, including Glenfiddich, Grant's and Tullamore D.E.W., as well as other iconic spirits brands such as Hendrick's Gin, Sailor Jerry and Drambuie.

As the Coronavirus situation unfolded, it became clear to us that we had the ability and capacity to make a difference. We decided that the best thing would be to produce ethanol that could go to specialist hand sanitiser manufacturers to help protect people around the world from coronavirus.

So we shifted production at three of our distilleries to supply about seven million litres of ethanol for the production of much-needed hand sanitiser.

We started at our small Tuthilltown distillery in New York State, then expanded to Tullamore in Ireland and Girvan in Scotland.

Our Girvan site is the largest grain distillery in Scotland which means we had the volume and capacity to produce ethanol for a range of hand sanitiser manufacturers. Our smaller-scale Tuthilltown distillery produced, packaged and distributed hand sanitiser to local health care providers.

It's been a significant change for our global teams. We've had to implement extensive health and safety and the relevant social distancing measures in our production sites as advised by local governments and the Scotch Whisky Association. We've had to adapt to ensure we can respond rapidly and it's not only been our production teams, but also the financials, supply chain coordination, logistics and so on.

Through this initiative, we can divert our technology and the skills of our people to contribute to the essential work of protecting people around the world from the impact of coronavirus.

Our teams are determined to do what they can to help at our distilleries and we are proud to have played our part in the worldwide fight against coronavirus. In 2020, we donated more than 34,000 litres of hand sanitiser to over 1,000 frontline groups and charities.

Stuart Watts / Distilleries Strategic Development Director

JOHN THOMSON
Actor & Comedian / West Didsbury

The thing about my line of work is that it's always feast or famine. My normal life is never 9-5 and so when Lockdown started, boredom was never an option for me. I'm quite used to having to cope with and be productive during downtime already.

We have so many resources available to us but I did also make sure I had back up for the internet going down! I did a lot of DIY, a lot of reading and I love cooking so I used it as a chance to hone my skills. I also made a point of getting out of the house regularly, just to escape the four walls. I was taking my recycling out one day and I saw an empty 'ring fit' box in my neighbour's bin so I decided to get one and I did that almost daily for over 100 days. I'd been feeling a bit lazy and that really helped.

And I also worked. For whatever reason, I'd had the foresight to convert the coal hole in my terraced house into a home studio a while back – so I've got this little 7ft x 3ft space, lined with foam and kitted out with a microphone and all the software, where I can do voice-overs. I narrate Ultimate Police Interceptors and this means I've been able to keep working which has helped to keep the wolf from the door. It's funny because although it's a massively different set up to a big studio, some of the technology we're using means it actually works just as well, if not better.

In some ways, I found Lockdown a breeze but I don't drink and I suppose you could say I went through my 'Lockdown' when I gave it up over 10 years ago. That was tough so I can see how, for many people whose social lives revolve around work or the pub, it must have been very difficult.

Obviously, I wasn't able to do any TV work for quite a while but we're now filming the second season of *McDonald and Dodds* for ITV and I'm so pleased to be back on set. It's different – we have to get swabbed by the paramedics every time we arrive on set, all the crew are masked and there's no socialising on the dining bus. Meals are all pre-ordered and delivered to us. We also all got given a little rucksack with our own masks and hand sanitiser in! The ladies in the cast had these funny little plastic visors, like they use at the hairdressers when they spray the hairspray, because that wouldn't wipe off their make up like the masks would.

We obviously have to be socially distanced which means the script and the shoot take a lot more organising. The cast are split into bubbles to work together and if we need to work across bubbles, we have to take a 10 day break first – so you can imagine that's led to some script rewrites to try and avoid that!

I've also got a work travel validation permit to show I'm travelling for work. It makes me feel like I'm in an old war film where the Gestapo would ask you to "show your papers"!

I am quietly baffled by how this thing is spreading though. It's not that hard to wear a mask or clean your hands. We've just got to follow the rules. People talk about the "new normal" but this is it and we should be getting used to it by now.

During Lockdown, being able to do the voice-over work was a godsend and now it's great to be back on set. In the last few weeks, I've also been approached for about 5 other jobs so I'm hoping that's a sign that things are starting to get a bit better for our industry.

> I'm quite used to having to cope with downtime but I'm so pleased to be back on set.

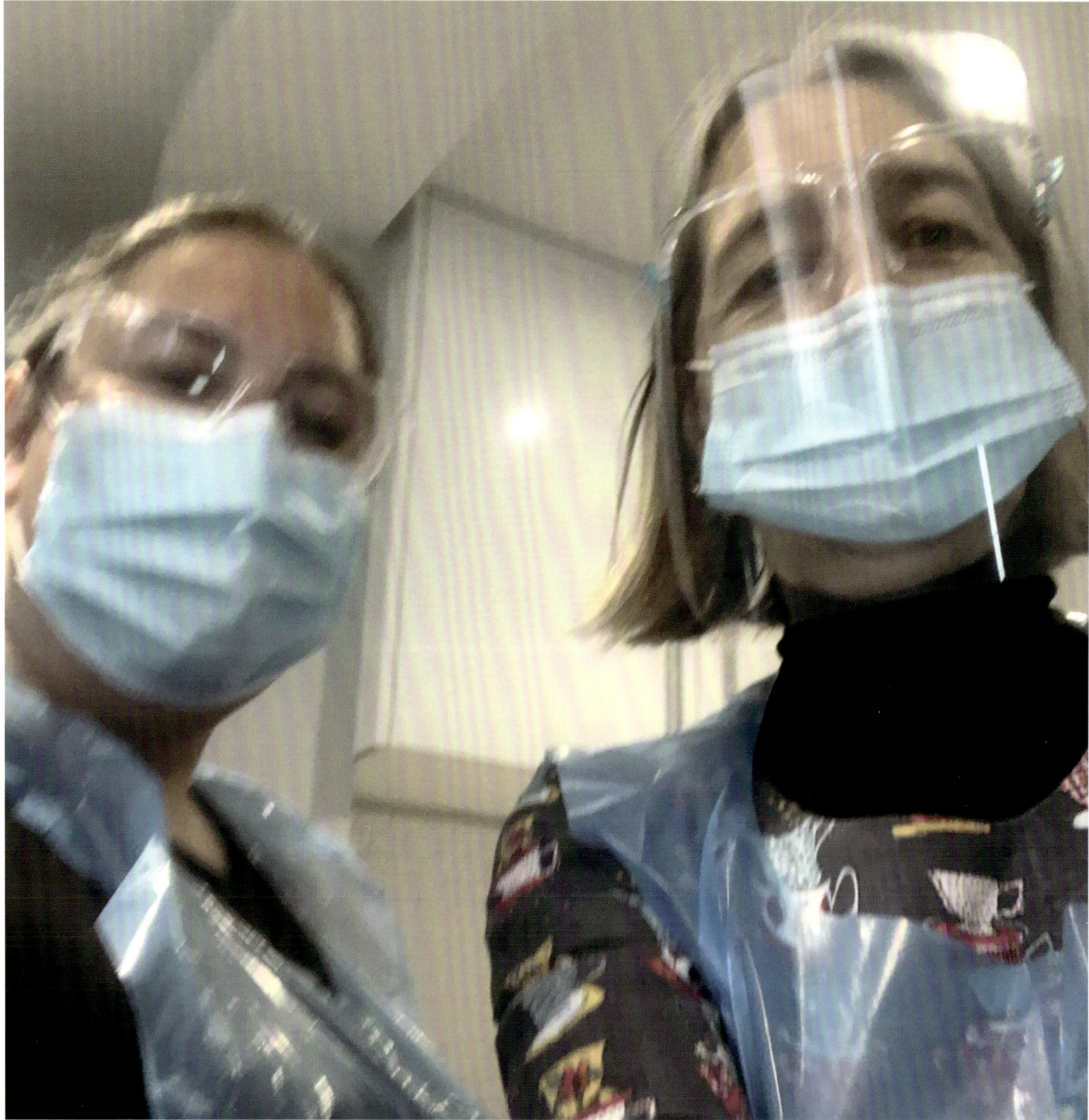

DONNA'S HAIR
Donna, Karen, Nicola & Cheryl / Cornwall

Donna's Hair was established in 1976 by my mum when I was 10-years-old. It's the longest-running salon in the market town of Helston and we have a mixed bag of customers of all ages with lots of elderly as well as three or four generations of the same family. Our clients are all very loyal and many have been coming to the salon for years. Some are like extended family and some we actually see more than our own families!

We had to shut completely on 23rd March and were closed for 102 days. I employ 3 stylists, who all started with my mum on Apprenticeships: Manager, Karen (36 years), Nicola (23 years) and Cheryl (14 years). They were all furloughed on 100% wages.

We diverted calls from the landline to our mobiles and had weekly phone calls from lots of of our elderly customers because they missed their weekly visits to the salon for a shampoo and set. Many said "it's not all about my hair, I'm missing the girls and a chat". I found that so rewarding. I learnt what the worth of my salon was and it's not financial, more welfare!

The support of our customers during the three months we were closed was fantastic. They sent cards and messages and booked and paid for haircuts in advance. One dear lady in her late 80s regularly phoned to check we were ok and to let us know how much she missed us. It made us feel very humble to think that all these people were thinking of us during these uncertain times.

Getting ready to reopen was a lot of hard work and getting hold of all the PPE required was like sourcing gold dust. We spent three days arranging appointments and not one person didn't want to come back or was worried about Covid. We were amazed. We honestly thought some would be concerned.

We were a little nervous about going back to work though and it was very different.

Physically the salon was different. It's only a small space so we could only have two stylists working. Some equipment was removed to support the safe distancing rules, we had markings on the floor and all products were put away into cupboards. We weren't allowed to have the radio on and gowns and capes were all disposable for a while, which made us sad as we all, as a nation, had been getting good at reducing plastic waste.

And it was different for us too. Getting used to all the PPE and trying to work with it all on was definitely a challenge. It gets very hot and the visors steam up, but we never let anything beat us and you do get used to it! So on with the aprons, gloves, masks and shields and back to work it was!

And then in came the "oh no look what I've done to my hair in Lockdown" stories! You think you've seen bad hair cuts but oh no, not like this. It didn't faze us though, we were just glad to be back at work and to have some sort of normality and routine.

Our clients were so glad to come back too, especially some of the older clients who hadn't been out for months. They always look forward to some chit chat, a cup of tea and a hair do (in that order!) and had really missed it. We have had amazing feedback on how everyone feels so safe.

Having just got back and used to working in a different way, it feels so so sad to now be heading into a second Lockdown but we do so knowing that our little business in this small Cornish town provides so much more than a good hair style and we'll be ready for those bad Lockdown haircuts once again!

> " We learnt the real worth of our salon and now know that we provide so much more than just a good hair style.

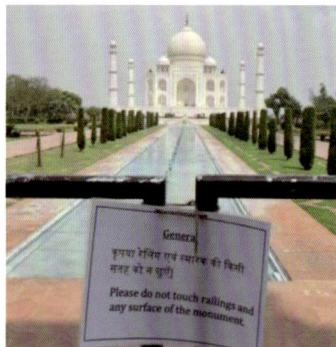

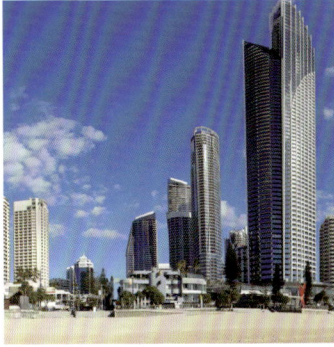

All around the world,
iconic landmarks and
tourist destinations
were deserted ...

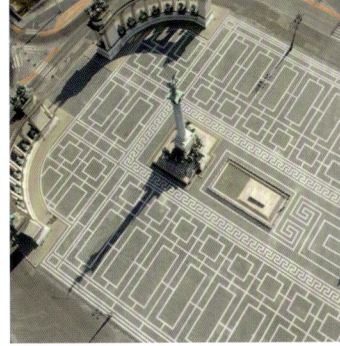

SIMON ABLETT
Refuse Lorry Driver / Blackpool

I'm a refuse lorry driver at Enveco North West. I'd always wanted to drive a wagon and find waste and recycling interesting. I'm normally awake about 5.15 a.m. for coffee and breakfast and then arrive at the yard for around 6.15 a.m. We pick up our work folders which detail the area we are doing that day and what crew we will have, then head to the wagon to do our daily wagon checks to ensure all is safe to use.

Since Covid, it's become very hard as social distancing measures are in place, so only drivers are allowed in the yard. We've got to pick up work stuff and wagon keys and then pick the loaders up en-route. In the cab where social distancing is impossible, we have been issued gloves and masks to wear and also have hand wipes and hand sanitizer, which we use an awful lot.

We have stopped collecting garden waste and are now collecting bottles/cans and general waste together every 2 weeks. We have stopped collecting the brown bags, which are used for paper/card recycling, as many people have been putting used tissues in them which, at this time, is a massive risk.

We'd normally finish around 3 p.m. but it's taking longer at the moment and is more tiring due to the extra bags we are collecting. The amount of waste has nearly doubled every day due to people staying home. Three extra crews have been put on every day to help out in taking streets off people, to help ease the day as best possible. We have CB radios in our cabs so we can talk to each other, which helps as we have banter with each other which is really helping during these tough times.

It's scary because we are interacting with the public and, although we wear gloves when touching bins, you don't know if someone has touched that who has Covid. I feel anxious about everything. Am I gonna come home having picked up the virus and pass it on to my family? I'm taking precautions by constantly cleaning my hands and the surfaces in the cab and I wash my work clothes and shower as soon as I get home.

I keep going because I love my job and feel great that I am doing something positive for people and helping them. We have received all sort of gifts from money to biscuits, chocolates and alcohol and we were even given a cuddly toy for the wagon! We've also had lots of children make us posters and lots of 'thank you' notes on bins which is amazing that people take the time to do this for us.

It makes us feel great and keeps us going knowing that just doing our job makes a difference to people. We have noticed a lot of people standing on their doorsteps clapping us which is lovely and we have not seen anything like this before.

The family at home are amazing, telling me to relax and my girls are doing stuff for me so I don't have to. My girlfriend Laura is also constantly checking I'm OK at work, as she knows I suffer with anxiety. Knowing I'll see them all at end of the day is what keeps me going.

> It's scary and I feel anxious about everything but it keeps us going knowing that just doing our job makes a difference to people.

WE WILL ROCK YOU

My band, The Slow Show, should have been on tour supporting the Pixies, but I've ended up in a classroom instead! The tour was cancelled and has been rescheduled, and it looks like it will probably have to be rescheduled again now. It's really sad but you have to do what's needed to keep people safe.

I also do some work in schools, teaching kids about music. This obviously got cut back too, although we still held some sessions for the keyworkers' children who were still in school.

We knew we wouldn't have the 'normal' run of work we usually do in the summer and we also knew that lots of kids would be sat at home, perhaps struggling with this weird situation. So we started thinking, "what can we do to help?", especially as parents began to go back to work and the holidays coming up. We decided to set up our own summer 'School of Rock'.

We set up the 'We Will Rock You' project, offering music lessons to kids and giving them the chance to learn and perform popular songs with the experts.

We had to take a Covid training course online to make sure we had everything set up properly and there's a lot of deep cleaning of equipment involved. It's difficult to maintain social distancing – kids want to play with their mates and it's been a challenge to keep their focus on washing their hands and giving each other space. It's been hard to get them into the habit but keeping them active has helped to distract them.

The kids get to play a bit of everything, from rock and pop to samba drumming. We've got electric, bass and acoustic guitars for them to try, as well as keyboards, drum kits and percussion. They get a full band experience and then they stream a live show to their family.

We also cover some mindfulness and a bit of art – we get them designing album sleeves and band logos.

We could see the good it was doing. The kids were meeting new people, working in teams and getting the chance to express themselves creatively. They loved it. We've had so many enquiries that we've had to extend it with a Saturday club too, and people have been donating space so we can gift places to kids from some of the more deprived areas.

Chris Hough / Founder

66

We could see the good it was doing.

EVANDER

The impact of Covid-19 on our everyday activity, our communities, our places of work and our ways of working is unprecedented and looks set to change the way we live for the foreseeable future.

We saw significant changes in the profile of demand passed to us in both our insurance and facilities management sectors. Around the country, there was a significant reduction in break-ins to respond to but we were working with more and more customers to take precautionary measures as businesses locked down and boarded up – we installed over 1,500 metres of preventative boarding on commercial properties.

We continued to do the day job. We made over 11,000 visits to homes and businesses during Lockdown, still attending 'safe and secure' visits, on average, within 150 minutes. We also prioritised almost 300 vulnerable customers.

We had small nucleus hubs working socially distanced in Head Office, supported by our customer experience and technical specialist colleagues working from home. Our service engineers were all equipped with precautionary and enhanced PPE and practiced Safe Systems of Work.

> " I just want to say a massive thank you for the herculean effort that is going on to board up our properties. I can't say how much it is appreciated in what are difficult and unprecedented times for us all.

We were really proud that some of our furloughed colleagues took the opportunity to support the NHS and local charities by volunteering – our "Furlonteers".

As the country began to return to work, many of our clients asked for our support in getting their business premises ready to reopen so we launched a range of new reinstatement services including preventative boarding, cleaning and disinfection, perspex screens and non-contact temperature monitors as well as Covid-19 adhesive graphics.

Over the past few months, we've remained flexible and agile, adapting our working practices in line with Government guidelines whilst remaining true to our commitment of prioritising the safety and wellbeing of our colleagues and customers and striving to make the places where people live and work safe, secure and smart. I am exceptionally proud of all our colleagues who have remained committed through difficult and challenging circumstances and I'm very proud of what we have achieved.

Receiving some amazing feedback from our clients and customers has been a real highlight for us all. It's lovely to know our hard work has been appreciated.

Whilst it's not really (or in fact at all!) in the job description, one of my favourite stories was the elderly couple who were isolating and needed food. They had no friends or family to turn to and couldn't get any deliveries for 3 weeks but were too scared to go out. In desperation, they rang their insurance company who put them through to our contact centre. Without hesitation, our team rallied round. We took their order, arranged the food parcel with a local supermarket and then phoned Ron, one of our engineers who was on a day off, and he delivered it to them.

They were quite emotional and wrote in to tell us: "We will always hold Evander and its wonderful staff in great esteem. Well and truly beyond the call of duty! Brilliant and much appreciated – a wonderful act of kindness and generosity".

That, to me, summed up what we're all about. We're busy delivering the service that our customers rely on us for but we're never too busy to care.

Paul Lewis / Managing Director

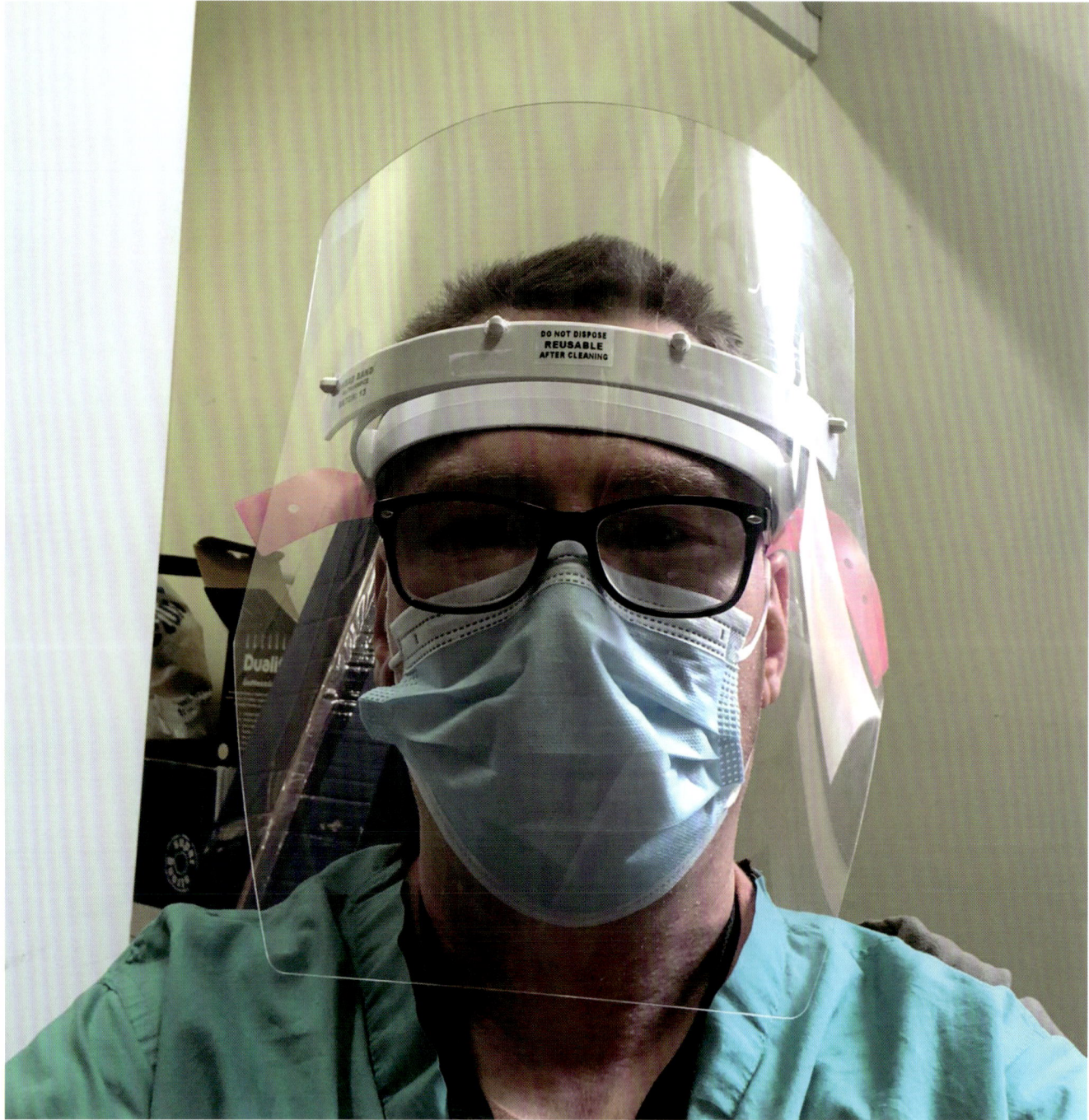

ALEXANDER (SANDY) DYKER
Consultant Physician / Newcastle

I'm a Consultant Physician at Newcastle Royal Victoria Infirmary and on a normal day, I'd be doing clinics and treating acute stroke patients. With Covid, I'm still doing that but we became far more concerned about the risk of infection – for patients and ourselves. Several colleagues got sick in short space of time at start of pandemic.

It's been challenging to juggle the anxiety, the reduced bed capacity, the worries about inadequate PPE and the additional time it takes to use the extra PPE needed but it has been rewarding to know we're surviving and still providing a 'normal' service to those that need us.

Outside of work, my wife and our French bulldogs Stewie and Meg have helped keep me going. Playing music also helps me feel better so I've spent a lot more time doing that and even set up my own YouTube channel!

> We're surviving and still providing a 'normal' service to those that need us.

TOM WALDEN
Camera Operator (Film & TV Drama) / Walthamstow

One of the greatest things about working in our industry is the sheer variety of things you do and places you visit. Every job I do has a different setting and aesthetic, which allows for a really rich variety in work and life. In 2019, I spent 5 months in India shooting the adaptation of Vikram Seths' 'A Suitable Boy' for the BBC. Spending this time immersed in Indian culture whilst also shooting a high-end production was simply a real pleasure.

When the pandemic hit, the British film and TV industry ground to a standstill. Overnight anything that was in production or gearing up to shoot went in to hibernation. For an industry that is predominantly filled with freelance workers who work from short contract to short contract, this was a really difficult period. Personally, I worked my last day in late February and didn't work again until the end of August: six months of the year when usually the industry is in full flow.

It wasn't the lack of work that I really struggled with, or the lack of income – although these began to weigh heavily as time went on. It was the not knowing when we might be able to go back to some normality, not being able to see the light at the end of the tunnel. I was able to be thankful for the chance to reset, reflect and rethink my outlook on what is important that the enforced time off gave me. I love my job and what it affords me, but sometimes it is at a cost of time with friends and family.

I also used the time to try and help a bit. I volunteered with an amazing local community cafe called the Hornbeam. It was called 'good deeds on bikes' and we delivered free meals and groceries to the vulnerable.

As time went on, there was so much talk of how productions would struggle to go back to normal. As a whole it was difficult to see the trees through the forest but, as well as my own personal reflection, the break also gave us as an industry a chance to reflect on structural inequalities, and how to make effective change for the future.

I am very lucky to have started work again, and it feels fantastic to be back in the hustle and bustle of set life. I'm currently shooting the third season of Netflix's 'Sex Education'. There was a lot of trepidation before the first day of shooting for a few reasons – not seeing anyone for months can create some anxiety when you are thrust back into a scenario with 100 other people, and not working for such a long period makes you a little rusty. Also with new protocols we weren't sure how we would be able to find our 'new normal'. Every day we have to complete a health questionnaire as well as having a temperature check. This is on top of having a Covid test twice a week and wearing face masks at all times.

On set we have separate 'bubbles' that are allowed to interact with each other. This is mainly for the actors who are not able to wear face masks. We also try to limit the amount of people on set at any time and have coloured zones. There were early discussions about shooting remotely, or having screens placed between the cameras and actors. Luckily there is relative sense of normality on set now, which seems to be working.

I genuinely love my job and feel so happy to be back at work doing what I do. We all have bills to pay and families to feed, and I feel grateful that I am able to provide whilst doing something I enjoy. Although working in the film and TV industry isn't the most vital thing in the world, I do believe it provides an escapism for people – and as we found during Lockdown – just how important arts, culture and entertainment can be as an outlet

It would be an understatement to say that 2020 hasn't been the best year but me and my partner Sally are expecting our first child early in the new year which I couldn't be more excited about so I'm sure 2021 is going to be a great year!!!!

> " It feels fantastic to be back in the hustle and bustle of set life although we weren't sure how we'd find our 'new normal'.

If this year has reminded
us of anything,
it is that the most beautiful
power we have
is the power to help
other people.

// MATT HAIG

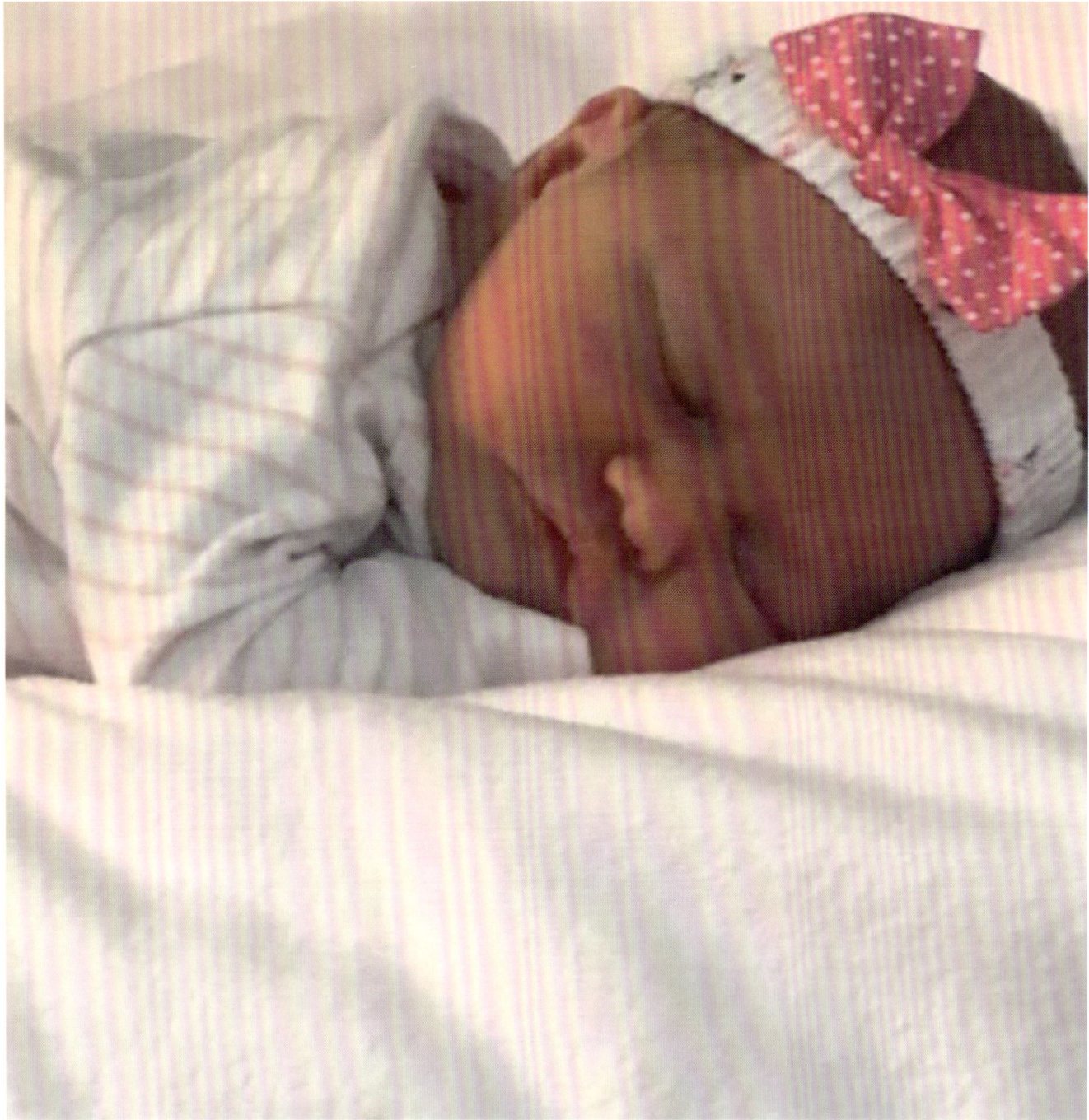

KAYLEIGH BARKHAM & BABY JOURNEY

'Lockdown Baby' / East Riding of Yorkshire

I was always going to be having a C-section with Journey as I have scar tissue damage from a C-section with my son and two other major surgeries on my stomach. My partner Stevie was planning on being there with me and staying with me until visiting time was over as this is what is usually allowed.

Due to Covid-19, I was aware that partners were only allowed at the delivery so was prepared for being on my own afterwards on the ward. Visitors were not permitted at any time on the ward I was on, as this would put all the women and babies at risk.

When we arrived, we got separated and I was left sat in a room on my own until it was time for the surgery. It was lonely and scary and I cried but the nurses couldn't comfort me because they had to have as little contact as possible. But in surgery, Stevie was there the whole while and got to spend time with her till my surgery was finished. The staff were brilliant and cheerful, trying to keep the mood light.

The nurses were great, but it was lonely and hard. I couldn't move to get her on my own and felt guilty having to ask nurses constantly as they have enough to deal with, so I felt I didn't get as much bonding time as I might have usually. Family and friends kept video calling wanting to see her and this was upsetting especially when my sons rang to see her and said they were missing holding her. The whole situation was was extreme compared to the happy memory of having Lincoln on the same ward in the same way 5 years earlier. I went home after 24 hours.

She is getting on brilliantly. She is so content and I find I'm sat willing her to wake up because it seems like ages since I held her. Her brothers Leo-Jay and Lincoln are brilliant with her, but soon lose interest because she doesn't actually do much! Having her at home with just us has been nice as we've been able to get into a nice routine without constant visitors but the reality of the situation is heartbreaking when we are stood meeting her Grandad and her aunties and uncles behind a window. It's only us that have held her so far and it may be a while before anyone else does.

There's a bit of a story behind her name. In 2016, I'd fallen pregnant but it was an ectopic pregnancy and I had to have surgery to remove one of my fallopian tubes. At the same time, my grandad was rushed into intensive care to have his bowel removed due to cancer.

My grandad beat cancer and I got better, but I didn't feel whole. There was always a piece missing and I struggled to cope. I attempted overdosing, self-harmed and pushed everyone away. I managed to pull myself out this hole by completing a mental health course and this helped me gain better understanding on how I was feeling. I got help, got better and continued learning. Then I got pregnant and unfortunately miscarried again. I struggled not to slip back into depression.

When I then got pregnant with Journey, I didn't let myself believe I would get to keep the baby, and every day I expected to wake up bleeding. But slowly the days crept by and I dared let myself get excited. Her name came so easily – I knew I wanted her to represent all this and to remind me of the journey I went through to get her. Her middle name is Ellise, which is an anagram of my grandad's name, Leslie.

To me, Journey being born amongst all this madness and scary times is proof that everything happens for a reason and this is hers – to come at a time when little rays of happiness and hope are needed.

> Everything happens for a reason and this is hers — to come at a time when little rays of happiness and hope are needed.

6 O'CLOCK GIN

HAND SANITISER

We're All In This Together

6 O'CLOCK GIN

To play our part during these uncertain times, we diversified and did what we could to help fight the spread of Covid-19 by making hand sanitiser.

Our hand sanitiser was made to the World Health Organisation formulation and came in a beautiful Bristol blue bottle, inspired by our 6 O'clock Gin award-winning London Dry bottle. The packaging is fully recyclable or can be rinsed and refilled with more hand sanitiser, soap or anything else that takes your fancy.

We initially just supplied local authorities, hospitals and nurseries with hand sanitiser in bulk. Then we made it available to our loyal 6 O'clock Gin fanbase and the general public on our website - and the entire batch of 175 bottles sold out in under two hours!

A social media post was shared over 120 times and demand created a frenzy of comments and requests for the new product. We actually had to ask all customers to be courteous and only purchase what they needed, in order to help us to supply as many homes and businesses as possible.

Key workers and others on the frontline were able to buy the hand sanitiser at a reduced, cost to produce price. And for every 250 ml bottle of our hand sanitiser sold we donated another bottle free of charge to the NHS on their behalf.

Covid-19 has brought with it a whole host of challenges for many UK industries and with pubs, bars and restaurants closed for our safety, the spirits industry was by no means exempt – although during Lockdown we actually recorded an 800% increase in online sales, thanks to our loyal fans' love of gin.

In the middle of March, with no end to Lockdown in sight, we had to take the difficult decision to cancel all of our distillery tours. We were delighted to, finally, be able to recommence them again in July, having had to postpone so many bookings over the past months. We were really excited to be able to show off our distillery in all its glory again whilst supporting social distancing, PPE, contract tracing and deep cleaning.

"We are doing everything we can to protect people in our community during the Coronavirus outbreak. I am extremely proud of my team and how they have rallied together to create a product that is very much needed at this time".

Michael Kain / Managing Director

> We did what we could to help fight the spread of Covid-19.

PATRICK BLAKE
Blake's of the Hollow / Co. Fermanagh

I am the third Patrick Blake to manage the Patrick Blake Group business. There is a fourth looming in the background, who has just completed his Masters in UCD in Dublin.

The Patrick Blake Group now comprises of six divisions – pubs, off-licences, fine wines, properties, agricultural holdings and funeral directors, so my normal working day is venturing into the unknown every morning! My real passion within the business is fine wine and we have built up relationships with some of the most prestigious wineries in Europe, with customers across the UK and Ireland as well as south east Asia, the US and the Caribbean. I am more than happy to devote as much time to our fine wine division and, of course, to engage in as much travel and sampling as possible!

'Blake's of The Hollow' is one of the most famous pubs in Ireland and has been in the Blake family since 1887. The business was founded as a typical Irish spirit grocer's shop, selling everything under the sun from one small location and, over the decades, it has evolved and expanded. The crown jewel is the Victorian bar to the front of the building, which has remained largely untouched for over 130 years and retains most of its original and distinctive architectural features. The building also contains a gothic-style bar spread over two floors, two food venues, as well as a sports bar aimed at the younger generation.

Since Covid, my job has changed considerably, not least in that our pubs were closed from 16th March to 23rd September during the initial Lockdown and closed again on 16th October.

> 66
> It's extremely frustrating to face another Lockdown but we look forward to welcoming customers back safely soon.

Supposedly we are reopening on Friday 13th November but we anticipate an additional two weeks to be added to this current Lockdown.

Blake's of The Hollow implemented an extensive and costly health and safety plan to protect our customers and staff as far as physically possible. One of the main challenges has been observing the health and safety protocols and social distancing necessary to create a safe environment in which to recommence business for the run up to Christmas, so it was extremely frustrating to face another Lockdown mid-October – just as staff, customers and the community in general were becoming acclimatised to protocols and conduct.

The other downside has been no foreign travel and no winery visits! France, in particular, is in the same boat as ourselves, but I am assured by our contacts at various wineries that production goes on as normal. Thankfully, vines are not affected by Covid!

As funeral directors, the hazards presented by Covid are ever-present for both families and staff. Complying with Department of Health guidelines is a complex but necessary requirement for funeral directors and next of kin. The funeral industry has had to cope with terribly sad bereavements, including funerals going directly to interment without a church service and others where a church service takes place but the coffin has to remain outside the church. Sadly, burials taking place within hours of a bereavement are now common place given the hazards surrounding Covid funerals. As funeral directors, we are in a paid profession, but equally important though is the recognition we receive from families for a job well done – often in very trying circumstances for all concerned.

Across all our divisions, we remain very much customer-orientated. Our head office remains in its original rural location; Blake's of The Hollow in Enniskillen is frequented by generations of the same families and is the meeting place of choice when family members return for festive seasons like Christmas and Easter. We look forward to welcoming them all back safely soon.

SNAG TIGHTS

We're lucky enough to have thousands of amazing NHS workers among our customers, who have supported us since we launched our unique size-inclusive brand two years ago – our super stretchy yarn ensures no snagging or sagging on a long shift!

We know how hard the people behind our NHS work at any time of year, let alone during a pandemic and we wanted to find a way for us and all of our customers to give a little something back to all the people in the NHS who are doing such an incredible job for the country right now.

We launched an initiative to gift frontline NHS workers with free tights, donating a pair for every customer order we receive. It's open to all NHS workers, from doctors and nurses to midwives, radiologists and ward clerks, who can receive the Snags of their choice in exchange for a snap of their NHS ID.

It's a thank you from Snag and our customers for everything our NHS workers do and to repay their extraordinary efforts amidst the Covid-19 pandemic.

We've already seen an overwhelming amount of NHS workers signing up, with more than 12,000 signing up in the first week and thousands more showing their support on our Facebook announcement. We're excited for the scheme to continue to grow.

Brie Read / CEO & Founder

66

This is amazing. I'm frontline NHS staff and this has put a huge smile on my face after a long stressful day. Thank you for supporting us.

RABBI LAURA JENNER-KLAUSNER
Senior Rabbi to Reform Judaism / London

As the Coronavirus crisis unfolds, there are increasingly fascinating conversations about whether there can be some positive effects of imposed isolation. Of course, we can only appreciate the positives of self-isolation in a physically and emotionally safe place as, for many people, it can be a living hell.

We are now using fewer natural resources, which is good for climate change and countering a dangerous depletion of the earth's precious assets. This is reminiscent of the concept of tzimtzum, which is used in Kabbalah for the theological idea that God began the process of creating by 'contracting' God's self and God's infinite light, to allow for finite realms to exist. It's pertinent not only to what may be happening to Earth because of Coronavirus but also to a specific style of leadership which enables other people, other forces of creativity, other voices, to shine. This is your chance to shine if you can step up within your community, organisation or even country.

A key element of my job is to embody an enormous amount of enthusiasm, positivity and hope. I call this 'rabbi as cheerleader'. "You're fine", "You're okay" doesn't necessarily mean that everything will be fine, nor that everything will get better. But it is a quick and effective tool for looking after others, emphasising that despite all this, they are valued and loved.

Pretending to be 'OK' can also be an incredibly useful resilience strategy. Pretending like this is not dishonesty. It's a mental framing exercise to make difficult moments more bearable. I pretend to be fine a lot of the time, in order to be fine. I gear myself up, put makeup on, wear a smile, tell myself I'm alright.

Whilst hand washing is not enough to free us from responsibility for our health, it does help us to protect ourselves from others and others from ourselves. The Hebrew Bible provides a compelling and universal truth, "They must wash their hands and feet so they will not die". We must wash our hands for self-protection but as a society, we cannot afford to wash the hands of each other. Now is the time to reach out to neighbours, to think beyond ourselves and to remember there are many creative ways to care for others which do not physically endanger ourselves.

During this Coronavirus pandemic, the threat is not just to our physical resilience but also emotional resilience and especially for the many people experiencing loneliness. Although much blame has been placed on technology for social distancing when we are not in enforced physical isolation, it is also technology that can help us proactively cultivate social closeness while we are having to be physically distant.

In a crisis, you may feel you have no choice but to dedicate yourself to being disciplined. You hold onto your emotions, you behave 'properly' and suppress your fury, terror and bad behaviour. Paradoxically, it may be harder to control yourself when you think it's over. It's not over until you have thoroughly processed what has happened, whether through talking about it, writing about it or laughing or dancing it out of your system. To remind you of the wisdom of Going on a Bear Hunt – "You can't go over it, can't go under it, you've got to go through it".

But this too, shall pass. In 1852, the fable 'Solomon's Seal' recounts a Sultan asking King Solomon for a mantra that would be true in both good and bad times. King Solomon answers him with "this too will pass away".

'Never waste a good crisis' is also a useful expression as it's an opportunity to encourage us to think in ways we may not be prepared to under normal circumstances, even though we wouldn't have wanted this situation to occur at all. Crisis opens up opportunities as people behave with unusual levels of solidarity and bravery, and are wiling to think creatively in a way that normal life might blunt.

In this Coronavirus pandemic, we have seen an explosion in volunteering. Thousands of people offering to help the NHS, local neighbourhood schemes burgeoning and one-to-one acts of kindness that are simply beautiful. We have shown our true selves to be generous, empthateic and resilient.

The question for after this period of isolation is over, is how we will sustain the positive dynamics. As Darwin wisely taught us, those who survive are not the strongest or the most intelligent, but the most adaptable to change.

> But this too, shall pass.

People used putting their bins out (and other household chores) as an excuse to get dressed up – in ball gowns, glad rags and fancy dress ...

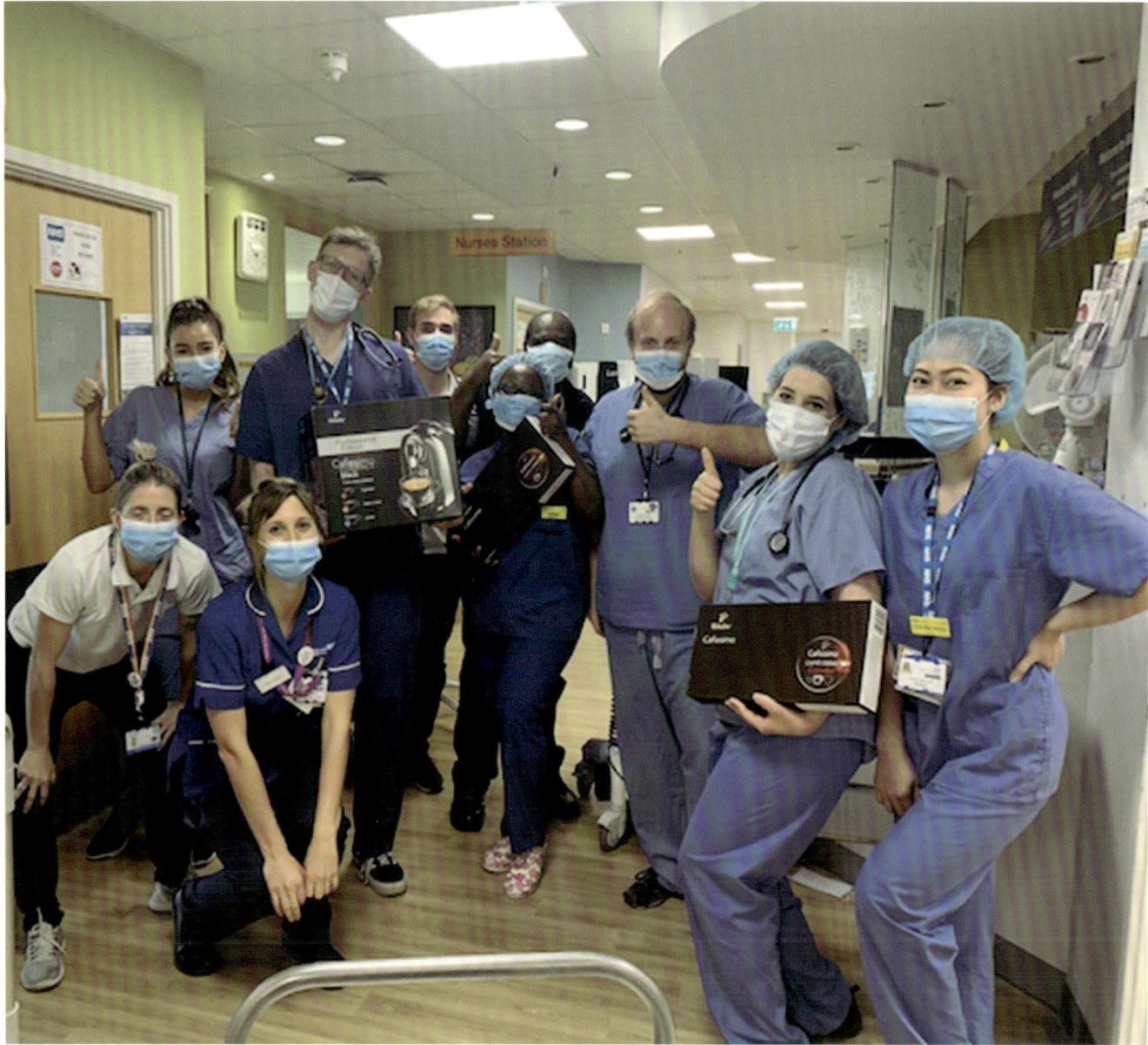

NHS COFFEE APPEAL

Just before Lockdown, I saw a link on Twitter to an LBC interview where an ICU Doctor, Jack, had called in to the show at the end of his tether. He was in absolute despair about what was happening and just happened to add that he'd love a decent cup of coffee.

I was moved to tears by this so I contacted the hospital and asked if I could buy a coffee machine for him and his colleagues. I hoped a small gesture might make a difference.

And then I called around some people I know – doctors and people that work in the NHS. They told me that most of the coffee shops in and around their locations have temporarily closed. Hardly any NHS wards have an espresso machine. Most have got one of those industrial tubs of instant, but they'd massively appreciate something that tastes better. It isn't the biggest thing they need, granted. But it is something that's easy to help with.

The demand was real. People were providing food but our NHS heroes would also like some proper coffee. When I contacted the local NHS Trust, they needed more than I could afford to buy on my own so I had a whip around amongst some of my friends, we sent out some machines and capsules, and the NHS teams seemed really pleased.

Then we set up this appeal to help members of the public and companies to sponsor a ward or donate an espresso machine and a supply of capsules to NHS staff working hard through the coronavirus outbreak throughout the country. If people can't afford to donate a machine, they can just order some capsules. Any donation, however small, will make a difference to our nurses and doctors.

Supported by members of the British Coffee Association (BCA) and the public, thousands of bags of coffee beans, pods, roast and ground coffee, filters, and espresso machines for those who need the extra boost, have been donated to NHS Trust hospitals and NHS teams nationally. That's enough to make almost 2 million cups of coffee.

I feel so lucky to have heard that original interview and to have been able to do something to help.

We are really heartened by these amazing donations but many more machines now need to be donated by individuals and companies, so we can ensure that every ward across the country that asks for help, receives a machine and some coffee.

Edouard de Guitaut / Founder

When the NHS Coffee Appeal contacted us about this initiative, we didn't hesitate to get our members involved. The work our doctors and nurses are doing deserves more than coffee but if it means they can enjoy a decent hot drink that helps them through a busy shift then we are thrilled to help out in any way we can. Our members have rallied to support the NHS Coffee Appeal, and several have also made their own donations directly to the NHS. To date this has meant almost 2 million cups of quality coffee for NHS staff.

Paul Rooke / Executive Director at the British Coffee Association

> We're turning clapping into coffee. Our brilliant NHS staff could do with a decent cup of coffee, so let's buy them one.

JEAN-MARIE HUGHES MBE
Lead Trade Improvement and Response Manager / Liverpool

In my role, we support all business functions and colleagues across retail in delivering the trade strategy at Co-op. The role is quite diverse role so each day is different but we are always very busy responding to feedback, influencing change based on that feedback and helping build strategies and plans that support our colleagues and customers for now and in the future. It's a very fast paced role but one that is very enjoyable and one where you can make a real difference.

Although safety always came first, Covid meant our role very much focused on keeping our colleagues, customers and members safe no matter what the cost. We stripped out lots of different processes to allow colleagues to simply serve our customers and help get them what they needed. I changed our working patters to make sure there was full coverage and support 24/7 so no matter what time of day or night it was, we were there to listen and respond. The role became much more intense and played a much more important role in the business as we acted as the voice of 55,000 colleagues and customers to make sure they were heard and protected.

At the time I felt like I couldn't do enough. We had colleagues who were scared for themselves, for their families, for their colleagues and I wanted to take all that away for them. The job became more than just delivering plans and ensuring stock was in store and more about reassurance, listening, supporting and ensuring we were focussing on the right things to keep our colleagues, customers and members safe.

I think we all, no matter what profession you were in across the world or what role you played in Co-op, just wanted to do what we could to help. In Co-op we all do truly care about doing the right thing and looking after each other – that's why I work for this business. I believe if you're going to do a job you should do so with the aim to make a positive impact to those you come in contact with.

I'm a single parent with two young children and everyone was asking how I managed to teach the kids, do my job and do shopping for vulnerable family. The answer is I have no idea! You don't realise just how much you can get done in a day until you

try. I was so proud of both my children, being so young they knew mummy had to work so school work was often done late or on weekends or split throughout the day but they worked so, so hard to help. Poppy, my little girl, and Alex, my little boy, both got star awards and those little things motivated me to keep going as it felt like everything we were doing was being achieved. The school was amazing in making sure children still felt connected.

Seeing that you are helping, colleagues telling you they appreciate your support, knowing that you have made a difference no matter how long your day is, keeps you going. Throughout I just thought what would I do if it was my daughter or son working in a shop and I would do everything I could to protect them. I often stopped during the day and just had a hug from them which also kept me going. My team are also amazing. We often just put a quick catch up in during the day to check how everyone was feeling and to support each other

When got the email to say I was on the Honours List, I thought it was a hoax. It honestly didn't hit home until the day it was announced and I still, to this day don't feel worthy of such an honour. I am so blessed, still very overwhelmed and extremely honoured to be rewarded in such a way – there are so many of us across the world who have done and will continue to do all we can to help.

> 66
> No matter what profession you were in across the world, we all just wanted to do what we could to help.

JOE FUREY
Coronavirus Test Centre Supervisor / Blackburn

A normal day for me would have been going to school and studying for my A-Levels, and playing basketball at the weekends. But schools closed, my A-Levels were cancelled and I started work at the test centre so my life was turned on its head. It was my first full-time job and I was working at the Manchester test site a few weeks after Lockdown begun.

I used to work part time as a kiosk worker at the Etihad on match days. They contacted me about the test centre role about three weeks into Lockdown. Despite my families concerns about the risks, I wanted to do something positive to help.

On my first day, I thought perhaps I would be helping make test kits and count PPE but by lunchtime I had collected the first self-administered coronavirus test in the UK.

> 66
>
> I collected the first self-administered coronavirus test in the UK. I never imagined I'd do a job like this but I felt proud of the work I did.

At first there were some teething problems as it was a completely new idea, so as a team we helped to offer advice and first-hand experience on how to make the process more efficient for the other sites opening in the UK.

When the test centre first opened in Manchester, it was extremely busy, collecting over 1,000 tests a day but as time went on it got quieter. However, I was then asked to help set up a new site in Blackburn, which was a hotspot at the time.

The shifts were extremely long, each one was 13 hours. There were also many difficult interactions with members of the public, especially when we had a limited number of tests to give out. Not only was it hard to say no, there were many people desperate for a test with symptoms who we simply had to turn away.

I never imagined I'd do a job like this. It was an unexpected opportunity that I thought would just last a few days.

At the start it was quite daunting, but over time it becomes normality although there are still occasions that arise where you remind yourself that it is a deadly disease.

I found the work stimulating and learnt lots of new skills. There were people from all walks of life working on the site and the conversations were often very interesting! My colleagues were always entertaining and supportive, making work enjoyable and the shifts go quickly.

I always felt proud of the work I did, and I know that in a small way I helped the national effort. My family were also extremely proud and the money I earned will now help fund me through university.

GARY WILLS
Furlearn & Talent Today Founder / Coventry

I've worked in recruitment for more than 20 years but in mid-April, I joined a large and rapidly growing club – I was furloughed. By the end of April, nearly 4 million people in the UK had been furloughed and by the end of May, it was more than 8 million.

Being furloughed is a very insecure situation. You don't know if you will be called back or made redundant, so people are really suffering right now. I've been in recruitment for so long, I've lots of connections and a good knowledge of how I can help people land jobs.

So, rather than sitting around twiddling my thumbs or worrying about what might happen next, I decided to do something positive – to make sure I made a positive contribution with my time off, helping people going through a challenging time. So I set up *Furlearn*, an online community for people like me who have been furloughed, or made redundant and are job searching.

The idea came to me when I was on the treadmill in my garage. I was doing the last bit of a 10-day charity challenge to run the equivalent of the 108 miles from NHS Nightingale Hospital Birmingham to NHS Nightingale Hospital London. My manager rang to say my furlough had been extended to the end of July and I came up with the idea for FurLearn.

I contacted a friend, Jade Johannsen, who works in marketing. She said it was a brilliant idea and wanted to come on board. So we founded Furlearn, based on the core pillars of personal branding, mental health, health & fitness and fun.

FurLearn offers a mix of things. It's a support network, with free advice and support. We also host regular online events, like webinars and masterclasses given by motivational and specialist speakers who give their time and expertise for free as an act of goodwill.

It can help people in many ways. It gives them practical advice and support at a time when they really need it. It motivates and inspires them, giving them a focus to look beyond their current situation. And perhaps most importantly, it boosts members' emotional, mental and physical wellbeing, partly through the content and support, but also because members are part of a community going through the same or similar experiences.

It has given people other people to talk to. They gather fresh ideas and realise they're not in it on their own. That makes a huge difference to people during the worry and stress of job searching.

Even though more people are landing jobs now, my concern is that there will be a lot of people who will be released from furlough at the end of October. Some companies won't be able to bring all that talent back to the business. You have to remember that this is a pandemic decision though, and people have to remember that, if they lose their job, it's not they who have been made redundant, it's the role.

We're really proud to be 'Covid Champion' finalists in The Learning Awards.

Having supported, trained and motivated 1,000s of jobseekers and hiring managers during 2020 it became clear to us that traditional recruitment was outdated, so we worked with the Furlearn community to change it and set up 'Talent Today' – a new technology enabled recruitment agency community.

> 66
>
> You have to remember this is a pandemic decision – it's not you who has been made redundant, it's the role. Furlearn can help in many ways.

TOMMY FERRIS & NANA JEAN
Self-isolating / Yate

I've been a postman since I moved in with my Nana. I used to work in hospitality but the unsociable hours meant it was a difficult role to balance with life here. As a postman, every day is different but I usually spend the first half of my day meeting a variety of weird and wonderful people. For every ten that moan, there is one that smiles and thanks you – and if one person can outshine ten others, it goes to show that kindness always wins.

I struggled with depression so taking on the honour of caring for Nana was my 'sink or swim' moment. My mum believed I needed a sense of purpose but I didn't think it was possible for me to care for another person when I was unable to care for myself. However, they say that your mother knows you like no other and, in my darkest hour, Mum assigned me a quest that ultimately saved me. I became stronger and channeled my pain into helping someone who needed it more than me.

Nana was orphaned at 13-years-old. A little girl in Scotland, she created the most beautiful and interesting life for herself against the odds. From being alone at 13, she now sits beside me as the mother of five, grandmother of twelve and great-grandmother of two (soon the be three). She has dedicated her life to helping others as a midwife and burns unit nurse and even in retirement, she continued her path of kindness by travelling across the globe to grasp the hands of children whose loneliness resonated with her own childhood. She is one of the bravest, kindest and purest human beings I've ever known.

Dementia is cruel, deceptive and often upsetting. I learned quickly to accept what's happening, to just enjoy Nana's company and cherish each moment she's fully connecting with me.

When Lockdown first began, I struggled immensely with being confined between these four walls. I love spending time with Nana and I began to feel guilty that I was craving time away from here. I'd lost what was a very vibrant social life.

It's been joyful and stressful in equal measures. We dance, we sing, we laugh. I wash her hair and I curl it. We watch quiz shows together and I cook for us. We speak of her childhood and she tells me of the gardener who wooed her, the man who saved her from a drain and about the love of her life – my Gramps. She tells me of how they met, created the largest family and how dearly she misses him. Endless, fascinating stories that I will never tire of. It has been a true honour that I will forever be grateful for.

But I'd be a liar if I said I didn't have moments of frustration. The challenges are constant. One moment it's a struggle to understand why people can't visit, the next it's an upset because she feels lonely when she's had family over and then misses them.

My Nana deserves the best 24-hour care this country can offer but we've had so many different people coming in and out, many with no PPE, and I've even had to prompt some of them to wash their hands! Nana dedicated her entire life to being kind and showing love to those who needed it most. The biggest challenge I've gone through is trying to understand how, in their final years, our elders don't always get the support and respect they've spent their life earning. The care service delivers such a delicate role and I'm passionate about wanting them to have the support they need in order to do the very best job.

In any given day, Nana is often vacant but when the Alzheimer's subsides and Nana shines through again, these are the moments I cherish. I've done it because it was the right thing to do. At the time, I had nothing to lose. I wanted to be better and the first step to achieving that was to do some good. With the guidance of my mum, I discovered the beauty of being selfless and it changed me. It healed me. Now I smile and feel proud of the man that looks back at me in the mirror. Living with Nana has taught me about kindness, closeness and the importance of family. Ultimately, I am a better man because of her and this worldwide pandemic.

I read a quote once that feels really relevant: "Being negative only makes a difficult journey more difficult. You may be given a cactus but you don't have to sit on it".

> 66
> We dance, we sing, we laugh. These are the moments I cherish and it has been a true honour I will always be grateful for.

REBECCA KENNELLY MBE
Director of Volunteering at Royal Voluntary Service

Royal Voluntary Service's main ambition is to mobilise and empower volunteers to support the health and wellbeing of vulnerable people. With the pandemic being arguably the biggest health challenge this country has even seen, we knew that we'd have a big role to play and we weren't wrong!

Royal Voluntary Service partnered with NHS England and GoodSAM on a scheme called NHS Volunteer Responders. The scheme mobilised an army of 360,000 on-duty volunteers to support those most vulnerable and at risk to Covid-19 with tasks such as shopping and prescription collection, transport to and from vital medical appointments, and supportive 'Check-in and Chat' calls. This is all made possible through a geo-targeted app-based system which matches the person in need to a volunteer close to them. This was really important to us as we know the importance of people getting help in the quickest possible time. We also wanted to make it as easy as possible for people to volunteer as we know how precious time is. The on-duty function means that people can volunteer as and when is convenient for them and it can fit around busy lifestyles.

Myself and the RVS team were also passionate about finding a way to support our existing Royal Voluntary Service clients at a safe social distance and our 'Virtual Village Hall' was born, supported by People's Postcode Lottery. The team turned it into something really beautiful and today our Virtual Village Hall is attended by thousands of people across the country who are brought together for activities and socialising from the safety of their homes enjoying online activities to support wellbeing, social connections, health and wellbeing.

When I first started my job at Royal Voluntary Service I could never have predicted that I would be doing what I am today! I know it's been said before, but the pandemic really was unprecedented, and I couldn't be more proud of the whole Royal Voluntary Service team for pulling together and working so hard. My skill set is around taking a challenging set of circumstances and turning them into something magical. The bits in the middle are always a bit complicated, but when they all sit together and work effectively, it's incredibly rewarding. I owe all of the success to the Royal Voluntary Service team who have been truly fantastic the whole way through. I must admit that there were times that it seemed we had an impossible task on our hands, but it was never

actually impossible with the team around. We are a team who pull together no matter what and that's exactly what the volunteers have done too. Proud is a total understatement!

Sometimes at the end of a long day when I have a meeting with my team, we are so tired that we just end up laughing. It's that team spirit that we all need when things get tough and I'm so lucky to have the best team in the world. Knowing that you're making a difference to people's lives does also make the late nights feel worthwhile, and when I read the feedback from the people we support and the volunteers who support them it reminds me that my job is part of something much bigger and it really does make me feel like all the hours we have put into this really are worth it.

I am also very lucky to have a fantastic husband and kids who are so supportive of what I do. Back at the start of the pandemic, I was doing my job as well as home schooling a seven and eight year old! If my children weren't absolute superstars at getting on with their home learning while their mum was working then it would have been much more difficult.

I'm still struggling to find the words about the MBE! It was completely breath-taking. It was quite funny because the nature of my job means that I frequently receive Government emails so I must admit I had to do a double take when it came through! When I processed the information (and it took a while!) I was completely humbled and overwhelmed. It sounds cliché, but I really do owe all the thanks to the team and all of the volunteers. This isn't just my award, it's a recognition of the work of every single person that has supported our Covid response. It really does take an army and the Royal Voluntary Service army is one that I am so proud to be part of.

> " We knew that we'd have a big role to play and we weren't wrong!

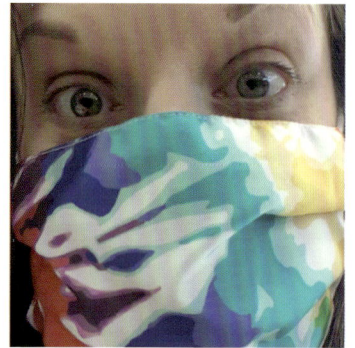

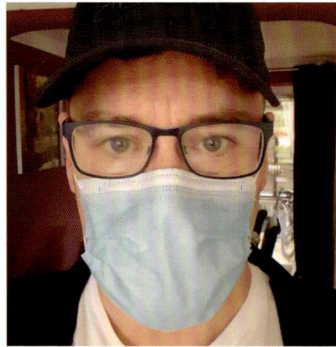

We wore masks, visors and face coverings (and quite often gloves too) in shops, on public transport and in bars & restaurants ...

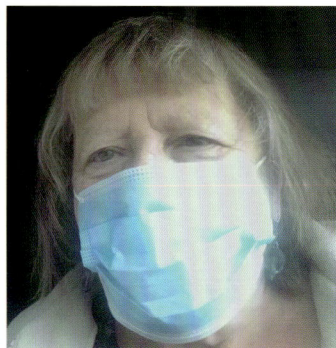

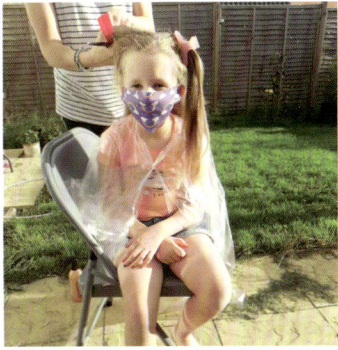

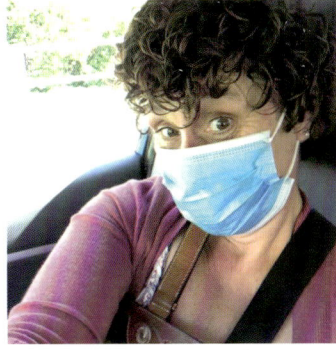

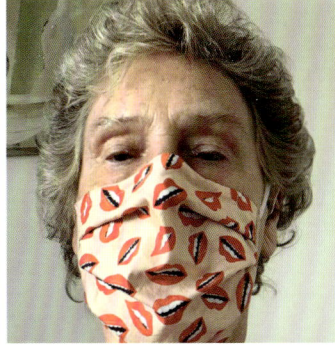

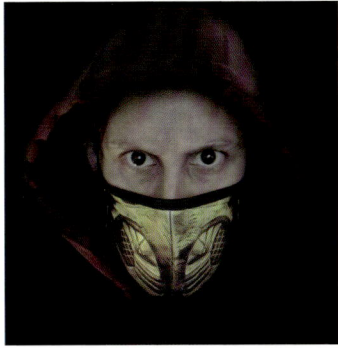

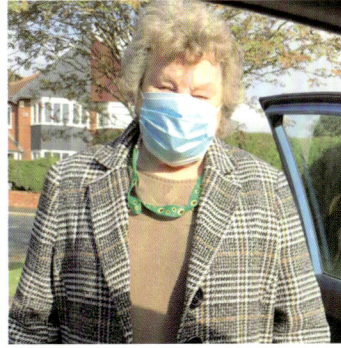

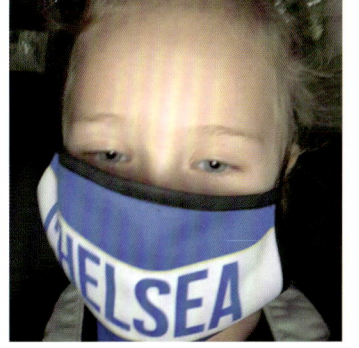

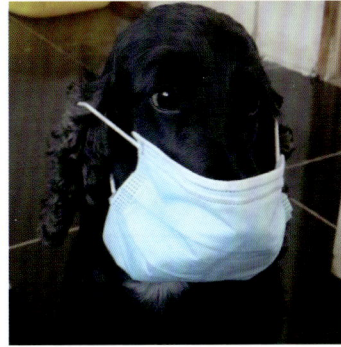

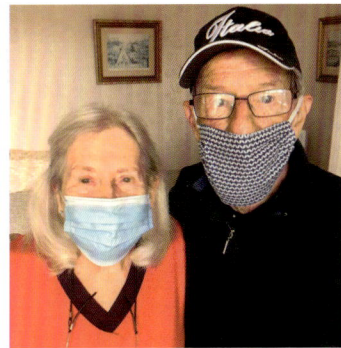

SMALL THINGS

Moments in your life don't get much bigger than this,
It's a milestone, like a wedding, or a teenager's first kiss.
But to be here in the finals is feeling slightly odd
It's champagne and caviar, I'm used to Vimto and battered cod.

And while this moment overwhelms me, the question must be asked
Do we sometimes miss the small things as life goes by so fast?
Mosquitos are only tiny but they can drive you mad
So never underestimate small things that make you glad.

Simon makes David happy and he'll be there when he calls.
He burst into his dressing room and realised it's just small

Things like
The last shoes in the sale are the right size for you.
A baby's expression when they're having a poo,
Looking in a junk drawer and finding a pen
Fitting a size 8 when you are usually a 10.

Small things that make you happy, small things that make you laugh,
Bubbles make kids giggle when they're trumping in the bath.
Aardvarks are happy when it's alphabetical,
Dogs will always wag their tails if they can lick their

Ballgames make kids happy when they're playing having fun
I wasn't happy when the schools closed and I had to teach my sons.
I was happy when Boris told me I could finally hug my Mum
But I was happiest in April finding loo roll for my bum.

Ant and Dec are happy when they take home an award
So they've been pretty happy since 1994.

You want to seize the moment, 'You just live once' I hear you say
But that's not true… you die once, but you must live every day.
Smile as if they've told you there's no need to quarantine
When you laugh in denim… happiness is in your genes.

Happiness is small things like being with our friends
Little things like when the Queen said we'll meet again.
On Thursdays, on doorsteps with pride inside our chests
Taking just a moment to clap the NHS.

And it won't be long before these masks are gone,
We'll be living life again to the maximum
And we'll remember people like Sir Captain Tom,
And in years our kids will be reminiscing, not about stuff that they've been missing
But that every day they got to play with Dad and Mum.
And we'll remember that we were strong when McDonalds was closed for so very long
And Britain's talent will be that we all carry on.
And Britain's talent will be that we all carry on.

To be here now, to get this far, for you to make me feel like a star,
For gratitude I don't know where to start
When Alfie asked me "What's it all about"
I thought I knew but I had my doubts,
But the answer is so simple and so smart:

You'll realise through it all, the moments that you thought were small,
Can take the biggest places in your heart.
And if you're lucky your family plays the biggest part.

// JON COURTENAY
WINNER OF BRITAIN'S GOT TALENT 2020

There is no 'normal' for us to go back to. People sleeping in the streets wasn't normal; children living in poverty wasn't normal; using other people's lives to pile up objects wasn't normal – the whole thing was absurd. Surely it's time to start imagining something better?

// FRANKIE BOYLE

CHARLIE MACKESY

I found a way of communicating with the people I've wanted to thank. All key workers. I think it's incredible we can make marks on paper that can somehow benefit someone somewhere else. It's been one of the greatest privileges of my live to discover that.

"They say there's a pot of gold there,"
said the boy.
"Yes – that's the nurses, doctors,
cleaners, carers and delivery people,"
said the horse "and you."

A MASSIVE THANK YOU

: to all the individuals and organisations featured – for what you've done and continue to do, for telling me your stories, for giving me your photos and for trusting me to share them all in this book. I hope I've done you justice.

: to the press and media teams that facilitated some of the interviews, and to all those who 'knew someone' and put me in touch.

: to everyone too numerous to mention (although I've listed some on the last page) who gave me their pictures for the photograph montages.

: to everyone whose story I didn't tell or photo I didn't use – I wish I could have included so many more, but I hope you find yourselves represented in here somewhere.

: to Roxanne, for so generously gifting the book its front cover illustration and for so perfectly capturing all the love and positivity packed inside. You can read more about her overleaf.

: to Lynn, for her eagle eyes and technical expertise – who knew there were (at least) three different types of hyphen?!? You are the knickers to my (fake) fur coat.

: to Gemini Print, for having faith in me and helping to turn the content into an actual book. I couldn't have made it this beautiful without your technical knowledge and support.

: to the organisations that agreed to stock and promote the book, giving it the best chance be enjoyed by as many people as possible and to raise as much money as we can.

: to my treasured family and friends for their support, encouragement, patience and nagging – and for the words of tough love when I doubted myself.

: and finally, to my Alexa – who was sneakily programmed to give me daily (and really quite bossy) reminders to "write the book". It worked, and I did.

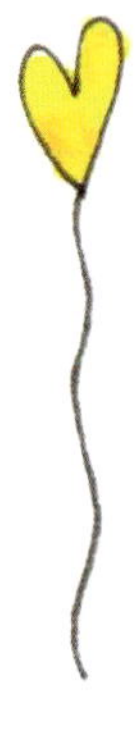

A little bit of me.

ROXANNE KNOTT
Illustrator & Artist

When people ask me "how did you get into drawing?", "Where do you get your inspiration from?" I always find it a little daunting trying to remember! But the truth is that there have been many factors and circumstances that have paved the way for my little artistic journey.

I have always had a love for illustration and take inspiration from books that I used to read as a child. After studying GCSE Art & Design I continued my learning, studying A-Level Art alongside Art History and Photography. It took a while to figure out which road I wanted to take but after the birth of my daughter, my love of book illustrations was rediscovered.

Sometimes it's been hard and, believe me, I've learnt a whole lot about what not to do, which I hope I have taken on board constructively. Having said that, I have been overwhelmed by the positive response I've received towards my drawings, so a big thanks to all who have filled me with positivity and spurred me on every step of the way.

My drawings are designed for all ages and you'll find some recurring characters throughout some of my work having their own little adventures! I really hope they bring a sense of cheerfulness to you all.

When Anna explained the project and asked me to design an illustration for her, I was delighted to be able to help – and a little starstruck to be on the front cover of a book with so many amazing people inside! I think it's really important that we all do what we can to help each other in these challenging times and I was only too pleased to be able to make a contribution in my own way.

www.roxanneknott.com

(She wasn't going to mention it but I wanted to tell you that the amazing front cover illustration is available to buy as a print from Roxanne's website. Get yourself a heart-warming keepsake and re-gift her some of her own generosity at the same time!)

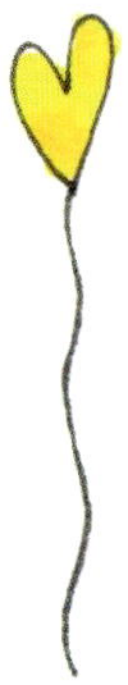

ANNA JAMES
Chief Storyteller

I am a corporate storyteller, working with organisations of all shapes and sizes to capture their stories and bringing together everything they need to deliver their key messages in print, on film and in person. I live in rural Somerset with my stonemason husband and love of my life, Andrew, our beloved and spoilt cockapoo, Leonard, and irritatingly patchy WiFi.

I donated my time to produce this book as a way to give a little something back during the Covid-19 pandemic.

In my day job (when it happened!), I produce commemorative books like this for organisations to celebrate their history, successes and key milestones. When Covid hit, my work came to a standstill. Like lots of other people, I was glued to the news and social media, despairing at all the worry and sadness but finding some comfort in the tenacity, humanity and community spirit that emerged all around the country.

After quite a few sleepless nights, I wondered if I should make one of my books to record some of the positive things we were seeing and hearing about as to well as to raise some money for charity – my way of contributing a little something to the national effort (our local farmers weren't desperate enough for my "help"!). Despite being woken at 3am to talk about it, my husband said he thought it was a great idea so I began asking people to tell me their stories and send me their photos.

That's how it started and now, I am humbled to have become the caretaker of this most amazing collection of stories from all these everyday heroes from every walk of life, which are heart-warming and heart-wrenching in equal measures. I just wish there were enough pages in the world to have included so many, many more. It's probably the book that none of us would ever have wanted but perhaps the one that we all need, to remind ourselves what a kind and generous bunch we can be.

www.jackanorycommunications.com

PHOTO ACKNOWLEDGEMENTS

The vast majority of photographs in this book were provided by the individual contributors and I'd like to thank them all for giving me permission to use them. Some pictures are a bit wonky, not that well lit or a little fuzzy around the edges – but I've purposely left them like that. I think they have a quaint charm that reflects the reality of the situations in which they were taken.

I was also lucky to be given some lovely professional photographs, provided by the featured organisations' press teams – thank you! These are all attributed to the featured organisation, unless otherwise noted. There are also some other professional photographers whose pictures appear on some of the montage pages that I wanted to acknowledge and thank here:

THE RAINBOW PICTURES: Contributors and Amazon / English Heritage / Longleat Estate

THE CLAP FOR CARERS PICTURES: Contributors and Eric Johnson Photography / Iain Tall / Michael Tubi / Sarah Bardsley / Sarah Lawrence

THE CLOSED SHOPS AND BUSINESSES PICTURES: 1000 Words / Al Robinson / Alena Veasey / Alex Daniels / Armani A / Ben Gingell / Cryptographer / Dani Berszt / DaveSmith1965 / Duncan Cuthbertson / Eddie Jordan Photos / EdinburghCityMom / Gareth Willey / Jam Travek / Jessica Girvin / Jordan Crosby / Life Reportage / Lorna Roberts / Maria Was / Mark D Bailey / Matthew Ashmore / Michael JP / OLG Photography / Oxford Shot / Private Event Photography / Red Carpet / Richard Johnson / Sandor Szmutko / Shaun Waldie / Three Eyed Raven Productions / Yau Ming Low / UAV4

THE EMPTY PLACES (UK) PICTURES: 21st Century Nobody / Agent Wolf / Christopher Keeley / Craig Russell / Cryptographer / EdinburghCityMom / Elizabeth Maher / Jez Night / Kasak Photo / Lortek / Marton Kerek / Mo and Paul / Phil Silverman / Quirky Badger / Ruth Ashmore / Sandor Szmurko / Sunfreez

THE NHS THANK YOU PICTURES: Contributors and Alena Kravchenko / Alla Bogdanovic / Ash Donelon (Manchester United) Castle Cary Rugby Club / Chris Dornay / Creative Circle Studio / De Vere Hotels / Govia / Jllze Kalv / John Gomez / Kathy Tomlinson / Lizzie Maher / Lubo Ivanko / Lucien Harris / Martin Bird / Moonstone Images / MrDoomits / Network Rail Scotland / Paddy The Golfer / Peter Fleming / Stapletons Tyres / Trevor Baker / Twickenham Stadium / Uncle Henry's Maize Maze / VV Shots

THE MAKERS PICTURES: Contributors and David Klien / EE / English National Opera / Hackney Scrub Hub / Laura Ralph / Make Town Photography / Poppyfield / Rebecca Gore / Somerset Scrubs

THE DOORSTEP PORTRAIT PICTURES: Photography by Anna Shtern Zhmaylik / Childsplay Photography / EKG Photos / Nick Beal Photography / Ryan Goold Photography / Stuart Fearn / Wedding Footeography

THE BLUE PICTURES (UK & WORLD): The #MakeItBlue Collective and Andrew Cuomo / Atlanta Braves / City of Waco / FedEx Field / Joseph Haubert / Kelloggs / Light Tick Photography / Millennium Park / Selfridges / SFGreat America / Texas Rangers / The O2 Arena / UCLA Football / Wisconsin Badgers

THE DIGITAL PICTURES: Contributors and UniLad / WhoHaha

THE OPEN MIC PICTURES: Contributors

THE CANCELLED EVENTS PICTURES: Akselierikerson / Anizza / Augustus Cethkauskas / Cowdens / Enrico Della Pietra / Graham Hartley / Gunter Hofer / Ian Fletcher / Ian Pudsey / Info84383 / Jane Kranendonk / Joe Kirby / Kasto 80 / Kmiragaya / Londongal27 / Luboslav Manko / Marcin Wos / Marina Endermal / Martin Applegate / Melinda Nagy / Mohammed Ahmed Soliman / Pakpoom Phumee / Petre Buguv / Pod 666 / Raw Pixel Images / Superjolly / Piero Cruziatti / Virgil Naslenas / Wirestock

THE EMPTY PLACES (WORLD) PICTURES: Adamkaz / Aleksandr Zotov / Carpin XO / Damijen Photography / Dub Dub / Em Campos / Eric Kitayama / FivePointSix / Frederic Legrand / Gabor Tokodi / Gekko Gallery / Get Coulson / Gordo / Ilze Kalve / Ishak Mutiarg / J Gillispie / Jorge Villalba / Kandl Stock / K Jarrett / Kemal Aslan / Kool99 ? Krill Neiezhmakov / Lensman / Manoej Paateel / Martina L / Matsicha / Mauvries / Mina You / Mzeta / Nizam Ergil / Ryosei Watanabe / Sergey Bezgodar / Shebeko / Souvmen Tarafder / Stock High / Tgor Salnikov / Trial / ViltVart / Zianlob / Zorro

THE BALLGOWN PICTURES: Contributors and the group Admin Team

THE MASK PICTURES: Contributors